THE LOST
ELEVEN

THE LOST ELEVEN

THE FORGOTTEN STORY
OF BLACK AMERICAN SOLDIERS
BRUTALLY MASSACRED IN WORLD WAR II

DENISE GEORGE AND **ROBERT CHILD**

CALIBER
New York

CALIBER
Published by Berkley
An imprint of Penguin Random House LLC
375 Hudson Street, New York, New York 10014

Copyright © 2017 by Denise George and Robert Child
Penguin Random House supports copyright. Copyright fuels creativity, encourages diverse
voices, promotes free speech, and creates a vibrant culture. Thank you for buying an authorized
edition of this book and for complying with copyright laws by not reproducing, scanning, or
distributing any part of it in any form without permission. You are supporting writers and
allowing Penguin Random House to continue to publish books for every reader.

CALIBER and its colophon are trademarks of Penguin Random House LLC.

ISBN: 9781101987414

Library of Congress Cataloging-in-Publication Data is available.

First Edition: January 2017

Jacket photographs: snowy landscape © Dirk Wüstenhagen/Westend61/Corbis;
soldiers © Bettman/Getty Images
Jacket design by Steve Meditz
Book design by Laura K. Corless

While the author has made every effort to provide accurate telephone numbers,
Internet addresses and other contact information at the time of publication, neither the
publisher nor the author assumes any responsibility for errors, or for changes that occur after
publication. Further, publisher does not have any control over and does not assume any
responsibility for author or third- party Web sites or their content.

148720106

In appreciation for the faithful service and great sacrifice of eleven black GIs massacred in Wereth, Belgium, on December 17, 1944.

And in appreciation for all African-American men and women who have courageously served in the U.S. military.

Freedom is not free. It is costly.

But for the compassion of a twelve-year-old Belgian boy, the tragic fate of eleven black American soldiers might have been forever lost to history.

TABLE OF CONTENTS

Part 3: Leaving Camp Gruber

Part 4: The Battle of the Bulge

Dear Reader:

The Lost Eleven will introduce you to eleven courageous African-American GIs in the 333rd Field Artillery Battalion who served heroically and sacrifically in the United States Army in World War II. While most black soldiers filled noncombatant support roles, these eleven mastered the complicated operation of the 155mm howitzer, one of the most important weapons in the war. In 1944, they traveled across German-occupied France with General Middleton's VIII Corps, providing support fire where most urgently needed. With their record-setting speed in loading and positioning the 155, and their extreme accuracy in firing, they helped prove the combat skill of black soldiers. This story, and the fate of the eleven, unacknowledged for half a century and left out of the Congressional War Crimes Report of 1949, is told here in book form for the first time.

The events in this book are true, gleaned from military documents, interviews, VIII Corps and 333rd Battalion after-action reports, and written verbal accounts. While accurate in content, some of it has been creatively retold. Some of the dialogue, unrecorded by history, has been created.

All the characters in this book are historical and use their real names, with the exception of "Jeb," the training instructor, and "Greta," the Langers' German-loyal neighbor who betrayed them, whom the Langers refused to identify.

This exciting true story of eleven black heroes will delight your spirit, give you rare first-person historical insights, and make you proud of America's devoted GIs. But be forewarned. While this story will *warm* your heart, it will also *break* your heart. Graphic and deeply moving, this story screamed to be written, and now yearns to be read by generations yet to be born.

It is with great honor that after seventy-two years, and within the pages of a book, we introduce you to the Lost Eleven.

Denise George and Robert Child
July 2016

A PARTIAL LIST OF CHARACTERS

THE LOST ELEVEN
Charley Battery, 333rd Field Artillery Division

Tech Sergeant William Edward Pritchett: from Alabama

Tech Sergeant James Aubrey Stewart: from West Virginia

Staff Sergeant Thomas J. Forte: from Louisiana, mess sergeant

Corporal Mager Bradley: from Mississippi

Private First Class George Davis: from Alabama

Private First Class James Leatherwood: from Mississippi

Private First Class George W. Moten: from Texas

Private First Class Due W. Turner: from Arkansas

Private Curtis Adams: from South Carolina, medic

Private Robert Green: from Georgia

Private Nathanial Moss: from Texas

333rd Field Artillery Division

Lieutenant Colonel Harmon S. Kelsey: commanding officer

Captain William Gene McLeod: C Battalion, commander

Sergeant George Shomo: Charley Battery, from New Jersey

Corporal Robert Rolland Hudson Sr.: Charley Battery, from St. Louis

American Officers

General Dwight Eisenhower: Supreme Commander of the Allied Force in Europe; headquarters located on outskirts of Paris, France

General Troy Middleton: commander, U.S. VIII Corps; headquarters located in Bastogne, Belgium

Major General Alan W. Jones: commander of the 106th Division; headquarters located in Saint Vith, Belgium

German Officers

Adolf Hitler: leader of Germany

General Sepp Dietrich: Sixth Panzer Army

Colonel Joachim Peiper: First SS Panzer Division

General Hasso von Manteuffel: Fifth Panzer Army

SS Major Gustav Knittel: First SS Panzer Reconnaissance Battalion

Field Marshal Walter Model: Army Group B

Field Marshal Friedrich Paulus: commander of the Sixth Army

Colonel Claus von Stauffenberg: chief of staff to Commander General Friedrich Fromm

Others

Mathias and Maria Langer: the Belgian family in Wereth, Belgium: Hermann, Tina, and the other Langer children

President and Mrs. Franklin D. Roosevelt: President and First Lady of the United States

Prime Minister Winston Churchill: Prime Minister of England

THE LOST
ELEVEN

PART 1

THE WORLD'S GREATEST DEMOCRACY

*"The world's greatest democracy fought
the world's greatest racist with a segregated army."*

STEPHEN AMBROSE[1]

CHAPTER 1

A QUIET FOREST

Snow falls from a tree branch in an odd, unnatural way. Sergeant Aubrey Stewart notices the slight movement in the trees on the edge of the Ardennes, the dark, almost mythical forest stretching out before him, miles into enemy territory. He shivers as he stands in snow, wearing worn-out boots and last summer's uniform, squinting his eyes, straining to peer through the heavy fog.

Nothing's happening at the "ghost front."

Sergeant Stewart and the black GIs of the 333rd Field Artillery Battalion, stationed at the Siegfried Line, are restless and bored as they wait for the war to end. For months, they have guarded the quiet Belgian-German border, Allied and Axis front lines separated by concrete dragon teeth, barbed wire, and land mines.

Stewart lifts his eyes when he sees another movement in the trees. Suddenly the predawn sky lights up with fireworks! Rockets from German Nebelwerfers scream as they sail from the east, exploding in treetops, shattering large branches, and sending the sharp, stabbing spears down onto the GIs. The 333rd artillerymen load the mighty 155mm howitzers, positioning them east toward the Ardennes, and launch deadly shells miles into the foggy distance. All morning, all day, and all night, the Germans' "Screaming Meemies" and mortars pockmark their campgrounds, wounding and killing the men of Able, Baker, Charley, and Service Batteries stationed near the front lines.

Early the next morning, the GIs are hurt, hungry, and exhausted from their nonstop firing. Their ammunition is almost gone. They don't know how much longer they can hold out. Suddenly, as if in a surreal dream, thousands of Germans clad in white winter gear run toward them, screaming as they burst through the fog-shrouded forests.

"We're under attack!" Stewart shouts to his comrades.

Before his eyes, streams of enemy soldiers emerge, attacking like feral animals, their eyes wide and wild, faces grotesquely distorted, yelling with an otherworldly, fanatical fury. They strike, setting up MG-42 machine guns, firing on the artillerymen and mowing them down.

Stewart bends over, grabs a wounded man, and hoists him onto his shoulders. As he bolts across the campground, he hears the sickening thud of a bullet slam into the skull of the man he carries. He feels the man's body jerk and then go limp. Blood trickles down his neck from the hole in the GI's head. Darting behind a tree, Stewart lays the lifeless soldier on the ground, the man's eyes open and fixed, brow and face bloody.

In a nearby foxhole, a GI stands up. His body is ripped in two by automatic weapon fire. Shells and mortar fragments sail overhead, exploding and sending shrapnel into men's bodies. Private Curtis Adams, the 333rd's medic, races from one fallen soldier to the next. Some he can help; others are already gone, blown apart, their body parts scattered on the ground.

Around Stewart are fellow GIs, caught unawares by the unexpected ambush, lying facedown, their arms and legs sprawled out on the icy ground.

Some are lifeless; others moan in pain, bleeding profusely. The mighty 155mm howitzers—the pride and firepower of the 333rd—sit eerily still and silent in the falling snow. Depleted of ammunition, their massive barrels and powerful shells are useless with the enemy so near.

Sergeant Thomas Forte, Private George Davis, and other GIs grab the few rifles and carbines available and fire until the ammunition runs out. The enemy continues to pour from the forests like water flowing from an endless fountain. Sergeant George Shomo finds a trench knife, then attacks, stabbing and killing two Germans. The 333rd, their ammunition gone, fight well-armed Germans in hand-to-hand combat, leaving both wounded and dead on the Ghost Front's battlefield.

Stewart, Forte, Davis, Adams, and the surviving GIs grab injured comrades and race to the waiting trucks at the corner of the campground. The drivers gun their engines as the GIs scamper into the backs of the trucks.

"Go! Go! Go!" they shout to the drivers.

German soldiers follow them to the trucks, shooting at them, grabbing arms and legs, and trying to pull them out. The drivers flatten the trucks' accelerators, and with tires spinning on the icy road, they race toward the Our River Bridge.

CHAPTER 2

THE BERLIN OLYMPICS

—BERLIN, GERMANY—
AUGUST 1, 1936

For the past two years, Berlin has dealt with torn-up streets and buildings wreathed in scaffolding as it prepares for the Olympic Games taking place in this city. Now, in the summer of 1936, the work is finally finished. The Germans stand back and admire their scrubbed and scoured city, decked out with newly planted trees and flowers and illuminated with rows of electric lights. They eagerly await the arrival of one hundred thousand visitors from around the world.[1]

The awarding of the XI Olympic Games to Germany, a benevolent decision made in May 1931 by the International Olympic Committee, has caused considerable international controversy. The world is aware of Nazi abuse of Jews and others they deem "racially undesirable." Most German Jewish athletes are excluded from Germany's sports and recreational facilities, having been expelled for racial reasons.

The IOC's invitation to Berlin comes as a goodwill gesture meant to publicly welcome Germany back into the world community after her humiliating defeat eighteen years before in the Great War. But Hitler cares little about sports, including hosting the prestigious Olympics.

"I do not want to have the games here," he tells Propaganda Minister Joseph Goebbels in 1931.

But the wily Goebbels convinces him to accept the award for Germany's sake.

"My Führer, we can showcase our 'new Germany' at the Berlin Olympics, demonstrating international goodwill, and perhaps changing the opinions of those who so strongly oppose us. It will give us an unrivaled opportunity to end all foreign prejudice against our Vaterland.[2] And just think of the money the event will bring when one hundred thousand internationals arrive in Berlin."

Hitler frowns, agreeing reluctantly to host the event.

"If nothing else," Hitler says, "perhaps the games will be a good opportunity to show off our Aryan athletes, demonstrating to the world their racial superiority."

After Germany makes the formal commitment to host the Berlin Olympics, Hitler's administration begins building a 325-acre sports complex 5 miles west of Berlin. The all-natural stone stadium seats 110,000 sports fans and costs the Reich a whopping 42 million Reichsmarks.

Not everyone favors choosing Berlin as the Olympic site. As late as November 1935, Hitler learns that Ernest Lee Jahncke, an American member of the International Olympic Committee (IOC), opposes the location.

"Neither Americans, nor the representatives of other countries, can take part in the games in Nazi Germany without, at least, acquiescing in the contempt of the Nazis for fair play and their sordid exploitation of the games," Jahncke writes to the International Olympic Committee.[3]

Shortly thereafter, the IOC expels Jahncke from the committee.

CHAPTER 3

THE BANNING

—BERLIN, GERMANY—
SUMMER 1936

As the opening day of the 1936 Olympic Games draws near, Hitler orders Berlin shopkeepers to remove racially discriminating signs and slogans from store windows. He also transports "undesirable" people from the city's streets. With open arms, Berlin waits for the hordes of international crowds to pour into their city, ready to welcome them with red-carpet enthusiasm, brown-shirted bands, lavish receptions, and a profusion of Olympic flags displayed beside swastika-emblazoned flags.

With few exceptions, Hitler bans Germany's non-Aryans from participating in the games, including Jewish athletes, Gypsies, people of color, and all those considered racially inferior, blatantly violating Olympic codes of participation equality. Because of this, Hitler learns that some nations will boycott the games. He clenches his teeth, loudly cursing each country that dares to boycott the Fatherland. After some time, however, most of the world decides to participate, including the United States.

At the end of July, Hitler welcomes the U.S. Olympic team: 312 athletes, including 18 African-Americans and 5 Jews.

When the International Olympic Committee officials demand that the Führer embrace black and Jewish participants, he narrows his eyes, begrudgingly assuring the committee: "Germany will treat the Negro athletes agreeably while they are here. And we will allow the *foreign* Jewish athletes to participate as well."

Hitler is angered when he learns that many of the world's Jewish athletes will boycott the competition, publicly displaying their disapproval and distaste for Hitler and his anti-Semitism. Most U.S. black athletes, however, decide to participate, arguing that their athletic victories will undermine Nazi Germany's myth of Aryan supremacy and, at the same time, foster a new sense of black pride at home.

Dark clouds form overhead when, on August 1, 1936, more than five thousand athletes from fifty-one nations march into Hitler's new stadium on the opening day of the Berlin Summer Olympic Games. Adolf Hitler, his head held high, leads Olympic and German officials, as well as prestigious international guests, to prominent stadium seats while three thousand Germans sing proudly the "Deutschland Über Alles" national anthem. In respect for their Führer, thousands of loyal Germans crowd the stadium, standing, thrusting their right arms forward in the Hitler salute, and shouting "Heil, Hitler."

The *Hindenburg* airship flies low over the stadium as Hitler stands and officially announces: "I proclaim the Games of Berlin, celebrating the eleventh Olympiad of the modern era, to be open!" The crowds roar with enthusiasm. Richard Strauss's "Olympic Hymn" plays triumphantly on loudspeakers throughout the stadium.

The Führer sits stiffly, his hands balled into fists, as he watches American track star Jesse Owens win multiple awards. "America's Black Auxiliaries," he calls the eighteen African-Americans who participate, as if they were second-class team members. German journalists refer to Owens as the "Negro Owens," the son of an Alabama sharecropper, and the grandson of a former slave. With each medal Owens wins, Hitler pouts, angry that the black Alabama-born athlete is publicly debunking his Aryan myth.

"And what is your reaction to this?" Hitler asks Joseph Goebbels.

"My Führer," Goebbels says, shaking his head in disapproval, "the victories by America's African-Americans [are] a disgrace."

Jesse Owens garners one medal after another, setting a new world record in the long jump and becoming an instant superstar in Germany. Fans chant his name when he walks into the stadium, and stop him in the streets begging for his autograph.

Near the end of the games, a reporter for the *New York Times* writes:

"One almost certain Negro champion [at the Berlin Olympics] seems to be Jesse Owens. 'Buckeye Bullet' strode through his 100-meter first-round heat . . . without pressing himself in the slightest degree [and] equaled the world and Olympic record of 0:10.3. . . . Victory for him tomorrow in the final seems to be his merely for the asking."[1]

But, unlike the white medal-winning athletes, the black U.S. Olympic star never has the opportunity to meet the Führer in person. Purposely ignoring expected Olympic protocol, Hitler storms out of the stadium after Owens's final win, refusing to personally receive him or the other award-winning black athletes.

"Hitler refused to shake Jesse Owens's hand or congratulate other black medalists," a reporter states in the *Baltimore Afro-American* newspaper.[2]

Almost five thousand miles away, Jesse Owens's wins make black people proud, especially one eighteen-year-old, Lil' Georgie Davis, a native of Bessemer, Alabama.[3]

CHAPTER 4

A WALL OF PHOTOGRAPHS

Davis and his only son, Lil' Georgie, sit in the front room of their small Bessemer house on the eve of Georgie's eighteenth birthday. Georgie clips a photograph of 1936 Olympic star Jesse Owens from the *Bessemer Herald*. In the picture, Owens is dashing across the Berlin Olympic finish line, winning the hundred-meter quarterfinal. Georgie pins Owens's snapshot on the front room wall that displays the Davis family photographs.

"He's gotta be the greatest athlete in the world," Georgie says, beaming with pride. "Daddy! Can you believe Jesse Owens won *four* Olympic gold medals?!"

"That Owens boy makes us black Alabamians proud," Davis says. "Guess he showed that Hitler monster a thing or two about colored athletes." He smiles, slapping his knee. "Wish I could've been a fly on Hitler's head when Jesse beat all those Krauts!"

The Davises, like other Alabama families still suffering the effects of the Great Depression, need some encouraging news. The nation's sudden economic collapse back in 1929 hit Alabama especially hard. Davis and his family, like other poor blacks in the southern United States, still endure Depression-caused poverty and find no relief in sight.

"Lil' Georgie," his father says, "it's good to see a poor sharecropper's son do so good in sports. I know his daddy's proud of him."

He points to the photographs of distant family members hanging on the wall. "His people, like ours, worked long, exhausting days. The Owens men worked the farms while our family's men toiled in Birmingham's coal and steel plants and on railroads. Not been easy for any of us, Lil' Georgie. We're still struggling to keep a roof over our heads. But it's good that the Owens boy's done so well."

"I'm gonna do good, too," Georgie says, grinning. "One day you're gonna be so proud of me."

"I'll always be proud of you, son, no matter what you do—or don't do. You've got nothing to prove to me."

That afternoon, alone in the front room, Davis reflects on his past, his family, and his son, Lil' Georgie.

I tried so hard to make sure Lil' Georgie got a good education, unlike most Alabama colored boys. At least my boy has three years of high school under his belt.

Even now, in 1936, Davis knows that education for Alabama's black kids is dismal, taking place in windowless schoolhouse shacks with dirt floors, heated by old coal stoves. In the early part of the century, when Davis was a boy, Bessemer parents "graduated" their children out of grammar school and put them straight into Alabama's pig iron factories. Every able-bodied person, no matter how young or old, was needed to help put food on the family table.[1]

Davis glances at the wall's photograph of Georgie on his first day of school. He's smiling big, ears clean, hair cut and combed, and wearing a crisp grade school uniform, a red plaid satchel held tightly in his hand.

You've been blessed, Lil' Georgie, to get educated. Few poor boys are so lucky.

Davis wanted his son to get a good education. Some of the more fortunate black children around Birmingham got to attend the better schools built and run by the Tennessee Coal, Iron, and Railroad

Company (TCI). But Davis didn't work at TCI, so Lil' Georgie wasn't eligible to attend. Davis looks to the ceiling and smiles. *Thank you, Lord, and thank you, Mr. Rosenwald.*

Davis had had the opportunity to enroll Georgie in one of the Rosenwald schools, built and funded by Illinois-born philanthropist Julius Rosenwald, the first president of Sears, Roebuck and Company. Out of the goodness of his heart, Mr. Rosenwald set up more than five thousand special schools for poor black children in the South's hard-hit rural areas.[2]

Davis looks down at his hands, rough and scarred from the intense heat of blast furnaces, a result of working year after year at steelmaking plants, converting iron ore, limestone, and coal into scalding liquid iron and casting it into pig iron.

The "Bessemer process," they called it. He rubs his knotted knuckles. *Ruined my hands, as well as my youth.*

He reflects on his childhood, a time of poverty, hunger, racism, and harshly enforced Jim Crow laws.

Not much has changed since then.

He tried hard to teach his small, innocent son to obey the segregation rules so brutally enforced in Bessemer, often warning him: "Lil' Georgie, use only the toilets and water fountains marked 'Colored,' and step off the sidewalks when a white person walks by. Stop and let 'em pass first."

"Why do I have to do that, Daddy?" Georgie had asked.

Davis recalls how his heart hurt when he tried to answer his son's question.

"Just do what I say, Lil' Georgie. Hear me? Don't ask questions. It's just the way things are."

He'd tried to explain to Georgie why he couldn't check out books from the Bessemer Public Library, or go to the moving picture shows in the town's theater, or shop for shoes in white-run department stores. He'd tried to explain why only black barbers could cut his son's hair, only black nurses could set his broken bones, and only white kids could swim in Bessemer's public pools. And he tried to explain why Georgie's baseball team had to play on dump-site vacant lots out of eyesight of the white boys' public ball fields.

Some things are hard to explain to a kid. Sometimes near impossible.

Even now Davis hates sitting in the backs of city buses. It hurts him even more to watch his wife and son forced to the bus's rear, or standing during a long bumpy ride when front seats are filled and a white person demands their back seats. But, even so, he keeps his mouth shut, and he obeys the unfair laws. But, at home, in curtain-closed private, he fumes aloud, pounding his fists on the arms of his chair.

Now that Georgie is a man, Davis worries about his son's adventurous personality, his playful innocence, his boyish immaturity, and his reckless, compulsive behavior. He has told him many times: "Son, I know you like girls, but you're eighteen years old now—a grown man. You can flirt with *colored* girls, but stay away from *white* girls. They're trouble."

Davis squeezes his eyes shut and shakes his head:

Oh, please, Lil' Georgie, don't look at them, don't talk to them, and for sure don't touch them, not even by accident. Colored men've been lynched for less.

Davis opens his eyes and looks at the newspaper picture of Jesse Owens on the family room wall. He recalls his son's promise to him: "One day you're gonna be proud of me, too, Daddy, just like Jesse made his father proud."

I am proud of you, Georgie. You're my only son, and you are precious to me.

CHAPTER 5

LEBENSRAUM

—BERLIN, GERMANY—
NOVEMBER 5, 1937

In September 1933, Germany's new leader promised the world, "We have declared a hundred times that we do not wish war with the rest of the world, nor do we want to incorporate anything that is alien to us. . . ."[1]

Four years later, on November 5, 1937, Hitler sits in the Reich Chancellery surrounded by his military and foreign policy leaders.[2]

"I have called this meeting," Hitler says, "because I have received complaints from Admiral Raeder that the Kriegsmarine is not receiving sufficient allocations of steel and other raw materials. I need not tell you that this lack of material threatens the entire Kriegsmarine building program."

"The program is in danger of total collapse," Admiral Raeder adds, nodding in agreement. "Neither the Luftwaffe nor the army is willing to decrease its steel allocations so that we might receive even minimal requirements."

"Without a strong Kriegsmarine, an even bigger problem faces us," Hitler says, swearing loudly. "Don't you understand? Germany has reached a crisis. Unless we wish a drastic fall in living standards, Germany must embark on a policy of aggression to provide sufficient Lebensraum. We desperately need more living space for future development."

"How do you plan to carry out this *policy of aggression*?" Field Marshal Blomberg asks.

Hitler's face reddens. He jumps from his chair. "We must seize Austria and Czechoslovakia! To secure and preserve the racial community, we must enlarge it." He begins to pace the floor, his movements jerky, cursing under his breath. "It's a matter of space for our eighty-five million people! That aggression may trigger war with the British and the French in the next five years or so, but to save the *Volksmasse*, we must seize Eastern Europe!"

"My Führer," Blomberg says, "the foreign policy you outline is far too risky. We need more time to rearm Germany before waging war, especially with *powerful* countries like Britain and France against us."

"I . . . I must agree with Field Marshal Blomberg," General von Fritsch says timidly. "My Führer, please understand that German aggression in Eastern Europe will likely mean war with France. You and I both know that Britain and France must not appear in the roles of our enemies."

"General von Fritsch is correct," Baron von Neurath interjects. "In a war between Germany and France, Britain will most certainly intervene. We are not at all ready for war on this scale."

Hitler is silent, beads of sweat popping out on his forehead.

"We have no *moral* objections to your strategy, my Führer," Blomberg says. "We are simply questioning the timing and wisdom of our imminent aggression."

"This is urgent!" Hitler shouts, pounding his fist on the table. "You can consider this policy my last will and testament! We must have more funds released for Germany's rearmament, and add Austria, Czechoslovakia, Lithuania, and Poland to the Reich." He rubs the back of his neck, sitting down in his chair. "We must go to war sooner rather than later."

"But, my Führer—"

Hitler stands, making no eye contact with anyone. "This meeting is over!" he states, and swears. "And each of you understands, of course, that you are sworn to secrecy regarding this matter!"

The men stand and salute the Führer, each nodding and affirming his personal loyalty and secrecy.

Hitler turns sharply, leaving the room. "Commander Göring, I must see you privately."

"Commander," Hitler tells Göring in a back room, "Blomberg, Fritsch, and Neurath must be removed. Immediately. And, in the near future, Raeder must be replaced as naval commander.

"We must silence these squabbling military commanders," Hitler continues. "The primary reason for this meeting was to pressure General von Fritsch to rearm the army. I am extremely dissatisfied with our rearmament progress. Very dissatisfied!"[3]

"Yes, my Führer," Göring says, saluting.[4]

CHAPTER 6

THE BASEBALL PITCHER
FROM PIEDMONT

"Can't believe our youngest boy is thirty-one years old tomorrow," James Stewart tells his wife, Emma, as they dress for Sunday morning worship service at the Waldon M.E. Church near their Erin Street home.

"At his age, he ought to be settling down with a wife and a bunch of children," Emma says. "Don't know why that boy doesn't get married and give us some grandchildren."

"He doesn't have time to be married and raising children, Emma. When he's not working at the paper mill, he's playing baseball with the Piedmont Giants."

"Aubrey can sure pitch," Emma says, smiling. "He throws better with his left arm than most pitchers throw with their right arm."

"Yep!" James says. "If Negro Leagues keep doing so well, one day the major leagues'll open their doors to them."

James and Emma Stewart's son, James Aubrey, ambitious and well liked, was born in the coal mining town of Piedmont, West Virginia, located at the foot of the Allegheny Front, the eastern edge of the Appalachian Plateau. Graduating from Piedmont's Howard High

School, he found a job at the local Westvaco Paper Mill, where he and his friends went to work after graduation.

The Stewarts are delighted their son works so hard and excels in athletics. Years earlier, they encouraged him to join the Piedmont Giants Negro baseball team. The Giants often play other local all-black teams, including the Moorefield Black Sox, the Frostburg Colored Federals, and the Cumberland Hurricanes.[1] Aubrey's friendly, engaging personality, plus his obvious pitching skills, brings him many friends and much respect.

"Don't you worry about Aubrey, Emma. He's ambitious. He'll find the right girl one day and settle down. I've got big dreams for our boy's future."

"So do I, James! So do I."

CHAPTER 7

THE MEETING
AT BERCHTESGADEN

— BAVARIAN ALPS —
FEBRUARY 12, 1938

On the cold morning of February 12, 1938, the chancellor of Austria, Dr. Kurt von Schuschnigg, meets with Hitler at Berchtesgaden, the Führer's fortified mountaintop retreat located high in the Bavarian Alps. Schuschnigg thinks the meeting will be private, and he is surprised when joined by some of Hitler's officials.[1]

"What a gorgeous view of the Alps and Austria," Chancellor von Schuschnigg says, smiling as he gazes out a plate-glass window from the second floor.

"We did not gather here to speak of the fine view!" Hitler snaps.

The chancellor catches his breath, surprised at Hitler's rude response. "Herr Hitler, I meant nothing impolite about—"

Hitler turns toward the chancellor, stepping within inches of his face.

"You have done everything you can to avoid a friendly policy!" Hitler yells at him, his eyes cold and glaring. "The whole history of Austria is just one uninterrupted act of high treason. And I can tell you right now, I am absolutely determined to make an end of this."

Schuschnigg takes a deep breath. "But, Herr Hitler—"

"The German Reich is one of the *great* powers," Hitler interrupts. "And nobody will object if we settle our border problems."

The chancellor looks directly into Hitler's eyes, staring hard for the next few seconds. *I will not allow Hitler to intimidate me, no matter how hard he tries!*

"I understood you to say four years ago," Schuschnigg says, "that Germany has no thought whatever of any aggressive act toward Austria and—"[2]

"Things have changed, Chancellor von Schuschnigg."

"In that case," the chancellor says, "we will do everything we can do to remove obstacles to a better understanding, as far as it is possible."

The Führer's nostrils flare and he swears. "I am going to solve the so-called Austrian problem one way or the other. Providence has destined me to do so. I have only to give an order, and all your ridiculous defense mechanisms will be blown to bits."

Without allowing the chancellor to respond, Hitler continues his cursing rant. "You don't seriously believe you can stop me, or even delay me for half an hour, do you? Don't think for one moment that anybody on earth is going to thwart my decisions!"

Hitler turns to his foreign minister, Joachim von Ribbentrop. "Give him the document!"

The foreign minister hands Schuschnigg a two-page document listing Hitler's demands, including the assimilation of Austria's entire economy into the German Reich.

"Sign the document immediately, or else," Ribbentrop threatens von Schuschnigg.

With trembling hands, the chancellor takes the document, scanning the papers and frowning. "I will consider signing it after I read it more carefully and understand what it is you are asking of Austria."

Hitler points his finger in Schuschnigg's face. "Chancellor, you will either sign it . . . and fulfill my demands within three days, or I will order the march into Austria."

Ribbentrop places a pen in the chancellor's hand. "Sign it," he orders.

Schuschnigg feels nauseated. He swallows hard. *If I do not sign this document right now, Hitler may not let me leave alive.*

He rubs his clammy hand on his coat and signs his name on the document.

"You will take this document to your president, Wilhelm Miklas, and make him cosign the agreement," Hitler tells him.

President Miklas will never agree to this outrageous aggression!

Without saying another word, Chancellor von Schuschnigg leaves Berchtesgaden, document in hand, feeling relieved to be alive and out of Hitler's presence.

When Schuschnigg returns to Austria, the Austrian president refuses to accept Hitler's demands.

"I will not sign this ridiculous agreement!" Miklas shouts. But later, he, too, intimidated by Hitler's threats, signs it.

In mid-February 1938, Schuschnigg promises Austrian Jews that in his government, they will have nothing to fear from Nazi influence. Minister of the Interior Dr. Arthur Seyss-Inquart agrees, reassuring the people that Austria will undergo no further changes.[3]

CHAPTER 8

INVASION!

—AUSTRIA—
MARCH 12, 1938

Hitler bounces out of bed before dawn, his heart racing. At daylight his troops will march into Austria, annexing the independent state into the Third Reich. He waits breathlessly to hear the initial reports of his invading armies.

"We have crossed the German-Austrian border with tanks and armored vehicles," the first report reads. "We have met little resistance. Some Austrians are even welcoming us, excited to join the new Germany."

Hitler dresses quickly and travels to his Austrian birthplace, Braunau am Inn. He visits his boyhood home in Linz. Traveling to Leonding, he lays a fresh wreath on his parents' graves.

He feels newly energized now to completely control his home country.

"If Providence once called me forth from this town to be the leader of the Reich," he tells his generals, "it must in doing so have charged me with a mission, and that mission could only be to restore my dear homeland to the German Reich."

After his armies enter Austria, Hitler half expects Britain and France to step in and stop the invasion. But, to his surprise and great pleasure, they do nothing. On Sunday, March 13, Hitler's law demanding Germany's union with Austria is approved. Austria no longer exists.

After conquering Austria, Hitler begins to make life more difficult for Germany's Jews under his Nazi rule. One in every four of the 150,000 Jews in Germany flees the country. After invading Austria, Germany gains 185,000 additional Jews. While most Jews make an effort to leave Germany, few of the world's countries will allow them to enter. Americans fear an influx of refugees will take the scarce jobs held by Americans, as well as overburden social programs.

Hitler reads an article in the *New York Times* by a reporter who addresses the refugee dilemma: "The immensity of the refugee problem was emphasized again today by an official estimate that 660,900 persons now in Germany and Austria must find homes in other countries with the least possible delay."[1]

Hitler smirks, remarking to his general, "I find it astounding that foreign countries so harshly criticize Germany for our treatment of the Jews, but none of them wants to open their doors to them."[2]

Upon learning of Germany's violent treatment of Jews, President Franklin D. Roosevelt calls for an international conference in France to discuss the disturbing problem.

In July 1938 the French resort of Evian-les-Bains welcomes Roosevelt, as well as delegates from thirty-two countries. They meet to discuss the Jewish refugee problem and to decide what to do about it. But they come up with few solutions, the leaders citing all the reasons why they themselves cannot allow Jewish refugees into their individual countries.

During this Evian Conference, with few decisions made, Roosevelt and the world's officials establish the Intergovernmental Committee on Refugees (ICR) to continue to work on the growing problem. When the conference ends a week later, only one country, the tiny Dominican Republic, agrees to accept Germany's Jews.[3]

CHAPTER 9

THE BELGIAN FAMILY

At home in the small farming hamlet of Wereth, Belgium, Mathias and Maria Langer listen in terror to the news told to them by Jewish friends in Austria.

"Those poor people!" Mathias exclaims, his face ashen. "I cannot believe that Hitler has stolen Austria before the eyes of the world! And that nobody has stopped him!"

"By doing so, he is breaking the Treaty of Versailles," Maria says.

"Yes, Maria. He is also rearming Germany to the teeth. Surely no one in Europe is safe from him and his Nazis."

Maria takes a deep breath and begins to cry. "The children, Mathias. What will happen to our *Kinder*?"

The Langers have eight young children in their home, ranging in age from one to thirteen. "What is to keep Hitler from invading and conquering Belgium, too, Mathias?"

"Many of our neighbors will wish for that to happen, Maria. They still hold deep German loyalties, admitting they will welcome and support the Germans."

As mayor of Wereth, Mathias grows more concerned with each day for his family, friends, and villagers as he watches the Germans escalate their abuse of Jews.

"They are humiliating, torturing, and destroying the people in their society whom they consider 'undesirable,'" he says. "Hitler has invalidated Jewish citizens' passports and is making strict new rules for their travel and emigration."

"I hear he has stolen Jewish property, Mathias, and is enforcing new regulations on the people."

"Has the entire world gone insane?" Mathias asks, shaking his head in disbelief.

Maria gathers her young children around her, holding them tightly. "What will we do, Mathias, if Hitler invades Belgium?"

"We will try to survive, Maria, protect our *Kinder*, and help Belgium's victims where and when we can."

In November, the Langers hear that anti-Jewish sentiment and violence has culminated into an event called *Kristallnacht* ("Night of Broken Glass").

"The Nazi regime has murdered ninety-one Jews and burned more than fourteen hundred synagogues across Germany," Mathias tells his wife. "Jewish-owned businesses have been robbed and destroyed. The Germans are blaming thirty thousand Jewish men for the violence. They have been arrested and sent to Hitler's prison camps."

Maria begins to cry, reaching to her neck, grasping and holding the small silver crucifix she wears on a chain, praying a silent prayer for her family's protection.

"I hear that three hundred thousand Jews are leaving Germany, trying to emigrate to the few safe places in the world that will allow them entrance," Mathias says. "And I fear it will only get worse."

"How will they survive this cruel abuse?" Maria asks. "I worry about our children's lives, Mathias, as well as our own."

"Do not worry, Maria. We are Catholic, not Jewish. Even if Hitler's armies invade Belgium, we will not be harmed. But I am concerned about our Jewish friends. Only God knows what will happen to them."

Late that evening, before Mathias and Maria tuck their children in for the night, they join hands at the feet of their beds, praying to St. Michael for protection.

". . . obtain for us from God a share of Thy sturdy courage. . . ."

"Are we in danger, Mama?" six-year-old Hermann asks, placing his small hand on his mother's hand.

"Do not worry, my dear Hermann," Maria tells him. "We will pray together daily for protection."[1]

In the United States, *Time* magazine chooses Adolf Hitler as its "1938 Person of the Year," posting his picture on the front cover of the January 2, 1939, issue. *Time* states boldly that Adolf Hitler wins this prestigious award because he is the public figure that has had the most effect on world affairs in 1938.[2]

The Third Reich's racial tension continues to increase with the Führer taking away the basic rights of those he deems "inferior races." He requires Germany's Jews to wear armbands identifying them as *Juden*, makes them register their wealth and assets, and forces them to live in ghettos and labor camps. He orders Jewish business owners to stop operating retail stores, dealing in trade, and providing goods or services, requiring most of them to sell their businesses at below market value prices. He bans Jewish children from the public schools, forcing them to attend segregated schools run solely by Jewish communities. Not long after, the government prohibits Jews from working as dentists, nurses, and veterinarians. Hitler determines that Germany shall be *Judenfrei* (Jew free).

Adolf Hitler, having become the Führer of the German people; commander in chief of the German Army, Navy, and Air Force; chancellor of the Third Reich; and *Time*'s "Man of the Year," tears the Treaty of Versailles to shreds right before the world's eyes, threatening world war and redrawing the map of Europe.

CHAPTER 10

THE WAR BEGINS

In September 1939, a *New York Times* reporter writes:

"The hours before dawn . . . saw the outbreak of Europe's second great war since 1914. At Adolf Hitler's command, German troops and planes crossed the Polish border. Two days later, in an attempt to stop Hitler from dominating Europe, Britain and France entered the struggle. By the end of the month, however, Poland was overrun and partitioned between Germany and Russia, and the world had had its first taste of a Blitzkrieg."[1]

On September 1, 1939, Hitler's unstoppable armies surge into Poland. Blitzkrieg becomes his signature attack, combined with extensive bombing that destroys the enemy's air capacity, rail system, communications, and munitions dumps. The German infantry then moves in, destroying everything in sight, silencing any remaining resistance. The Führer sends his highly feared SS "Death's Head" regiments to terrorize the country's civilians. He builds concentration camps to enslave and exterminate all opposition.

The Polish Army, whose military forces are antiquated—with some cavalry still carrying lances—proves no match for Hitler's modern mechanized panzers. Poland collapses within weeks. Great Britain and France declare war on Germany.

Meanwhile, the Nazi newspaper, *Der Stürmer*, focuses on racial rather than military goals: "The Jewish people ought to be exterminated root and branch. Then the plague of pests would have disappeared in Poland at one stroke."[2, 3, 4]

Hitler's aggression continues unchecked. On May 10, 1940, he attacks Holland, Belgium, and France. German armor and infantry plow through the dense Ardennes Forest, his armies pushing north, surprising the Allies, who believe it impossible to enter Belgium through the thick, almost impassable woods.

Hitler knows that memories are short. The Germans came the same way in ambush in 1870 and 1914.[5]

Mathias Langer tenses on hearing that Germans have invaded his cherished homeland. The Belgian and French governments, warned that this might happen, failed to take Germany's threat seriously. Much time had passed since Hitler conquered Poland, and all had been quiet in the west.

Hearing of the invasion, Mathias's wife, Maria, collapses. He helps her to a chair and then hurries outside to gather his children.

"*Hilf mir!* Quickly! Help me!" he calls to Tina, who is working with livestock in the large cow pasture a short distance from their house.

"Find *unsere Kinder*, and bring them inside. Quickly!"

Tina and her younger brother, Hermann, gather the frightened children into the house, locking the door. The baby, eleven-month-old Therese, senses something is amiss and begins to cry. Papa takes the baby in his arms, kissing and rocking her back and forth until she quiets.

"Papa," Hermann asks, "what is wrong?"

The rest of his children gather around him and listen.

"The Germans have invaded our country," he says, "as well as the Netherlands and Luxembourg. No one thought it would happen."

"But we are a neutral country, Papa," Tina says.

"Yes, we are neutral, Tina. But that means nothing to the Germans. But do not worry, my *Kinder*. God will protect us."

The Langers' worst fears have come to fruition. The madman has violated Belgian soil.

W hen the Germans invade, Belgium's military is sorely unprepared to defend its homeland. The Belgian Army, deployed along the French and German frontiers, lacks enough muscle to stop Hitler's assault. They are overpowered by Germany's new strength—attack by air. While Belgian troops wait on the ground, German airborne forces, with freight-carrying gliders, land near the Meuse River. General von Reichenau's Sixth Army successfully disables the guns of Belgium's twelve hundred armed troops, taking hundreds of Belgian prisoners and seizing the two key bridges. In a stunning move, German air forces land on top of the impregnable fortress, Eben Emael, dropping explosives through the roof and quickly silencing all resistance.[6]

The Allies fight hard, but Wehrmacht forces encircle and defeat them, cutting lines of communication and crossing the Meuse River defense line. In just ten days, the Germans drive the reeling Allies into the sea at Dunkirk. Hitler now controls all access to the English Channel and the Atlantic Coast. Belgium surrenders on May 28. Germany demands the immediate abdication of King Léopold III.[7]

T he United States and other nations rebuke Hitler's actions. On the day following the invasion, the *New York Times* announces:

"The envoys of the Netherlands and Belgium today condemned in scorching terms what they declared to be the unprovoked German attack upon their peaceful countries . . . despite the official German pledge of October 13, 1937, to respect the inviolability and integrity of Belgium."[8]

By June 17, 1940, the world has witnessed Poland's occupation, followed by Denmark, Norway, Holland, Belgium, and France succumbing to German armies. Nazi forces prepare further invasions, Hitler's dreams of conquest coming true.

CHAPTER 11

THE BAKER'S SON AND
THE BUTCHER'S APPRENTICE

— FRANCE —
JUNE 1940

The future SS-Sturmbannführer Gustav Knittel lies on a bloody French battlefield, awaiting rescue, his leg severely wounded. Son of a Bavarian baker in Neu-Ulm, born during the early days of the Great War, Knittel has impressed Hitler with his bravery and leadership. Since childhood, Knittel has dreamed of a military career, joining the Nazi Party on May 1, 1933, at age nineteen. He has served loyally with various SS units, becoming adjutant of SS Reserve Battalion Ellwangen in August 1939.

Shortly before the invasion of France, Knittel was transferred to the famed First SS Fifteenth Motorcycle Company of the Leibstandarte, and awarded the Iron Cross Second Class for action in combat at Wormhoudt and Bollezeele. But while leading the attack on the small wine-producing village Saint Pourçain-sur-Sioule, he is wounded.

When medics find him, they transport Knittel to a field hospital in Troyes and then move him to the SS hospital in Hohenlychen, Germany. For his service, he is awarded Germany's Infantry Assault Badge and the Wound Badge in Black.[1]

On May 28, 1940, his forty-eighth birthday, while inspecting the Second Battalion in Wormhoudt, Joseph "Sepp" Dietrich and his companion Obersturmführer Max Wunsche come under a storm of heavy machine-gun fire from British troops in the Gloucestershire Regiment. Diving beneath their burning Mercedes, they try to shield themselves from the violent weapon assault.

Pop! Pop! Pop! Pop! Pop!

As British troops approach the vehicle, Dietrich and Wunsche roll into the muddy drainage ditch on the side of the road.

"The petrol!" Dietrich shouts as he watches the car's fuel tank ignite, sending a trail of flaming petrol into the ditch.

"Cover yourself with mud!" Dietrich calls. The men slather themselves with the wet sludge, protecting their skin and clothing from the flames.

From the distance, Dietrich sees elements of the Second Panzer Brigade coming toward the Gloucestershire Regiment, firing weapons and overtaking British troops. Within minutes, both men are rescued.[2]

While on the outskirts of Wormhoudt, Sepp Dietrich captures eighty or ninety Allied prisoners and marches them to a barn. On the way, his men thrust bayonets into prisoners, later shooting the survivors in groups of five.[3] Dietrich is savage, brutal, and admired by many soldiers, including Adolf Hitler.

On July 5, 1940, Dietrich receives personally from Hitler the Knight's Cross of the Iron Cross for his distinguished service in mercilessly driving the Allies to Dunkirk. It is Germany's highest award, given for courage in conquering France.[4]

Dietrich, like Knittel, is proud of the way his SS units have performed during the French Campaign, pushing westward to the sea, battling the Allies, and sweeping aside hordes of fleeing civilians.

An old Nazi hand and Hitler's favorite general, Dietrich proves his total allegiance to the Führer when on August 1, 1928 he joins the

SS and is appointed an officer at the party's national headquarters in Munich. As Hitler rapidly gains power in Germany, he taps Dietrich to command his personal bodyguard, the Stosstrupp Adolf Hitler (Shock Troops of Adolf Hitler).

After the French Campaign, Dietrich, the former butcher's apprentice, rises quickly in SS ranks, eventually attaining the rank of general der Waffen-SS. The general becomes part of Hitler's inner circle, one of his closest and most trusted associates. He accompanies the Führer on outings and engagements, lunching, dining, and spending time talking with him during late-night meetings.

"I can express my opinions and views to the Führer," Dietrich brags to others. "He listens to me when he listens to few others."[5]

Sepp Dietrich is infuriated, however, when Great Britain resists Hitler's attack in July 1940. He watches the British grit their teeth, unite, and bravely resist the Blitzkrieg bombing of their island home. German bombers and fighters sustain heavy casualties. Germany's navy is no match for the British, and the English Channel proves to be an insuperable natural barrier. Hitler postpones his intended invasion of Britain, Operation Sea Lion, on September 17, 1940. It proves a first significant defeat for the Führer.[6]

SS-Obersturmbannführer Joachim Peiper is also a member of the elite Leibstandarte-SS Adolf Hitler, a protection squad that guards Hitler, commanded by General Dietrich. Peiper joined the Hitler Youth as a young boy. In 1934, at age nineteen, he applied for admission to the prestigious Waffen-SS. Sepp Dietrich reviewed his application, accepting him into the Leibstandarte-SS. His training taught him to be ruthless, taking immediate and aggressive action with little forethought, and using extreme tactics to cause terror.[7]

In 1938, Peiper becomes an aide, and later a personal adjutant, to Reichsführer-SS Heinrich Himmler. A dashing, tall, slender, blond-haired, blue-eyed man with Aryan features and noble Germanic looks, Peiper might easily have been a poster child for Waffen-SS recruiters. On his wedding day, Joachim and his bride, Sigurd, receive from Hitler a black leather-bound copy of *Mein Kampf* nestled inside a wooden box, the top carved with oak leaves, acorns, and Nordic runes.[8]

Peiper is a persistent and ruthless man who does whatever it takes to get things done. He impresses both Dietrich and Hitler with his courage, brutalty, and sheer joy of killing.[9]

CHAPTER 12

THE TRIP TO PARIS

— PARIS, FRANCE —
JUNE 23, 1940

One of Hitler's most delightful conquests is the capture of Paris, on June 14, 1940, after only six weeks of fighting.

"When our German tanks rolled down the Champs-Élysées," Hitler laughs with his generals, "the French prized Paris so much that, in order to save their beautiful city from destruction, they permitted us to take it without firing a shot."[1]

"Not even the Maginot Line could protect the French against our invasion," a general agrees. "And how fitting that yesterday we should make French officials surrender to Germany in the same Compiègne Forest railroad car that we were made to surrender in 1918 after the Great War."[2]

Today, on June 23, Hitler's forces march proudly through the streets of Paris as stunned Parisians wail with loss and sadness.[3]

When Hitler's plane lands at Le Bourget Airfield near Paris, he steps into a large black Mercedes. The Führer sits beside the chauffeur, thrilled to inspect his captured "City of Light." He is anxious to see the Paris Opera House, which he has long admired.

"I am fascinated by the opera's beauty," Hitler says as he enters Charles Garnier's great neobaroque building, his eyes lighting up with excitement. As an attendant escorts the party through the rooms,

Hitler opens his wallet, taking out a fifty-mark note and handing it to the attendant. But he refuses it. "I'm just doing my duty," he says, unsmiling and with downcast eyes.

The Mercedes whisks the Führer down the Champs-Élysées, the Trocadero, and then to the Eiffel Tower, while a photographer snaps pictures. When the party arrives at the tomb of Napoleon, Hitler stands beside it, still and quiet for a long time, as if secretly worshipping and personally identifying with the legendary French emperor. After inspecting the Pantheon, the tour ends at the church of Sacre Coeur on Montmartre, where Hitler stands surrounded by his escort squad. He watches silently as unsmiling French worshippers move in and out of the church, seeming to purposely ignore him.

"I know they recognize me," he curses as churchgoers walk quickly past him, their eyes staring straight ahead.

At day's end, Hitler takes a deep breath, smiles, and exclaims, "It was the dream of my life to be permitted to see Paris. I cannot say how happy I am to have that dream fulfilled today."[4]

Hitler spends three hours in Paris that morning, posing before flashing camera bulbs with the Eiffel Tower in the background, celebrating the height of his capture and triumphs and claiming his spoils. He had previously planned to destroy the city, but after the exhilarating tour, he changes his mind, leaving Paris intact for the Reich's future generations. As he departs, never again to return, Hitler remarks to his companions, "Wasn't Paris beautiful? But Berlin must be made far more beautiful. When we are finished in Berlin, Paris will only be a shadow."[5]

On June 22, 1941, under the code name Operation Barbarossa, Hitler invades the Soviet Union. Disregarding the mutual peace pact, German forces overwhelm Soviet defenses, surprising them with a three-pronged attack along a broad front that stretches from the Baltic Sea in the north to the Black Sea in the south. At the Führer's

urgings, the highly mechanized invaders storm eastward like a wide
fan for six hundred miles.[6, 7, 8]

Hitler sends his trusted Gustav Knittel, now fully healed from his
wounds, to invade the Soviet Union. In July, the Führer receives reports
that he and his soldiers have attacked the city of Zhytomyr, on the
Teterev River in the Ukraine, a settlement of thirty thousand Jews.
Like a killing machine, they murder four hundred of the city's Jews. In
August, they kill another thousand Jews. With Hitler's encouragement,
German killing sprees prove common as Knittel and his troops push
deeper into the Soviet Union. In the midst of battle, Knittel takes a
bullet through his right armpit.

In September, the Führer receives word his troops have forced all
remaining Jews into a ghetto on the outskirts of the town, and that
many have died of starvation and disease. The six thousand remaining
Jews in Zhytomyr are rounded up by German soldiers and executed
outside the city.[9]

Hasso von Manteuffel, another of Hitler's favorites, joins Gustav
Knittel in the attack upon Zhytomyr during Operation Barbarossa. Impressing the Führer with his loyalty years earlier, the war-
rior joined the Imperial German Army on February 22, 1916, at age
nineteen. After his service with the Fifth Squadron, Third Hussar
Regiment on the Western Front, the descendant of Prussian aristocrats,
deeply rooted in politics and military affairs, was promoted to lieutenant. He rose through the ranks to Oberleutnant on April 1, 1925;
to Rittmeister on April 1, 1934; to Major on October 1, 1936; and to
Oberstleutnant (lieutenant colonel) on April 1, 1939.

The pale-faced, slightly built Hasso von Manteuffel had been severely wounded in the Great War, on October 12, 1916. He lay on a
French battlefield, his right thigh bleeding profusely, deeply penetrated
by shrapnel, the pain proving almost unbearable.

Waiting among the wounded near the Albert–Baupaume road, and listening to the cries of dying comrades, Manteuffel had focused his eyes on a faraway statue.

"Someone will come and rescue me," he whispered with sincere assurance as he gazed upon the Golden Virgin tenderly holding her Child atop the basilica in nearby Albert. "I will endure the pain bravely and wait for them," he said aloud.[10, 11]

As Manteuffel waited and suffered, he gazed up at the misty autumn sky, his right hand grasping his thigh, and reflected on the summer before. With the loss of few men, he and his fellow Germans had defended their positions north and south of Albert, a village quietly tucked between Gommecourt and Fricourt. Ever focused on the Madonna and Child, he smiled, recalling his troops cutting down, wounding, and killing tens of thousands of British troops.

"We blew those Tommies apart with our machine guns and rifles," he reflected. "I will never forget the thick smoke that filled the French skies on those hot summer days in the Battle of Albert."

Help finally came to young Manteuffel as he lay looking at the Golden Virgin. Plucked from the muddy grave site of the German field army, he received medical treatment in a hospital and soon recovered enough to return to the battlefields.

On August 25, 1941, Hasso von Manteuffel takes over the Sixth Rifle Regiment of the Seventh Panzer Division after its commander is killed in action, and heads his troops to the Soviet Union. He is promoted to Oberst (colonel) on October 1, 1941, the highest staff officer rank in the German Army.[12]

During the first days of July 1941, after two weeks of German aggression in the east, Joseph Goebbels writes a newspaper article, explaining to the German people the reason for Hitler's June 22 attack on the Soviet Union.

"The war that we are waging against Bolshevism is a war of moral humanity against spiritual rottenness," he writes, "against spiritual and physical terror, against criminal policies whose makers sit on mountains of corpses in order to see whom their next victim will be."

He places his pen on his desk, sitting still and pondering his next words.

They must be powerful as well as honoring of our soldiers. He picks up his pen.

"The Führer's order to the army on the night of 22 June was an act of historic magnitude. . . . The soldiers obeying his order are the saviors of European culture and civilization. . . . Germany's sons once again are defending not only their own land, but also the whole civilized world. . . . They hold in their hands a torch that will keep the light of humanity from going out."[13, 14]

CHAPTER 13

THE EINSATZGRUPPEN

Before dawn on the morning of June 22, 1941, Hitler attacks the Soviet Union by surprise with three million men, three thousand tanks, seven thousand guns, and three thousand aircraft.

"The German Air Force is the terror of our opponents," Hermann Göring tells Hitler after the successful invasion. "And it will remain so."[1]

Leaving a trail of blood and littered body parts, Hitler's troops push eastward toward Moscow, covering a five-hundred-mile-wide front, encircling and capturing millions of Soviet soldiers. The Einsatzgruppen, Hitler's killing units, massacre everyone who crosses their paths, soldiers and civilians, and they imprison massive numbers of Soviet Jews.[2]

"You only have to kick in the door and the whole rotten structure will come crashing down," Hitler boasts.[3]

German bombers raid Moscow at night, killing civilians, demolishing buildings, and even damaging the Kremlin. But the Führer is surprised by the Soviets' resistance, when their army of nine million armed men, and another five hundred thousand in reserve, fight back, overcoming the German forces. The fighting during summer and fall proves brutal, each side experiencing both successes and failures.[4, 5]

Hitler has counted on taking Moscow before winter, but the Red

Army proves a fierce adversary. In December, when temperatures in Moscow drop to minus thirty-six degrees Fahrenheit, German troops run out of food, medicines, and supplies. Supply trains loaded with desperately needed provisions break down, the water tanks in locomotives freezing in the subzero temperatures. The men, still in summer uniforms, are ill-prepared for such weather. Their fingers and toes begin to rot, succumbing to frostbite. They are freezing, starving, dying of disease, and trying to fight the vicious Red Army. Operation Barbarossa, Hitler's brainchild, fails as Soviet forces not only hold, but stage continual deadly counterattacks against, the miserable invaders.

During the first week of December 1941, the Germans are surprised by yet another unusually strong Soviet counterattack. Dug in on the outskirts of Moscow, trying desperately to take the city, they are pushed back by fresh, well-fed Soviet troops from Siberia and the Far East. Clad in white winter-camouflaged uniforms, the Soviets bring new supplies and attack the Germans with T-34 tanks and Katyusha rockets.[6]

Upset at having failed at Moscow, Hitler realizes that Germany is now required to fight a prolonged struggle on the Eastern Front, a war he knows will consume much of the army's manpower and resources.[7, 8]

PART 2

THE WORLD AT WAR

"Thank God that the lonely months of 1940 are over,
with the United States now standing by Britain's side. . . ."

PRIME MINISTER WINSTON CHURCHILL,
CHRISTMAS 1941[1]

CHAPTER 14

THE SURPRISE ATTACK

—USS *WEST VIRGINIA*—
PEARL HARBOR, HAWAII
DECEMBER 7, 1941

On the other side of the globe, African-American Doris "Dorie" Miller, mess attendant third class, aboard the USS *West Virginia*, works in a steam-filled kitchen belowdecks on the predawn Sunday morning of December 7, 1941.

The *Wee Vee*, as the ship is affectionately dubbed, is moored at Battleship Row with other navy vessels along the southeast side of Ford Island.

For some time that early morning, Dorie has been hearing noises. *Coast artillery practice*, he thinks.

Suddenly, at 0755, Dorie hears a shipmate scream, "The Japs are attacking us!"

Dorie races to the ship's bridge. He sees a squadron of planes above him, the sky blackened by antiaircraft smoke. Japanese fighter planes fly low and dip, their noisy propellors clanking, making a loud, distinctive racket. They drop bombs and nose-dive at the navy's ships. Dorie feels the *Wee Vee* list sharply to her port side, hears loud explosions nearby, and sees the harbor engulfed in flames.

Glancing about, he spots the skipper, Captain Mervyn S. Bennion, lying on the bridge, bleeding, motionless, and moaning in pain.

Shrapnel has gashed his belly. Dorie pulls the captain to safety. Then manning a nearby .50-caliber antiaircraft gun, he aims it at the oncoming aircraft, firing repeatedly until he runs out of ammunition. Hitting several planes, he watches them crash in an explosion of fire.

"Abandon ship!" someone screams. In the midst of billowing black smoke and fiery chaos, he sees several small boats approach the sinking *West Virginia*, coming to rescue survivors still on board.

As a black man serving in a noncombat role, Dorie has had no prior weapons training. He is a mess attendant, period. Later that day, when reporters ask him how he managed to shoot down enemy planes, he shrugs and replies, "It wasn't hard. I just pulled the trigger and she worked fine."

That afternoon, Miller hears that Captain Bennion has died from his wounds, along with 130 shipmates. Dorie closes his eyes and sighs. He also learns the *West Virginia* had been hit with at least six torpedoes and two bombs on her port side.[1]

On December 7, 1941, in Washington, D.C., President Franklin D. Roosevelt sits in his study with his top adviser, Harry Hopkins. Around one thirty p.m. Navy Secretary Frank Knox bursts in, interrupting their conversation and telling the president that Japan has attacked America's naval base at Pearl Harbor.

Roosevelt is silent. Beads of sweat form on his forehead. He purposely tries to remain calm as he hears the horrifying news: Twenty naval vessels destroyed. Two hundred airplanes demolished. Dry docks and airfields devastated. Two thousand American soldiers killed and many more injured during the two-hour enemy siege.

Late that night, Roosevelt meets with his cabinet and congressional members to discuss the situation.

"This is probably the most serious crisis any cabinet has confronted since the Civil War," he tells them, wincing, his right hand massaging his jaw.

Roosevelt asks Congress to declare war on Japan. He admits it will take time for the United States to build up its military. But he promises victory. Congress approves his declaration with just one dissenting vote. America has finally joined World War II.[2]

CHAPTER 15

THE NEWS AT WOLFSCHANZE

Hitler scans a map of the Soviet Union in his small windowless bunker, the Führer's headquarters, hidden deep in the woods of Rastenburg, East Prussia, one of the Third Reich's most fortified districts. He spends more time at Wolfschanze than any other place. Close to the Kętrzyn Forest, he can personally supervise his assault on Stalin and the Soviet Union.

He feels safe in his new fortress, built the previous summer. The buildings are far from any major roads. Thick concrete walls and ceilings protect the Führer and his large assortment of military staff, guards, and support personnel. On the grounds and roofs, densely planted trees, both natural and artificial, blend the bunker into the forests, camouflaging it from enemy aerial reconnaissance. The Great Mazurian Lakes to the rear of the fortress hinder enemy attempts to invade by land. Antipersonnel explosives and land mines encircle the entire expansive property, providing maximum security.[1]

When the Führer hears the morning's new battle reports, he is stunned.

"The Soviet Thirtieth Army has attacked our German Third Panzer Army at Lkin," an intelligence officer announces. "And the Soviet Fiftieth Army has attacked our Second Panzer Division near Moscow. Our units are making hasty withdrawals, abandoning immobilized equipment, and running for their lives."

Hitler's face turns to steel, and his eyes grow fiery. "You tell them to hold their ground!" he orders. "German soldiers do not run for their lives. They fight to the last bullet and the last man!"

"Yes, my Führer. I will tell them."

Hitler leashes his beloved dog, an Alsatian named Blondi, and stomps from the bunker to take his morning walk.

"I do not wish to be disturbed," he tells the head of the Reich Security Service (RSD), the team responsible for his protection. They gather around him and then quickly spread throughout the grounds far from the Führer's sight.

After his one-hour walk, he looks through the morning mail delivered each day by aircraft or courier train, and then meets with his closest consultants. At noon, Hitler eats his usual vegetarian lunch in the bunker's casino, inviting only a few close friends and associates to dine with him.

"My Führer," an aide says, walking in and interrupting Hitler's meal, "I have just received news that Japan has attacked the United States base at Pearl Harbor, destroying their battleships and aircraft. The air attack has killed thousands of Americans."

Hitler's face goes pale. He had no idea Japan was planning such an attack.

"Where in the world is Pearl Harbor?" a general asks. The room goes silent.

"Bring me a world map!" Hitler snaps. After he has located Pearl Harbor on the map, Hitler's lips curl in a devious smile.

"Now we can't lose the war," he says, rising from his seat, infused with new optimism and energy. "We have an ally who has not been defeated in three thousand years of history!"[2]

Hitler races back to Berlin, spending several days in deep thought, trying to decide the appropriate response.

Hitler has little respect for America or President Roosevelt, calling the multiracial United States a "mongoloid" nation far inferior to Germany's

Aryan, purebred nation. Nazi Germany, Imperial Japan, and Fascist Italy had earlier entered into an agreement that promised to provide military help if one of them was attacked by a nation not already in the war. Hitler had hoped the powerful Axis pact might intimidate America, discouraging her from helping lonely Britain.

"It seems it didn't," Hitler mutters.[3]

"If America joins the war," Hitler has told his generals repeatedly, "the U.S. Army's military forces will never measure up to Germany's fighting strength. We will be victorious in Europe, and Japan will conquer East Asia and the South Pacific."

He grins and rubs Blondi's head.

"After this attack on Pearl Harbor," he says, "America will need to focus her primary war efforts in the South Pacific. She will be forced to stop interfering with North Atlantic shipping lanes and protecting British convoy supply ships."

He stands and looks out the window, his eyes lighting up with dreams of the new Germany.

"I look forward to giving my U-boat commanders unrestricted access to destroy all U.S. warships. We shall cut off Britain from her main supply source. The great British lion shall starve!"

CHAPTER 16

THE DATE THAT WILL
LIVE IN INFAMY

—BESSEMER, ALABAMA—
SUNDAY AFTERNOON, DECEMBER 7, 1941

Twenty-three-year-old Lil' Georgie Davis relaxes with his family at home in Bessemer, Alabama, listening to music on an old Zenith radio while resting up from a lengthy church service, and the heaping plate of fried chicken and peach cobbler he put away at dinner.

"Preacher sure went on long this morning," Georgie's dad says. "Somebody needs to buy him a Westclox Big Ben. With an extra-loud double-bell alarm. Wouldn't be so bad if his sermons weren't dry as wood shavings."

"Don't say unkind things about Pastor in front of Lil' Georgie," Mrs. Davis says, giving her husband an annoyed look. "Pastor's been good to our son."

"Well," he says, "you have to admit—"

"We interrupt this program . . . ," the radio announcer cuts in with an excited voice, telling the nation about the Japanese surprise strike on Pearl Harbor, an attack still in progress.

Georgie's mother clasps a hand over her mouth, springs from her chair, and wraps her arms around her son's shoulders, holding him tightly, protectively, as she listens to the radio announcer's terrifying words.

The Davis family goes to bed that night wondering what news the next day will bring. The next morning, Monday, December 8, the family turns on the radio and listens anxiously to the speech made by the president of the United States.

"Yesterday, December 7, 1941, a date which will live in infamy, the United States of America was suddenly and deliberately attacked by naval and air forces of the Empire of Japan.[1]

"The attack yesterday on the Hawaiian islands has caused severe damage to American naval and military forces," he continues. "Very many American lives have been lost. . . ."

"Does this mean we're going to war?" she whispers to her husband as she wipes her eyes with the edge of her apron.

"Listen!" her husband says. "President Roosevelt'll tell us."

"Since the unprovoked and dastardly attack by Japan, I ask that the Congress declare a state of war between the United States and the Japanese empire."

"Yep!" he says. "That's exactly what it means."

"Meaning Lil' Georgie'll have to go fight the Japanese?" she cries.

"Nah, Lil' Georgie's not going. President Roosevelt'll call up white boys for service, not black boys. Anyway, Lil' Georgie's too short and scrawny for the army. He'd never pass the physical."

Georgie jumps from his chair. "Dad! Black soldiers have been fighting in every war since the American Revolution. And a five-foot-four-inch man's not that short. Scrawny or not, I'm gonna pass the army's physical, hands down. If it means fighting to defend my country, I'm signing up!"

"No, you aren't!" his father shouts. "If you sign up, you'll be cooking the white boys' food or digging their nasty latrines. And they'll not allow you to eat in their mess halls or sleep in their barracks. I remember the Great War, son, and nothing's changed for us coloreds since then."

"But, Dad, we gotta protect our country's freedoms! We've been attacked."

"You have no business fighting the white man's war," his dad says, his hand forming into a fist. "You don't need to fight for freedoms you don't even have! Let the white boys go. They're the ones who are free. Not us!"

Mrs. Davis sits in her rocker, closes her eyes, and starts to sing with a strong voice and a steady rhythm: "Roll, Jordan, roll. Roll, Jordan, roll. I wanter go to heav'n when I die, to hear ol' Jordan roll. . . ."

Georgie has heard the old Negro spiritual many times during his twenty-three years, sung by his grandmother at family funerals, and by choirs at tent camp meetings. The tune always seems to calm his mother when she gets worried or anxious. "Roll, Jordan, roll / Roll, Jordan, roll / Oh, keep my Georgie safe / O Lord / Roll, Jordan, roll . . . ," his mother sings, each refrain becoming louder, faster, and sung with more deeply felt emotion, the lyrics changing with each stanza as she personalizes them.[2]

Georgie's dad spends the rest of Monday afternoon sitting in the front room, fretting over the war and worrying about his son.

That boy's far too innocent and risk-taking to be turned loose into such a dangerous world.

Mrs. Davis has kept her son close to home in Bessemer most of his life, and that has suited Mr. Davis just fine.

It's a dangerous place for a black boy outside the walls of his home. Sometimes he's not safe inside, neither.

"So Lil' Georgie wants to go to war?" he says aloud, shaking his head. "What's wrong with that boy? Can't he see how white folks treat us here in 'Bama? Let Uncle Sam kill off Jim Crow first, and then maybe we'll be more likely to go. No way my only son's gonna fight this white man's war!"

Two years earlier, Davis had hoped Frank M. Dixon, Alabama's promising new governor elected in '39, might bring positive changes for Alabama's black population. Governor Dixon, a lawyer and second lieutenant with the Royal Canadian Air Corps in the Great War, lost a leg in France. The one-legged former airman quickly endeared himself to Alabama's white residents, especially its veterans.[3]

But it turned out Governor Dixon was an active and open advocate of white supremacy, supported the Ku Klux Klan, and boldly opposed the idea of a rumored federal antilynching bill. As did his political friend from Barbour County, Alabama, Chauncey Sparks.

"It's dangerous, unwarranted, and unwise," Dixon stated publicly when the government suggested the new law would fine and jail policemen and Klan members who gang-lynched a Negro.[4]

Mr. Davis rises from his chair. *Tried my best to protect that child all his life long. Got him up to twenty-three years old. Don't want to lose him now on some foreign battlefield. I don't care what the boy wants. Lil' Georgie'll enlist in Uncle Sam's army over my dead body!*[5]

CHAPTER 17

THE CHANGING WORLD

Two weeks before Christmas 1941, Hitler broadcasts a speech on live radio around the world. Standing at the podium, a huge golden eagle in a frightening predatory pose behind him, he mocks President Roosevelt.

"I will pass over the insulting attacks made by this so-called president against me," he says. "That he calls me a gangster is uninteresting. After all, this expression was not coined in Europe, but in America, no doubt because such gangsters are lacking here."[1]

The listening crowds at the Reichstag cheer the Führer wildly during his speech, showing their wholehearted belief in him, as well as their total support.

"Overt acts of war against Germany," Hitler shouts, "declare that under these circumstances brought about by President Roosevelt, Germany, too, considers herself to be at war with the United States, as from today."[2]

Hitler is now at war with America, Britain, and Russia.

Joseph Goebbels sits at his Berlin desk, writing the lead newspaper article for the December 21, 1941, issue of *Das Reich*.

"It is astonishing, hardly believable, how the state of the world can change entirely within a short time," he scribbles.

He tells the German people that war is inevitable, that Japan suffers from the same problems that plague Germany: The population has no room to grow, and both countries need more raw materials and economic prospects "for space, work, food, and life itself." He writes that unless Germany and Japan wish to give up their dreams of becoming great world powers, they must "follow the laws Fate ordains."

Goebbels assures the people that the military powers of the Axis—Germany, Japan, and Italy—are far better than the Allies' forces, and that Germany's army is much better prepared now than it was in 1914 at the start of the disastrous Great War.

"We've now defeated France," he writes. "The Balkans are no threat, and the Soviet Union is no longer a decisive factor in the war."

He ends the article on an encouraging note: "The day will come when the enemy begins to crumble. No one can predict when that will be, but we all know that it will come."[3]

A few days before Christmas, on December 22, 1941, and three weeks after the Pearl Harbor attack, within the walls of the White House, President and Mrs. Roosevelt have an altercation. The quarrel is a quiet one, but nonetheless significant.

Roosevelt has failed to tell his wife, Eleanor, that he has invited a number of guests to the White House for the holidays, including British prime minister Winston Churchill and his party. And even worse, he now tells Eleanor they plan to arrive within a few hours.

"You should have told me! Why didn't you tell me?" Mrs. Roosevelt says, staring at her husband. She shakes her head. "If only I had known."

On Christmas Eve, Roosevelt and Churchill stand side by side on the White House balcony, watching the annual lighting of the National Christmas Tree and addressing more than twenty thousand listening people bundled in overcoats and standing on the White House south lawn.

"Our strongest weapon in this war is that conviction of the dignity and brotherhood of man which Christmas Day signifies," Roosevelt tells them.

Once the president has concluded, Churchill begins to speak in his deep, familiar British accent. "I spend this anniversary . . . far from my country, far from my family, yet I cannot truthfully say that I feel far from home. . . . [T]his is a strange Christmas Eve. Almost the whole world is locked in deadly struggle and, with the most terrible weapons science can devise, the nations advance upon each other."[4]

CHAPTER 18

THE CHRISTMAS EVE MESSAGE

——GERMANY——
DECEMBER 21, 1944

A sad, dark Christmas holiday is dawning for the German people. The war has brought uncertainty, heartache, and a serious lack of food and supplies to the families of the Fatherland.

On Christmas Eve 1941, Joseph Goebbels speaks by radio to the German people, telling them that Germans "must withstand the storms of the age until victory is ours."

"We have sent our Christmas candles to the Eastern Front, where our soldiers need them more than we do," he says. He apologizes for the lack of Christmas gifts the people will have to give and receive during the holidays, explaining that "dolls, castles, lead soldiers, and toy guns" will not be produced this Christmas, that the materials must be used for "our troops . . . our first priority."[1]

Goebbels then turns his listeners' attention to the soldiers spending Christmas deep in Russia on the frigid Eastern Front, sadly aware that Operation Barbarossa continues to rage on and on with no end in sight, marked by massive human suffering on both sides. He explains the Fatherland is losing her finest soldiers at an alarming rate as Hitler pushes the "Slavic subhumans" out of the land Germany needs to occupy.[2]

In closing, the minister of propaganda reminds his listeners, "We must thank those who defend us, our sons, fathers, and brothers, who have learned only in distant lands among foreign peoples how dear their Vaterland and their people are."[3]

A t his annual Christmas dinner, Hitler sits down to a bountiful and festive meal. Behind him stands a beautiful, large Tannenbaum tree decorated with shiny ornaments and silver tinsel streamers. Heinrich Himmler, commanding officer of the Nazi Secret Police, along with dozens of generals, officers, and soldiers, join him around the food-laden, candlelit tables.[4]

O n that same day, German families sit quietly around their Christmas Day tables staring sadly at the number of empty chairs where husbands, fathers, sons, and brothers once sat. The women and children have little food to eat, no decorated trees, and few if any Christmas gifts.

O n Christmas Day in Washington, D.C., the president and Britain's prime minister attend a service at a nearby Methodist church. During the afternoon, the Roosevelts, Churchill, and their guests dine on oysters, turkey with chestnut dressing and giblet gravy, beans, cauliflower, and sweet potato casserole. After dinner, Roosevelt and Churchill put their heads together in another part of the White House, talking, drinking brandy, and smoking until two or three in the morning as they try to figure out ways to crush their common enemies. Night after night for the next two weeks, they drink, smoke, and talk until nearly dawn. Mrs. Roosevelt interrupts them often with subtle hints about bed.

"We must begin building up our military and resources," Roosevelt tells Churchill. "Our production goals must drastically increase. We need airplanes, tanks, antiaircraft and machine guns, as well as tons of merchant shipping and supplies.

"I must tell Secretary of War Henry Stimson: 'We must not only provide munitions for our own fighting forces,'" Roosevelt says, "'but vast quantities to be used against the enemy in every appropriate theater of war.'"

"And your army's ultimate mobilization goal?" Churchill asks.

"At least ten million men," Roosevelt responds.[5]

"Who is the greater threat to the United States," Churchill asks, "the Germans or the Japanese?"

"You are asking who will we fight first?" Roosevelt asks. "We must put the war in the Pacific second to victory in Europe. We will first fight Hitler."[6]

During his stay at the White House, with Roosevelt at his side, Churchill tells reporters, "Thank God that the lonely months of 1940 are over, with the United States now standing by Britain's side, just as [I stand] beside its president."[7]

From Washington, D.C., President and Mrs. Roosevelt watch American life drastically change after the Japanese attack. The United States is sorely unprepared to go to war. The army numbers only 1.6 million men with 120,000 officers, many not combat-ready. Military equipment and ammunition are scarce, with only forty-five modern fighter planes ready to protect the West Coast, and fifty-four army fighter planes ready on the East Coast.[8]

Now at war with three formidable adversaries, the president must prepare America to fight on two distant fronts. He knows the country must quickly build strong military forces for combat in Japan and Europe as well as prepare the homeland defensively for a possible invasion by an enemy.

Back in September 1940, already concerned about having to one day enter the war, Roosevelt and Congress narrowly approved the nation's first peacetime military draft. By Christmas 1941, America's military has grown to 2.2 million soldiers, sailors, airmen, and marines, consisting mainly of citizen soldiers—men and women recruited from civilian life. Many are volunteers, but most enter the military through the draft and are assigned to the army.[9]

In 1941, America's armed forces have fewer than four thousand African-Americans serving in the military. Only twelve are officers.[10]

Civilian life segregation practices have spilled over into the United States military, demanding that "the white and colored militia shall be separately enrolled, and shall never be compelled to serve in the same organization. No organization of colored troops shall be permitted where white troops are available. . . . Colored troops shall be under the command of white officers."[11]

Though officially segregated, many African-Americans answer the call to duty, eager to enlist. Many, however, are turned away, refused by some all-white draft boards.

The black soldiers are assigned to noncombat units and are relegated to service duties and menial labor far behind the action, even though they yearn for active combat.[12]

CHAPTER 19

THE LOUISIANA RIOT

The weary residents of Louisiana are still quaking after learning of the Pearl Harbor attack the month before. They express great angst about their sons leaving home to fight on foreign fields, many of their boys enlisting, others getting draft notices or already drafted, and all undergoing basic training at one of the three army camps located within a few hundred miles of Alexandria.

Most Louisianans are also still reeling over the discovery, several years before, of massive corruption in Governor Richard W. Leche's administration. Leche's illegal involvement in the highly publicized "Louisiana Scandals" has landed him in prison on a ten-year sentence.[1]

Hoping for some normalcy to return to their troubled lives, Alexandria's white citizens, who can pay the $4.40 admission and train prices, buy tickets to the annual Pasadena, California, Rose Bowl game, scheduled for January 1, 1942, with Duke University playing Oregon State. Like Alexandria, the city of Pasadena, Jackie Robinson's boyhood home, enforces strict Jim Crow laws, allowing Southern whites to feel comfortable attending the games, watching segregated college teams play in the Rose Bowl.

But at the last minute, jittery Rose Bowl officials cancel the game in Pasadena, fearing the Japanese might invade the Pacific coastline, fewer than thirty miles away, and attack the packed stadium's fifty thousand loyal fans.

To placate the angry sports enthusiasts, Duke University steps up, offering their Durham, North Carolina, stadium and agreeing to host the game. No one suggests that the Germans might attack the Durham stadium from the Atlantic coastline, only 140 miles away. Their generosity accepted, Duke borrows extra bleachers from the University of North Carolina and North Carolina State to accommodate the thousands of fans arriving on trains from every corner of the country.[2]

At the time of the Durham Rose Bowl, young Thomas Forte has been drafted and in basic training for almost ten months. Back home, some three hundred miles away, his bride-to-be, Angelina, a divorced woman five years his senior, anxiously awaits the wedding planned to take place that month.

No one in Alexandria, Louisiana, knows who started the racial riot on Saturday night, January 10, 1942, in Thomas Forte's hometown.

Rumors are that the Lee Street Riot started in "Little Harlem," a small, segregated, four-square-block area in the city's "Negro section." Thousands of black soldiers in basic training at nearby Camp Livingston, Camp Beauregard, and Camp Claiborne gathered on narrow Lee Street to dance and drink at the popular halls and liquor joints during their liberty weekend.

After the riot, Thomas Forte telephones a friend at Camp Claiborne to find out what happened.

"The army's hushing it up," he tells Forte. "I heard a fight broke out at the Ritz Theater. A white policeman supposedly beat up a colored soldier. When the other black soldiers got wind of it, they got upset. The MPs and local police attacked them with clubs, tear gas, and sawed-off shotguns. Of course they fought back. After all, the army's teaching those boys how to fight. Lots of folks got hurt. Don't know how many got killed. Everybody blamed the riot on the colored Yankee soldiers, who don't know to obey the state's seg' laws."

"Looks like somebody oughta tell the Yankee soldiers about Jim Crow," Forte says. "Those boys don't know how they're supposed to act around whites in Louisiana."

"They've already caused a stir with the city's whites," his friend says. "Some won't sit in the back of city buses. They say, 'We're not sitting in the back when we pay the same price for a ticket as the white man who sits in the front!' Others walk right through the front doors of city restaurants, refusing to go round back to the 'For Coloreds' door."

"They've got a lot to learn," Forte says. "I hear Fort Benning's been havin' some race problems, too."

"Yeah. Someone told me a white man hanged a Negro private on a tree outside Benning. And at Fort Bragg, two coloreds were left dead after a fight between white MPs and Northern blacks." He pauses, sighing. "If coloreds don't get killed overseas, they get killed right here at home!"[3]

On January 19, 1942, ten days after the mysterious Lee Street Riot, Thomas Forte marries Angelina. His eyes light up when he sees her handmade wedding dress in the candlelight ceremony. He slips a thin tin ring on her finger, promising to buy her a real diamond wedding ring when he can save up the money. He vows to love, comfort, honor, and keep her for better or worse, for richer or poorer, in sickness and health. On their wedding night, Thomas and Angelina talk about their future together and the children they plan to bring into their family.

At the end of the month, Thomas reads a letter published in the *Pittsburgh Courier* written by twenty-six-year-old African-American James G. Thompson from Wichita, Kansas.

Forte, a grammar school grad, reads the letter slowly and deliberately, stumbling over some of the words. In the letter, Thompson demands that African-Americans fighting for their country overseas receive full citizenship rights at home. He includes some thought-provoking questions for his readers to chew on.

"Would it be demanding too much to demand full citizenship rights in exchange for the sacrificing of black lives?"

"Should I sacrifice my life to live as a half-American?"

"Will things be better for the next generation of Americans in the peace to follow?"

"Will America be a true and pure democracy after this war?"

"Will colored Americans continue to suffer the indignities that have been heaped upon them in the past?"

Thompson ends his letter assuring his readers of his love for America, telling them he is willing to die for the America he knows will someday become a reality.[4]

By the time Forte finishes reading the letter, his nostrils are flaring. Over the next few weeks, Forte sees huge consequences stemming from Thompson's letter.

He hears that the *Courier* is giving it wide promotion and starting a nationwide "Double V" campaign, designing a recognizable "Double V" logo, and calling for immediate democracy for African-Americans: "Victory at Home, Victory Abroad."

He watches his friends in black communities sport the "Double V" lapel pins, display giant posters, and sing catchy songs supporting the cause.

Forte and Angelina attach pins to their own lapels, learn the lyrics, and jump on the "Double V" campaign bandwagon, along with the nation's civil rights leaders and the NAACP. They flood the White House, Congress, and courts with postcards and letters demanding equal rights action.[5, 6, 7]

CHAPTER 20

DRAFTED!

Five months after Pearl Harbor, Mr. Davis's worst nightmare comes true when his only son, Georgie, is drafted into the army. Georgie packs his bags, prepares to leave home for the first time in his life, and heads to Oklahoma. The army's new military cantonment, Camp Gruber, has just opened.[1]

Before he leaves, Georgie dresses in his Sunday suit, stands tall and erect, his shoulders pushed back, his chest thrust forward, and has his picture made for his parents. He kisses his mother good-bye, shakes his father's hand, and promises to make them both proud of him. Before he leaves, his father slips a small box into his hands.

"This is the railroad pocket watch your granddaddy gave me long ago," he tells Lil' Georgie with tears in his eyes. "I want you to have it, son."

His mother hugs him one last time. "Lil' Georgie," she says, "every time you look at that watch, please think about us and remember how much we love you."

Before he leaves, Georgie takes the newspaper photograph of Jesse Owens off the family room wall and puts it in his pocket.

———————

Mr. Davis sees how excited Georgie is about serving his country, but he and his wife are devastated. For months after Georgie leaves home, Mr. Davis tries without success to comfort his distraught wife. But she will not be consoled.

"He's all we've got," she tells her husband. "Our only son. Doesn't the army make an exception if he's a mother's only son?"

Day after day, he watches her sit by the radio, listening to war news, holding the photograph of Georgie, sobbing pitifully for her boy, and humming the tune that always seems to encourage her—"Roll, Jordan, roll, O Lord," she sings, "keep my boy safe, please keep my dear boy safe."

"He'll be back to us soon, safe and sound," Mr. Davis assures her. "I came back from the war. So will he. Anyway, he'll be safe because the army's not putting colored boys in combat."

But even as he says the words, a sense of doom fills this father's grieving heart. And deep within his soul, he knows his son will not come home again.

CHAPTER 21

THE RISK

Maria and Mathias Langer live in constant fear during the two-year German occupation of Belgium. By early summer 1942, they hear more and more accounts of the Nazi persecution of Belgium's Jews.[1]

Mathias has kept his own family safe so far, but he worries about the safety of other families in Belgium, especially the country's Jewish families, many of them his friends. He hears frequent and appalling reports of German and secret military police seizing the homes and businesses of Jews, forcing them to wear the yellow Star of David patch, arresting them in the streets, and deporting entire families to Poland.

He knows he must do something to help them.

"Maria, we must be willing and available to help the Jews. They are enduring unthinkable cruelty, and I believe life will become even worse for them."

"But, Mathias, you know what will happen to us and our children if we try to help them. We will be punished."

He glances at the old wooden crucifix hanging above the dining room door. "As devoted Catholics, Maria, we cannot stand idle while our Jewish friends suffer."

"Yes, I know. But what can we do?"

"We have the cellar. Several families could hide down there."

Maria takes a deep breath, closes her eyes, and exhales slowly, loudly. "The Germans are constantly searching our neighborhood, offering money to informers who turn in Jews and the people who hide them. It is a tremendous risk, Mathias. We could face deportation . . . or even death."[2]

"Yes, it's true. Many eyes are watching us, and we could face severe penalties if we are caught. But, Maria, if we do nothing, we are helping the Germans destroy Belgium's Jewish families. We must take a stand against such crimes."[3]

"I understand," Maria whispers, staring at the floor.

Late one night, Mathias answers a knock at his front door. A member of the Belgian Resistance asks him to hide a Jewish man. Mathias agrees, but at the same time, he feels his stomach knot with concern for his family's safety. He arranges for the man to arrive late the next night. On the dark, moonless evening, Mathias quietly ushers him inside, hiding him in the cellar.

The look of horror on Maria's face is hardly surprising.

"I know how you feel about it, Maria. But we must do this."

Maria says nothing, closes her eyes and crosses herself, and scurries to make a pallet bed with thick blankets. She prepares their guest a plate of gray bread and nettle soup, the main meal eaten by the Langers.

That night Mathias explains the rules of the household to the frightened but grateful young man.

"You must remain quiet at all times. Some of our neighbors are German sympathizers who will not hesitate to report you and us. This area was part of Germany until the Versailles Treaty was signed. They still think of themselves as German loyals."

"Yes, Herr Langer. I understand."

"Please call me Mathias, as you are our guest. Please know that

German soldiers stop by often, requesting food and supplies. And they are always searching for Jews."

The man reaches into his pocket, pulling out a few coins. "Please sir . . . uh . . . Mathias, take this money. I would give you more, but it is all I have. I so appreciate your kindness to me."

"Please, son, keep your coins. You will need them when you are free again."

The guest swallows hard, nods several times, and walks down to the cellar.

During the following days and weeks, other resistance members bring more Jews to the Langer home. The family works hard to feed and care for all of them. Maria spends most of her waking hours washing and cooking, trying to stretch the sparse food to feed an increasing number of mouths. The older Langer children help with the work, collecting eggs, milking the cow, watering and harvesting crops. German soldiers often stop by to help themselves to the scarce vegetables growing in the Langers' small garden.

Maria cries often, confessing to Mathias her fear for her children should they be betrayed.

"And I fear, too, being deported to work in Germany's factories. Whole families have been deported or . . . or killed for much lesser offenses. If that happens, who will care for our children?"

"We will be fine, Maria. God will protect us. We are in His hands now."

The Langers never refuse anyone in need. They invite many to sit around their large wooden table, feeding them eggs, milk, bread, soup, and potatoes. They hide and protect many Jewish families, often for months. But soon the food runs out, and they can no longer feed themselves or their hidden guests.

Week by week, Maria watches her children lose weight, some falling ill from poor diets. She fears for them, panicking whenever she sees a German Schwimmwagen stop at a nearby house, frantic that a neighbor might have learned of their Jewish visitors.[4]

One morning, after Maria has made breakfast for the household, she hears a knock at the door.

She races to the window, drawing back the curtain slightly, looking outside. *Thank God! No Schwimmwagens.*

She hesitates before opening the door.

"Maria," one of her neighbors, Greta, greets her. "I have come to visit you. May I come inside?"

Maria sucks in her breath, trying to keep a calm expression on her face. She thinks about the Jewish men, women, and children hiding in her cellar, waiting quietly for the eggs, bread, and milk on the kitchen table. *Why is Greta here? She never comes to my house. I have never trusted the woman. She must suspect I am hiding Jews.*

"Yes, Greta, please come inside. Would you like a cup of milk?"

"No, thank you. You have food on the table, Maria. Are you expecting guests for breakfast?"

"No, Greta. May I offer you some breakfast? I have some to spare."

"No, Maria," Greta says, and sits at the table.

Maria holds her breath and bites her bottom lip. She fears one of the babies in the cellar will cry, or a man or woman will speak or stumble or drop something. *Please don't make a noise! Our very lives depend upon your silence.*

Maria hears a slight movement coming from the cellar.

"What is that noise, Maria?" Greta asks, looking down at the floor.

"What noise, Gre—"

At that second, Hans, Gertrud, and Leo run into the kitchen, laughing loudly and sitting down at the table.

"Greta, I must feed my family now. I will say good-bye, but please come visit another time."

When Greta leaves, Maria exhales, closes her eyes, and touches the cross on her necklace. *Thank you, dear God.*

That evening Maria is still upset and shares her fears with Mathias.

"Greta came to our house unexpectedly. She seemed suspicious, as if she expected to find hidden Jews here."

Mathias takes Maria's hand. "I'm sorry, Maria. It is the chance we must take. We must consider the lives we are saving."

"But, Mathias! By harboring Jews and deserters, we endanger *our Kinder.*"

Mathias looks into her eyes. "But, my love, we are helping to protect *their Kinder,* who are just as loved by their parents."[5]

CHAPTER 22

THE ARMY'S JIM CROW

—CAMP GRUBER, OKLAHOMA—
SEPTEMBER 1942

Thomas Forte leaves his new bride at home in Louisiana and moves to Camp Gruber, located on Highway 10, eighteen miles east of Muskogee, Oklahoma. Forte becomes a mess sergeant with the 333rd Field Artillery Battalion, an all-black, segregated battalion activated on August 5, 1942, and a sister battalion of the 969th. Sergeant Forte forms friendships with other black GIs in Charley and Service Batteries, including privates first class Georgie Davis, Jimmie Leatherwood, and Due Turner; privates George Moten, Nathaniel Moss, and Curtis Adams; Technical Sergeant William Pritchett; Staff Sergeant James Aubrey Stewart; corporals Robert Green, Mager Bradley, and Robert Hudson; and Sergeant George Shomo.

Sergeant Forte isn't surprised when the black soldiers are billeted in separate barracks from the white soldiers, or that the battalion's two commanders, Lieutenant Colonel Harmon S. Kelsey and Captain William McLeod, are both white.

"What did you expect, Forte," Green asks, "what with you being a Louisiana boy, and me being from Georgia? You thinking we'd be rubbing shoulders with the white guys or getting colored officers?"

"Guess I was thinkin' things would be different in the army, Corporal."

"Well, Sergeant, I reckon you're wrong about that. From what I hear, we'll be doing everything separate—sleeping, eating, training, everything. Doesn't surprise me."

"Yeah, they must be thinkin' we're just a bunch of yardbirds."

Thomas Forte and the other men of the 333rd Field Artillery Battalion don't care much for their CO, Lieutenant Colonel Kelsey, a forty-nine-year-old California native and tough career officer. It's obvious that Kelsey resents being assigned to a black battalion, and that he wants to prove to the brass he can "whip those colored boys into shape."

They stand at attention, listening with apprehension as Colonel Kelsey makes his initial welcome speech: "Don't even think of getting out of this outfit, boys. The only way you will get out of here is to *die* out of here. There. Are. No. Transfers."

Forte isn't surprised when Kelsey works them long and hard, pushing them to their physical and emotional limits and publicly criticizing Captain McLeod for his easygoing attitude and visible compassion.

Everyone smiles but Forte when Private Georgie Davis mutters, "That guy gives me the heebie-jeebies."

One afternoon, Forte overhears Kelsey and McLeod talking: "For crying out loud, Captain. If you don't toughen up those Negro boys, you're going to make me look bad and get them all killed on the battlefield."

"They've already been 'toughened up,'" McLeod says with as much dignity and respect as he can muster for his superior. "Most of them grew up in the South with Jim Crow!"

Sergeant Forte and his battalion like Captain McLeod, the kind, caring Oklahoman. They appreciate his encouragement and support. But Forte has a hard time adjusting to the segregated battalion, and he carries out his kitchen duties with clenched teeth.

"I wanna fight," he tells Corporal Green. "The last thing I wanna do is cook and wash pots."

"We all wanna fight, Sergeant. But I don't reckon colored GIs'll ever get to. Even if they let us, the war'll be over before we get the chance."

C aptain William McLeod, twenty-one, can't sleep that night. He worries about the men of the 333rd. He knows how tough basic training will be, especially at Camp Gruber, with the deep inbred societal tensions between whites and blacks.

He stares at the ceiling in his darkened room and thinks about his father, Howard McLeod, a World War I veteran and now a state penitentiary warden.

He's a wonderful man and a tough old bird! I hope I can accomplish a fraction of what he has done in his life.

He reflects on the stories his father told him years ago.

"I was born in Granite to pioneer parents in pre-Oklahoma Indian Territory," he said. "Your mother, Ruby, taught school near Granite until we married. But she had to quit because only single women could teach. Then you came along, our firstborn child."

McLeod recalls the excitement he felt when, at sixteen years old, he began his own military career, enlisting in the "French 75" Field Artillery Battalion in the Forty-fifth Division of the Oklahoma National Guard. Later, as a sergeant, he entered the Field Artillery Officer Candidate School, where, just this year, 1942, he is commissioned second lieutenant, earning the respect and admiration of his father, as well as his fellow officers and men.

I had good opportunities growing up. I'm fortunate I'm white.

He turns on his side and glances at the clock. *Oh two hundred. Why can't I sleep?*

He feels concern about his black troopers, the ridicule they will endure from white officers and enlisted men, the menial jobs they will be given, the sense of second-class separateness they will most likely feel, and the lack of respect they'll receive no matter how well they train and perform.

It won't be easy for my men. Jim Crow feelings run deep in the military. Somehow I must keep these young men safe and train them to be first-class soldiers.

McLeod thinks about his men—Sergeant James Aubrey Stewart, the baseball pitcher from West Virginia, an older man blessed with ambition, intelligence, compassion, and good common horse sense.

He'll do well. Seasoned with life experience. Hard worker. Has become something of a father image to the younger guys.

Private Curtis Adams, the young medic, a new husband and father from South Carolina.

Adams just wants to get home in one piece to his wife and baby. His initiative, training, and natural compassion will make him a good medic.

Private Georgie Davis, a fun-loving, adventurous, but immature kid from Bessemer, Alabama. Davis's main ambition is to fight the Germans, become a hero, and make his parents proud. McLeod smiles as he thinks about the newspaper picture of Jesse Owens that Davis carries in his pocket.

I wish the men wouldn't call him Lil' Georgie. It's belittling. We need to build his confidence. Grow him up. Treat him like an adult, not like some kid.

When McLeod thinks of Sergeant Thomas Forte, he closes his eyes and shakes his head. Forte—angry, resentful, and never smiling—wants to fight the enemy, not feed the battalion.

Hope I can get him through basic training without too many incidents with the white boys. I fear Forte will be a handful.

Before he goes to sleep, McLeod thinks about some of the other men in the 333rd: Leatherwood, Pritchett, Bradley, Moss, Moten, Turner, and Green.

All Southerners. They'll be no trouble. They understand the strained relations between blacks and whites, as well as the seriousness of the South's Jim Crow laws.

He is concerned, however, about Sergeant George Shomo, the young man who grew up with white friends in a desegregated New Jersey neighborhood.

No doubt he'll have a hard time dealing with harsh racial rules enforced in Oklahoma and the military. It'll be a shock. Hope he can handle it.

CHAPTER 23

THE GI FROM
PONTOTOC COUNTY

At twenty years old, Jimmie Lee Leatherwood leaves his boyhood home in Mississippi, arrives at Camp Gruber, and joins the 333rd Field Artillery Battalion. Born in Tippah County, Jimmie Lee has grown up in Pontotoc County, near Tupelo, home to two thousand residents. As a boy, Leatherwood loved history and enjoyed impressing his friends and family members with his knowledge of Pontotoc County's historic past.

"Chickasaws named this place," he'd brag to them. "Pontotoc means 'Land of Hanging Grapes.'" True to its name, Pontotoc County had long produced good wine.

Jimmie Lee also loves baseball. His family follows the Memphis Red Sox and the Birmingham Black Barons, members of the professional Negro League. His hero is Cowan "Bubba" Hyde, a fleet base stealer for the Memphis Red Sox who later joined the Birmingham Black Barons.[1]

At Gruber, Leatherwood hears Sergeant Stewart has been a talented left-hander for the black, semipro Piedmont Giants. From then on what few free hours Leatherwood has he spends talking baseball with

Stewart, describing in tedious detail baseball players, history, and development over the years.

"Baseball's more than jus' a fun game," Stewart tells Leatherwood. "It builds skills and develops character. Boys need to learn both early on in life."

"Think us coloreds'll ever be playing with the white boys, Sergeant?"

Stewart scratches his head. "Jus' not sure, Private. I sure do hope so. Bring together the best of both of them, and you'd have one tough ball club."

Captain McLeod notices the grimace on the colonel's face when he enters Kelsey's office to discuss the battalion's new training agenda.

"I have just been ordered to train the colored men of the 333rd to operate the new 155mm howitzer," Kelsey sighs. "What is the army thinking? For crying out loud, the 155 is one of our most powerful weapons, and extremely difficult to load and fire. It demands speed and accuracy. Those boys will never get the hang of it."[2]

Captain McLeod raises his eyebrows but stays quiet. He knows about the new 155mm howitzer that has recently replaced the old World War I model.

"That's quite a vote of confidence for the men of the 333rd," McLeod says. "The new howitzer has done well in North Africa, and they're saying it's the best weapon of its class."

"That's right, McLeod. Now you tell me how these *green* colored boys are going to learn to operate such a weapon. Most of these birds are just off the farm or fresh from the street. No military experience at all, especially with modern artillery. I can't believe the army wants to turn them loose with the 155!"

Kelsey drops his head in his hands. "So far in this war, we've been able to limit the Negro's participation—mostly truck drivers, cooks, and laborers. But not artillery, not combat."

"Well, sir," McLeod replies, "I've gotten to know the men in the 333rd. I believe they'll do well with the artillery, and I'm confident that—"

"McLeod!" Kelsey yells, slamming his fist on his desk and swearing. "Stop taking up for them. Everybody knows coloreds will never cut it in combat. They're not as smart as white soldiers, and they're cowards—everybody knows that. They're not an asset, but a drain on the army's resources. And when the 333rd fails to master that weapon, my career will be history."[3]

"Sir, I respectfully disagree," McLeod says softly, swallowing hard. "I think you underestimate the potential of our black GIs. You've heard about Dorie Miller getting the Navy Cross at Pearl Harbor—"

"Yeah, yeah, the navy's black poster boy," Kelsey snaps.

"His courage saved lives on the *West Virginia*," McLeod says.[4]

"He was a laborer, McLeod, a cook, for crying out loud! In the right place at the right time, that's all."

"Sir," McLeod persists, not wanting to argue with his overbearing CO, "I'll work with these men day and night, and make sure they master the—"

"Well, you better, Captain," Kelsey interrupts. "They start training on the 155 pronto."

"Yes, sir," McLeod says.

"By the way, Captain, how are the coloreds being treated by the white soldiers? I've heard some confusing reports."

"Not so good, sir," McLeod responds. "Many of the whites resent them being here, have little to do with them, and call them degrading names. There's a lot of disrespect shown to the blacks."

"No surprise there," Kelsey says. "I hear it's the same on other bases."

"Perhaps things would be different, sir, if the army desegregated Camp Gruber instead of keeping them separate," McLeod says. "That would certainly be a better use of resources, rather than duplicating barracks and facilities."

"Never happen, Captain!" Kelsey says, standing erect, his arms crossed. "Always said that mixing white and colored units would be like a running sore. Just won't work."

"Sir, I don't mean to seem argumentative," McLeod says, clearing his throat. "But just this month, the *eighth* class of Negro pilots graduated from flight training at Tuskegee. And I hear the airfield plans to slowly desegregate its facilities."

"Maybe so, Captain," Kelsey says, frowning and looking McLeod squarely in the eye. "Let's just see how those colored pilots do overseas when battle-seasoned German pilots start shooting at them! I'll be the first one to say 'I told you so.'

"Dismissed!" Kelsey barks.

Captain McLeod salutes, turns, and leaves.

"I think the 333rd just might surprise you, Kelsey," McLeod says, chuckling, as he hurries down the hall. "Then we'll see who has the last laugh."[5, 6]

CHAPTER 24

CHRISTMAS OF '42

For the past year, President Roosevelt has been rapidly building military strength, putting every able-bodied American to work producing armaments and ammunition, and shouldering a war with troops on two different fronts. He has also watched some thirty-six million patriotic Americans register for military service, a decision allowing them to choose their desired branch of service.

Those selected from the draft lottery, instituted on September 16, 1940, are required to serve at least one year in the armed forces. But once the United States enters the war, draft terms extend through its duration.[1]

By Christmas 1942, hordes of young Americans have moved to military camps, undergoing rigorous physical and combat training and learning strict military discipline.[2]

But even after a year of war, the country's military is still segregated. At times, the GIs fight one another as they learn how to fight the enemy.

On November 9, 1943, President Roosevelt studies a report written by Brigadier General Benjamin O. Davis, U.S. Army, the first African-American inspector general in the U.S. Air Corps.[3]

General Davis has been asked to investigate the role and treatment of African-Americans in the military. In his report, he describes the military's segregation, noting a big difference in the morale and attitudes of soldiers from Southern states, in which he notes "great dissatisfaction and discouragement." He claims that African-American soldiers are denied the rewards resulting from good behavior and proper performance of duty—that upon completion of basic training, the colored combat units are not sent to theaters of operations but are transferred to service units. "The field artillery units," he writes, "are showing low morale, and don't hold out much hope for combat opportunities." He states that when new colored units are activated, few commanding officers, if any, are chosen from the colored field officers.

The general reports that colored men in uniform in the South are the target of hostility from community officials, and suffer humiliation and mistreatment from white citizens, fellow white soldiers, and white police. The black GI is made to live under harsh Jim Crow laws in the Southern states; sit in the backs of buses, streetcars, and trains; and use segregated public restrooms, alternative restaurant entrances, et cetera.[4]

One afternoon, Eleanor Roosevelt writes an article for the *New Republic*. A civil rights activist since her move to the White House in 1933, the First Lady travels nationwide, speaking out against rampant racial discrimination.

She smiles, recalling a comment made by FBI director J. Edgar Hoover. So offended by her racial views and close association with the NAACP, he once exclaimed, "Mrs. Roosevelt must have black blood."

Her pen scratches across paper: "Civil rights is the real litmus test for American democracy. There can be no democracy in the United States that does not include democracy for blacks."

Putting down her pen, she picks up a copy of *Top Secret War College Report of 1925—Use of Negro Manpower in War*. She begins to read:

"It is believed to be of such value in lieu of further study by the

General Staff, as to furnish a basis for the employment of the Negro in the next war. Compared to the white man, he [the Negro] is admittedly of inferior mentality . . . inherently weak in character. . . . If he makes good, he will have the opportunity eventually to fight in the war with all-Negro organizations."

She places her hand on her stomach, feeling slightly nauseated. *To think a major general in the army penned such derisive words!*

She continues to read: "He [the Negro man] has not the initiative and resourcefulness of the white man. . . . [H]e is by nature subservient . . . most susceptible to the influence of crowd psychology, and cannot control himself in the fear of danger. . . . In the process of evolution, the American Negro has not progressed as far as the other sub-species of the human family. . . . All officers, without exception, agree that the Negro lacks initiative, displays little or no leadership, and cannot accept responsibility."

She stops reading the report, written seventeen years earlier. Closing her eyes, she recalls reading the recorded views of other officers: "The Negro does not desire combat duty under conditions of present day warfare. That if, when drafted into service, he was given a choice of assignment to a combat organization or to a 'Labor Battalion,' the majority would choose the less dangerous service."

She raises her eyes to the ceiling, shaking her head. *I am continually frustrated with America's segregation, and white America's refusal to see how segregation mocks American values.*

She smiles as she remembers her visit with the Tuskegee airmen at their Alabama air base, as well as her trips to other U.S. military bases. *How eager the black GIs are to serve in active combat protecting their country's freedoms and values! Inferior mentality? Weak in character? Lacking in initiative, leadership, and acceptance of responsibility?! Hogwash! Everywhere I've gone, I have witnessed just the opposite!*

"Surely," she says aloud, "we white Americans should have progressed more intelligently in our views since 1925! Oh, how I deplore segregated schools, restrictive housing covenants, employment discrimination, literacy tests, and unfair voting procedures. I must continue to try to change the status quo."[5, 6]

She stands, pacing the room, stretching and thinking. She reflects on the day in 1941 when she visited the Tuskegee Air Base. She remembers every detail: talking with wounded black soldiers in hospital beds, opening an integrated canteen, flying in a plane with a black pilot . . .

She laughs. *Those photographers had a field day when I took off into the air with Charles Alfred Anderson, a black trainee airman. I couldn't wait to get those photographs developed and back to the White House, hoping I could use them to convince my stubborn husband to send the Tuskegee airmen into North Africa and Europe. Oh, and the criticism I received after that. . . . Seems like Americans love to criticize everything I say and do.*

She recalls asking Franklin to let her visit American troops and speak out against racial discrimination.

"I give you that freedom, Eleanor," he had told her, but quickly cautioned, "You must, however, be careful. The Negro situation is too hot."[7]

CHAPTER 25

THE 155MM HOWITZER

—CAMP GRUBER, OKLAHOMA—
JANUARY 1943

Lieutenant Colonel Harmon Kelsey dreads the day the 333rd Field Artillery Battalion will begin training on the 155mm howitzer.

"They'll never learn it," he tells Captain McLeod. He picks up the War Department's *Field Artillery Field Manual* on firing the howitzer, waving it in the air. "This manual is a hundred and ninety-eight pages of deep technical information *just on firing* the 155. Just *one* part of the entire process. It's much too complicated for these men. Some of them just have a grammar school education."

"It's a lot to learn, but I have faith in these men, sir," McLeod says.

"Well, they better learn it," Kelsey snarls. "If they don't, I will have a lot to answer for."

Kelsey and McLeod watch the men of the 333rd assemble for the class. The instructor and his men pull up in a Diamond T truck carrying the massive weapon, ammunition, and equipment.

Kelsey shakes his head forlornly.

"This will be a disaster," he mutters.[1]

P rivate Georgie Davis's eyes widen when he sees the sheer size of the weapon.

"That's what we'll be shooting?" he asks.

"Don't you worry, George," Stewart says. "We'll get it. There's nothing we can't learn."

The colonel overhears the men talking, and barks at Captain McLeod, "Your people better shut up and pay attention!"

The instructor gathers the men around the huge weapon, explaining its history and how it operates.

"Men, the old M1918 155 was copied from the French 155 Canon Schneider used in the Great War. Lots of the features haven't changed."

"What's a Canon Schneider?" Georgie asks, wiping sweat from his forehead.

Private Green frowns, hissing, "Quiet, Lil' Georgie. He'll explain it. Nobody knows anything about this weapon yet."

The pair receives a baleful look from their captain.

The instructor continues: "The government has just produced four thousand of these 'Long Toms.' They can fire a distance of sixteen thousand yards, three thousand yards farther than the old model. That's *nine miles*—a really long reach. The army has supplied us with Diamond T trucks and M5 High Speed tractors to transport the 155s, along with projectiles packaged in metal canisters."

"Look at the size of those shells!" Georgie whispers. "They must weigh—"

"Shhhh!" someone says.

"The howitzer has separate loading ammunition," the teacher continues, "that includes a projectile, a bag of powder propellant charge, a fuse, and a primer. The HE—high-explosive shell—weighs about one hundred pounds, but some shells weigh much more. In order for the weapon to be efficient in battle, the loading, positioning, and firing should be done *in less than five minutes*. After each round is fired, the powder chambers of the 155mm tubes must be cleaned and inspected. If not, the powder residue builds up, causing the barrel to possibly explode. Of course, this can't always be done in the midst of battle when you must fire round after round without stopping."

He continues. "Another safety hazard with the 155mm is the powerful hydropneumatic recoil system. It's the job of the gunner corporal and assistant gunner to keep the men away after firing. The forceful impact of the recoil can kill a man. When you hear a man shout, 'Stand back!' get out of the way quickly."

The GIs stare at the enormous weapon, two large wheels attached to each side of the barrel.

"The 155mm barrel sits atop a mounting that supports the recoil cylinder. The top and bottom carriages include a single axle, double-tired with steel rims and rubber wheels. The M114 155mm howitzer weighs six and a half tons and has a running length of twenty-four feet, a width of eight feet, and a height of nearly six feet. It requires an eleven-man crew to operate it, including a unit commander, gun layer, loaders, ammunition handlers, and others."

The instructor pauses. "Any questions so far?"

"We have no questions," Colonel Kelsey barks.

"Okay, then, let's continue," the instructor says, patting one of the large shells. "The 155mm shell comes in many flavors." He smiles, as if trying to ease the men's visible tension. "They come in high-explosive, chemical, illumination, and smoke."

Georgie overhears Kelsey tell McLeod, "This is so above their heads they're probably not getting a single word of it."

The instructor continues. "Each shell contains its own individual elements; for instance, the muzzle velocity of the high-explosive, chem-ical, and smoke rounds are about eighteen hundred and fifty feet per second. The illumination round is somewhat lower, at eleven hundred and sixty feet per second. The high-explosive and chemical rounds manage the longer engagement range—out to sixteen thousand, five hundred and fifty-five yards. The smoke round manages a nine thou-sand, seven hundred–yard range; the illumination round peaks at seventy-one hundred yards. Each of these projectiles is loaded with a bagged charge."

"I'm lost," one soldier exclaims loudly enough for everyone to hear. "Are we supposed to remember all this?"

"Best be listening," Green says, eyeing the colonel. "We need to know all this stuff before we can fire these things."

"Men, notice the carriages on the 155," the instructor says, pointing to the gun's supporting steel frame. "This carriage is a split-trail type that can be closed for transport and opened to support the firing process. The breech incorporates a two-step, slow-cone interrupted screw."

"A what?" Georgie asks. He shuts up when he sees the colonel look at him, roll his eyes, and shake his head.

"The gun mounting allows for an elevation of minus-two to plus-sixty-three degrees and traversal of twenty-five degrees right or left," the instructor explains, pointing to the mounting and directional wheel. "Now that I've explained it, let me show you how it works."

The instructor demonstrates how to secure the howitzer, spreading wide the two rear steel braces. A firing jack supports the front of the weapon when in firing position and all wheels are off the ground. Several men step forward, picking up the heavy shell, sliding it into the powder chamber, and then ramming it with a six-foot rod. Another man shouts a series of numbers. The gunner turns a large metal wheel, adjusting the barrel's angle and height, and places a powder charge in the chamber. After inserting the primer and firing lock, the instructor shouts, "Stand back!" A gunner pulls the firing cord, and the shell launches with a deafening roar, sending a huge ball of white smoke skyward.

Georgie claps his hands to his ears, unprepared for the sudden eardrum-splitting boom. He stares transfixed at the instructor.

"Nothing like a few fireworks to create a learning situation," the instructor laughs.

"As you now see," he says, "firing this baby is no simple task. Everything must be loaded perfectly and separately—the projectile, bag of powder, fuse, and primer. My crew can load, adjust the target, and fire in five minutes. That's record time. Of course, they are well trained and highly experienced. Once you people learn to use this weapon properly, you can kill a lot of Nazis."

Someone hands out copies of *Field Artillery Field Manual* on firing. "Don't just read it," the instructor says. "Memorize it!"

He passes out another War Department manual. "And when you finish that one," he says, "memorize this one, too!"[2]

Georgie Davis thumbs through the 198-page manual. *I've got to memorize all these pages?*

He sees Kelsey turn to McLeod, smirking and exclaiming loudly, "Captain, you still think these boys can load and fire that in five minutes? If so, you're dreaming! More like five hundred!"

Georgie waits to hear the captain's response. McLeod shows no expression, and says nothing.

CHAPTER 26

THE EARLY MONTHS OF '43

—EUROPE—
JANUARY–FEBRUARY 1943

Hitler's anxiety deepens as he continues to hear discomforting news from the Eastern Front. The brutal battle rages on and on, already in its sixth month. German soldiers engage in bloody combat on bone-chilling cold battlefields, struggling to survive in waist-deep snow, below-freezing temperatures, and with little food for their empty bellies. The Fatherland's faithful sons lie dead and dying on Soviet battlefields, the medical care inadequate, and the ground too frozen to dig proper graves. Hitler knows that Stalingrad is proving to be such a wartime disaster that not even Joseph Goebbels can make the situation appear hopeful. In late January, Hitler receives news that the Soviets have taken Stalingrad's last airfield.

"Troops can no longer receive food and ammunition," his advisers tell him. "Without the airfield, no supplies can be delivered."

But the Führer remains stubborn. "I demand the troops defend themselves to the last!"[1]

In Poland, at the beginning of 1943, Jewish wives and mothers, still alive in the filthy Warsaw ghetto, mourn the deaths and deportations of almost 350,000 of their family members and friends. For the past three years, they have watched their loved ones suffer and die of disease and starvation in the closely guarded, 1.3-square-mile, sealed-off city, surrounded by ten-foot-high walls and topped with rows of barbed wire. Those who have survived now wait to be executed or shipped off to the Treblinka extermination camp.[2]

But the Polish Jews are not yet defeated. When they hear that the Germans plan to enter the city, deport the rest of them, and destroy the ghetto, they somehow find new strength, weapons, and ammunition. On January 18, they stage an uprising against them.

After four days of battle, they run the Germans out of their city. When, after April 19, the Germans reenter the ghetto, the Jews have rearmed and are waiting for them. For three weeks, they defend themselves until they can fight no longer. The soldiers raze and liquidate the Warsaw ghetto.[3, 4]

In mid-January, President Roosevelt and Prime Minister Winston Churchill travel to Casablanca, Morocco, where they meet with other world leaders. They call for Adolf Hitler's unconditional surrender, one in which no exceptions are given to Germany. Most agree it is the only way to ensure postwar peace.[5]

At the end of January, sixty-four B-17 Flying Fortress and B-24 Liberator long-range bombers take off from their bases in England, for the first time dropping bombs on Germany. Both the RAF Bomber Command and the U.S. Eighth Air Force target and bomb Germany's Wilhelmshaven Naval Base. Planes demolish factories and warehouses, seeking to impair the German military. For two nights, the Royal Air Force bombs Berlin.[6]

CHAPTER 27

THE URGENT MESSAGE

—WOLFSCHANZE, EASTERN FRONT—
JANUARY 1943

Hitler buries his head in his hands when a messenger delivers the morning battle reports from the Eastern Front. *Can the news get any worse?*

"My Führer, our troops in the Soviet Union are freezing, starving, and dying of disease. Frostbite is causing many casualties. They are begging us for more supplies."

"I am told the Luftwaffe is supplying them by air," Hitler snaps. "Are we not dropping seventy tons of supplies a day to our troops there?"

"Yes, my Führer. But freezing weather and Soviet fighters have taken their toll on our troops. Seventy tons of food and supplies is not adequate. Our men need at least three hundred tons a day to survive. They are so hungry they are killing and eating their horses."

"They must do on one-third of their normal rations," Hitler demands, waving his hand and dismissing the messenger.[1]

That same morning, Hitler receives an urgent message from General Friedrich Paulus, one of his most experienced generals and the defender of German forces surrounded in Stalingrad. Paulus served on both the Eastern and Western Front during the Great War. His message is tense:

Army requests immediate permission to surrender in order to save lives of remaining troops.[2]

For the next few minutes, Hitler sits quietly, reflecting on the trusted leader who has served him so well. Commander of the Sixth Army and recipient of the coveted Knight's Cross, General Paulus has performed with distinction in the invasions of Poland, Belgium, and France, and has led the Wehrmacht in battle at Dnepropetrovsk in Russia.

"General Paulus wants to surrender? No, I will not permit it! I have promised my people that nobody will drive us out of Stalingrad."[3]

Hitler dictates a firm response to the general.

"Supreme Commander to 6 Army, January 24, 1943. Surrender is forbidden. 6 Army will hold their positions to the last man and the last round and by their heroic endurance will make an unforgettable contribution towards the establishment of a defensive front and the salvation of the Western world."[4]

Hitler awards Paulus the Oak Leaves of his Knight's Cross and promotes him to field marshal. "No field marshal has ever been captured," he reasons. "I expect Field Marshal Paulus to fight to his death, to the bitter end."

The next day, Hitler receives word that, despite his orders, Field Marshal Paulus and the Sixth Army have surrendered. He also learns that most of Paulus's army lies dead or dying on frozen battlefields, and the rest have been taken to Soviet POW camps.

"Paulus is still alive?" Hitler shouts.

"Yes, my Führer," a messenger responds. "We have learned he is alive and collaborating with the Soviets, urging our other troops in the east to surrender."

Hitler finds it hard to breathe, his face losing its color. "Paulus chooses surrender over suicide!" He curses, ranting uncontrollably about Paulus's betrayal.

The messenger trembles as he stands at attention, waiting to receive instructions.

"Committing suicide is the only response to such a humiliating defeat of this magnitude," Hitler fumes. "Find Field Marshal Paulus's family and imprison them in one of our concentration camps!"[5]

To Hitler's disgust, the Battle of Stalingrad officially ends on February 2, 1943. The defeat proves a deep humiliation to the Führer, and a turning point for Germany, her army now in full retreat, and more than ninety thousand of her troops taken prisoner.

Two days later, Hitler announces a three-day period of national mourning. Not to mourn the men killed or captured at Stalingrad, but to mourn the shame Field Marshal Paulus has brought to Germany.[6, 7]

In the face of such high casualties, Hitler cancels hundreds of thousands of military exemptions, demanding that every German man between sixteen and sixty-five years of age, and every German woman between seventeen and fifty, mobilize and prepare to fight.[8]

Hitler has a firm message for the German people this year, the tenth anniversary of his accession to power.

"The National Socialist state will continue the fight with the same zealousness that the movement has called its own from the moment when it began to take power in Germany."

He calls for total war for everyone in Germany, an all-or-nothing struggle.[9]

In early spring, Hitler learns that one of his trusted leaders, Claus von Stauffenberg, has been seriously wounded while serving with Field Marshal Erwin Rommel's Afrika Korps at Sebkhet en Noual, south of Mezzouna in the North African desert.

"Von Stauffenberg has served me well in Poland, France, Tunisia, and the Soviet Union," Hitler says. "What happened, and what is the extent of his injuries?"

"Allied fighters strafed his Horch staff car," the messenger reports. "They pitted his body with shrapnel. Von Stauffenberg lost an eye, his right hand, and the last two fingers on his left hand."

"Was anyone else injured in the incident?" Hitler asks.

"Yes, my Führer. An officer sitting in the backseat was killed."

"Make sure Claus receives the best medical attention," Hitler orders. "When he recovers, I plan to promote him to chief of staff to Commander General Friedrich Fromm. Claus von Stauffenberg is truthworthy, and this promotion will give him direct access to me and to my briefing sessions. I need more loyal men like him."[10]

CHAPTER 28

THE TRAINING MANUALS

Private Georgie Davis rubs his eyes and closes his copy of *Field Artillery Field Manual: Tactics and Technique*.

"What's wrong, George?" Sergeant Stewart asks when he walks by Georgie's bunk.

"I don't understand a word of this," he says. "It's Greek to me."

"Yeah. I know what you mean. It's about as clear as mud, George. But we have no choice. We have to learn this one, and the other manuals, too."

Stewart sits down beside Georgie, takes the manual from his hands, and opens it to page three.

"George, I just finished studying this section," Stewart says. "It describes 'considerations affecting delivery of artillery fire.'" He begins to read aloud: "'Range, field of fire and dead space, observation, signal communication, character of ground at emplacement.'"

"What does 'dead space' mean?" Georgie asks.

Sergeant Stewart runs his index finger down the page. "It says 'dead space' is 'the terrain between the mask and the points of impact of trajectories just clearing the mask.'"

"Oh," Georgie says. "Well, that clears that up."

Stewart smiles. "We've both got a lot to learn, George. Maybe we can learn it together."

After the next training session, Georgie receives another manual: *Field Artillery Tactical Employment.* Again he is told to memorize it.

Davis opens the manual and reads the first paragraph in Section 1 on the role of field artillery: "Field artillery is a supporting arm for relatively long range combat. Massed artillery fire possesses great power of destruction and neutralization."

Georgie rubs his forehead and continues reading: "It contributes to the action of the entire force by giving close and continuous fire support to infantry (cavalry) (armored) units and by giving depth to combat by counterbattery fire, fire on hostile reserves, fire to restrict movements in rear areas, and fire to disrupt command agencies."

He shakes his head. *Looks like I've got my work cut out for me. How will I ever learn all this stuff?*[1]

Sergeant Stewart meets with Georgie Davis almost daily, reading and studying the manuals together. They soon realize how complicated positioning, loading, and firing the 155s will be. They learn about camouflage, field fortifications, communication systems of field artillery units, offensive combat, defensive combat, retrograde movements, ammunition, and maintenance. In the field, they practice repeatedly all the steps involved in operating the howitzer.

"It seems we've got to learn how to load and fire the 155 quickly," Stewart says as he studies the firing manual. "And at the same time, be deadly accurate."

Stewart reads aloud from the manual: "Accuracy in the performance of individual duties must be stressed; it is obtained by insistence upon exactness from the beginning. Speed acquired by prompt performance of individual duties in regular sequence must not be stressed at the expense of accuracy."

"How is it possible to be accurate when we'll be firing at targets nine miles away?" Georgie asks.

"That's what we've got to learn, George."

"There's also a long section on precautions in handling ammunition," Stewart says.

"Meaning that handling the ammo is dangerous," Georgie says.

"I'd say 'deadly.' It tells us not to toss, roll, or drop ammo; don't smoke cigarettes around it; don't tamper with it; don't expose it to gas," Stewart says. "With pieces using separate loading ammunition—like our 155—it says 'primers are not inserted until after the breechblock is closed and locked in its recess.'"

"Do you know what a primer, breechblock, and recess is, Sergeant?"

"Not sure I do, Private."

Day after day, the 333rd trainees meet with the howitzer instructor, learning more and more about operating the colossal weapon. They are each given specific jobs: section chief, gunner, assistant gunner, loaders, rammers, ammunition bearers, forward observer, and others. Everyone is taught to perform his job—in the loading, swabbing, cleaning, positioning, and firing process. The gun crews are instructed to be disciplined, to observe safety rules, to be aware at all times and in all situations, and to keep equipment properly maintained and ready to fire.

"Carelessness is not tolerated," they are told. "If you set the fuse improperly, cut the fuse too short, drop the fuse on the ground, or jam it against the side of the breech, it can explode. Watch your hands and fingers, or you'll lose them."

Throughout the long days, the instructor teaches the 333rd trainees about the jobs of the sergeant, corporals, telephone operator, linemen, recorders, chief mechanics, and sentinels. He instructs the men who will be in charge of resupplying ammunition, improving emplacements, concealing the howitzers from enemy ground and air observation, announcing fire commands, and on and on. He passes out cotton balls to place in their ears to protect their hearing.

During practices, the battery commander sends the data to the executive:

Instrument direction left 146, 3,800.
Base deflection left 150.
On No. 1 Open 3.
Shell MK. I.
Fuze quick.
Battery one round.
Zone 5 Mils.
Quadrant 115, 125.

The process is complicated and highly specialized, each man working with concentrated speed and striving for one hundred percent accuracy.

At the end of the training session, the instructor tells the men the 333rd will be attached to individual divisions, moving with them and supplying them with direct support.

"That means we'll be assigned to give additional fire support where it's most urgently needed," Stewart explains to Georgie. "Our CO can move us every twelve to twenty-four hours. Looks like we'll never be staying in the same place for long."

"So we're the ones who'll step in and rescue the others?" Georgie asks.

"Pretty much, George. We've all got an important part to play in the overall operation. Seems like a big responsibility."[2]

CHAPTER 29

THE BABY

— MUSKOGEE COUNTY, OKLAHOMA —
FEBRUARY 1943

On a cold, blustery morning, Catherine Adams carries her infant son, a brand-new fountain pen, and a small black Bible, and boards a Greyhound bus in Columbia, South Carolina. She settles into a backseat and heads west to Muskogee County, Oklahoma. She wants to surprise her husband, Curtis, who is currently undergoing basic training at Camp Gruber, introducing him to his son, Jesse.

Catherine and Curtis married eight months before Curtis enlisted in the army in October 1942. He was first sent to nearby Fort Jackson. Catherine worried when he was reassigned to Camp Gruber, almost a thousand miles away. She hoped he'd still be at Fort Jackson when the baby came.

She wraps another blanket around Jesse. "Little guy, you're gonna meet your daddy tomorrow. You're gonna love him. He's got a real tender heart."

Catherine touches her son's chubby milk-chocolate face. "Jesse, you look just like your daddy! He'll be so proud of you. And so surprised to see you!"

The journey proves long and difficult for the young mother, who has never traveled far from home. The bus stops at every major city: Augusta, Atlanta, Tuscaloosa, Tupelo, Memphis, Conway, Fort Smith, and finally Muskogee County. At each stop, Catherine finds the "Coloreds" toilet and sink, changes Jesse's diaper, washes and feeds him, and then returns to the back of the bus. She quickly averts her gaze when some white men wink at her.

"Here I am, holding this baby, and those old flirty men think— Lord have mercy!" she mutters.

The Dust Bowl of the southern Great Plains greets her with hills and rolling plains. Oklahoma has been a state for only thirty-five years. Before that it was "Indian Territory," the new home of the displaced "Five Civilized Tribes" of Cherokees, Chickasaws, Choctaws, Creeks, and Seminoles, who were marched to the federal reservations two or three decades before the Civil War. During the 1870s, the government moved an additional twenty-five tribes to Oklahoma.[1]

Stepping off the bus in the small town of Braggs, Catherine thinks she has landed on another planet. When she asks a white woman where Camp Gruber is located, the woman points her finger northeast, frowns, and mumbles something Catherine can't understand.

"Thank you," Catherine says, dropping her gaze to the ground in an effort to protect herself from the woman's hateful glare.

"We'd probably gotten a warmer welcome from wild Injuns," Catherine whispers to Jesse when out of the woman's hearing.

A guard at the front gate escorts Catherine and Jesse through the wide stone entrance pillars and into Camp Gruber. She is taken aback by the enormous size of the base, its vast parade grounds stretching for two miles, rows and rows of white barracks trimmed in green, the impressive headquarters building topped with an American flag. As she walks down the gravel sidewalks, all she sees are soldiers, tents, trucks, tanks, jeeps, planes, and barracks. In the background, she hears the loud, strong voices of men marching and singing: "Over hill, over dale, we have hit the dusty trail, and those caissons go rolling along. . . ."

Private Adams's mouth drops open when he first spots his wife holding the small bundle in her arms. He bounds toward her, gasping her name, and takes her in his arms.

"Curtis," she says, tears streaming down her face, "this is Jesse, your son."

Curtis takes the baby in his arms and for a long time hugs the boy to his chest, whispering over and over, "He's beautiful, Catherine. My very own son! And he looks just like you!"

"I knew you'd be proud," Catherine says. "I just couldn't wait for you to meet him."

Catherine follows the proud new father as he carries his son around the camp, introducing the child to some of the 333rd troopers.

"A fine boy, Private Adams," Sergeant Stewart says, holding out his hands to take the baby. "Mind if I hold him?"

"Of course not," Adams says, handing him the baby.

"I hope to have a child one day," Stewart says, grinning and turning to Catherine. "Mrs. Adams, I sure am glad this boy looks like you, and not like his daddy."

Sergeant Stewart gently takes Jesse's tiny right hand in his own, staring at it for a long time.

"Your boy's got a pitcher's hand," Stewart says. "Bet it won't be long till he's throwing a baseball!"

Adams refuses to let Georgie hold his baby.

"No, Lil' Georgie," Adams says. "You'll drop him."

When Colonel Kelsey meets Catherine and Jesse, he is polite but tells Private Adams that Camp Gruber is no place to bring a baby. Captain McLeod, however, takes the child in his arms and smiles at Adams.

"You must be proud, Private," McLeod says. "You've got one strong, fine son here. Why, there's no telling how Jesse might one day change the world."

When Catherine and Curtis have a few hours alone, Catherine opens her purse and pulls out two small wrapped gifts.

"I brought you my Bible, Curtis," she says. "It's the one I've had since I was a little girl."

Curtis takes the small black Bible in his hand, kissing his loving wife. "I'll treasure it, Catherine."

She hands him the second gift, smiling as he unwraps it.

"You always wanted a real fountain pen," she says. "I saved up my money and bought you a Sheaffer."

"It's beautiful, Catherine. Never thought I'd ever have a Sheaffer pen! I promise to write you every day with it."

Catherine finds everything she needs at Camp Gruber during her stay: guesthouse, beauty shop, laundry, sports arena, lodge, and lake. She has a pocket-sized picture of herself and Jesse made at the photo studio on base and gives it to Curtis.

Two days later, Catherine and Jesse board the bus, walk to the backseats, and begin the long trip home.

Looking out the window, she watches the southern Great Plains disappear from view and thanks God her man is serving under the nice Captain McLeod.

Looking down at her sleeping baby, she whispers, "Won't be long till this war's over, Jesse, and your daddy'll come back home to us."

CHAPTER 30

TRAINING

—CAMP GRUBER—
EARLY SPRING 1943

In the training fields of Camp Gruber, Sergeant Stewart stands beside Captain McLeod as they watch the 333rd GIs struggle to learn military maneuvers quickly and efficiently.

"These boys are from farms and factories, and have no experience in the ways of war," Stewart tells Captain McLeod. "They're doing okay now, but I worry about them when they land on battlefields and face experienced, seasoned armies."

"I have the same concerns, Sergeant," McLeod says, rubbing his chin. "You are older, more experienced, and have more than your share of good common sense. Please help them where and when you can."

"Thank you, sir. I will."

During his training at Camp Gruber, Stewart watches with amazement as thirty-five thousand troops take demanding classes covering a litany of military subjects, including weapons, drill tactics, care of equipment, military discipline, hand-to-hand combat, and physical training—all the skills needed to prepare them for combat. The training begins every morning with shaving, dressing, and reporting to a parade field for thirty minutes of hard calisthenics. After breakfast, the men run to their classes.

The classes are varied and intense. The men struggle with tearful, burning eyes from tear gas despite wearing gas masks, long hours on the rifle range learning to handle weapons, and a host of other skills they must master.

Stewart watches the soldiers, who, in the squatting position, learn to operate the .30-caliber Springfield rifle. They are taught to assemble and disassemble the rifle, clean, and care for it. They learn about ammunition, spare parts and accessories, and personal safety precautions. Marksmanship training includes range practice and rifle fire techniques, firing at moving targets on the ground—vehicles and personnel—and in the air—antiaircraft marksmanship.[1]

At Green Leaf Lake, Stewart sees teams build bridges across the lake using pontoon boats, making them strong enough to support Diamond T trucks loaded with heavy howitzers.

The men also learn practical and needed skills such as water purification, sanitation responsibilities, and personal hygiene. Their instructor is a sad little man, his shoulders stooped and his voice monotone, dull, and irritatingly squeaky—like fingernails clawing a blackboard.

"You've got to stay healthy," Jeb, the instructor, tells them. "You must be in fighting shape at all times. Did you know that, in other wars, disease knocked out more soldiers than battle casualties? The danger of disease is always around the corner. You men will be crowded together in camps, coming in contact with unfamiliar and sometimes contagious germs. We often deal with respiratory, intestinal, and venereal diseases like syphilis and gonorrhea. Bad stuff. Many of these diseases can be avoided with good health and sanitation practices."

Georgie Davis's eyes begin to glaze over. George Moten tries to suppress a yawn. The instructor continues. "Before you came to Gruber, each of you was vaccinated against smallpox, typhoid fever and paratyphoid fevers, and tetanus. To keep you from getting sick, these immunizations will be repeated at regular intervals during your military service. In the meantime, cover your nose and mouth when you cough or sneeze, don't use common drinking cups and canteens, and for heaven's sake, don't spit on the floor or ground."

Several of the men laugh. Jeb clears his throat, his face reddening.

"You can laugh now," he says defensively, "but when you end up with 'gyppy tummy,' diarrhea, dysentery, and other bacterial food or excrement poisoning, I doubt any of you will be laughing then."

"'Gyppy tummy'?" Davis whispers. "Yuck."

The instructor raises his voice, his expression overly serious. He avoids making eye contact with the men, keeping his eyes focused on a distant wall.

"Now, men," he says, "I don't need to tell you about all the venereal diseases lurking out there. To stay safe, you must avoid promiscuous sexual intercourse altogether."

The men laugh loudly and shout, "Booooooo."

"There are ways to avoid venereal diseases," he says, ignoring their laughter and shouts.

"What are those ways?" Sergeant Forte asks with a serious expression.

"Well," Jeb says, "if you don't want to avoid promiscuous sexual intercourse altogether, here are some suggestions."

"Wait a minute!" Forte says, unsmiling. "Let me write these down."

The instructor shakes his head, raises his eyes to the ceiling, and with a deadpan expression continues. "Don't have sex with infected women, protect yourself by using adequate prophylaxis—we'll supply you with free adequate prophylaxis—and stay away from houses of prostitution. We can cut down the VD rate considerably by being careful."

"Is this information really necessary?" Private Adams whispers to Sergeant Stewart.

Stewart smiles. "He's not near finished yet, I'm afraid."

The instructor moves from venereal diseases to human waste disposal.

"I know you'd rather be learning how to fire a rifle than how to dig a cat hole," he says. "But you must know how to dig a proper and effective latrine. In doing so, you'll be able to control flies and prevent fly breeding and avoid contaminating water supplies."

For the rest of the afternoon, the men are bombarded and deathly bored with details about digging and designing mound latrines, bored-hole latrines, pail latrines, straddle latrines, deep pit latrines, Otway pits, soakage pits, and urine troughs.

"I hope we never have to see or hear this guy again," Forte says. "I can't stand much more of 'Mr. Monotone.'"

Upon overhearing Forte's insult, the inspector looks the sergeant in the eye, and for the first time he curls the corners of his lips.

"Tomorrow," Jeb says, still staring at Forte, "I will teach you *everything* you need to know about controlling eye gnats, blackflies, chiggers, fleas, roaches, ants, lice, mites, bedbugs, ticks, and rats."[2]

CHAPTER 31

THE HELPER

—CAMP GRUBER, OKLAHOMA—
SPRING 1943

Private Curtis Adams reads the *Medical Field Manual*, struggling to figure out how to splint a broken bone, trying to use his own leg as a model. Sergeant Stewart walks by and sees the young medic starting and stopping and making no progress.

"Need a leg?" Stewart asks.

"Sure do!" Adams says.

After successfully splinting Stewart's "fractured femur," Adams places the opened manual on the ground.

"Now," he says, "I need to evacuate you from the active battlefield and transport you to a medical installation."

"Good luck, son," Stewart says, smiling. "How are you gonna do that?"

"I'll have to carry you, of course," Adams says. "Lie down."

Adams picks up the book, flipping through pages of illustrations. "I can carry you in several different ways, Sergeant," he says. "There's the arms carry, the saddle-back carry, the fireman's carry, and the two-man packsaddle carry."

"I'm a pretty big man," Stewart says. "Not sure you can pick me up. Wouldn't it be better to use a litter?"

Adams turns to the section of the manual that describes putting together a makeshift litter if no stretcher is available. "Says here that I can transport the injured using a camp cot, door, bench, or ladder."

Turning the page, he reads aloud. "Here's another way to make a litter: 'The barrel of a rifle is inserted through each sleeve of an overcoat turned inside out and buttoned, sleeves inside, buttons down, collar toward the rifle butts.'"

"Very creative," Stewart says. "Just hope one of the rifles don't go off and shoot the man carrying the litter. Then you'll need another litter and three more men to carry them."[1]

During the afternoons, the men have some recreational time. Stewart is amazed at the huge sports arena equipped for basketball, volleyball, boxing, weight lifting, and badminton. He also enjoys the three swimming pools, fishing lake, four theaters, and especially Gruber's ten baseball diamonds. The camp also offers the men some special events to entertain them.[2]

"In December, the camp has scheduled a boxing exhibition with heavyweight prizefighter Joe Louis," Stewart tells Forte.

"Oh yeah!" Forte says. "The 'Brown Bomber.'"

"That's the one," Stewart says. "Louis is the son of Alabama cotton pickers. Do you remember when German heavyweight Max Schmeling defeated and humiliated Louis?"

"Yep! And the 'Bomber' challenged him again in 1938 and won, knockin' him out in just two minutes and four seconds."[3]

"With that defeat," Stewart says, laughing, "Louis, the Alabama Negro, dealt Hitler a damaging and embarrassing blow."

One afternoon, Stewart watches Private Moss try, without much success, to master the art of throwing a dummy hand grenade. Time after time, he fails, his movements clumsy, the grenade slipping through his fingers and falling to the ground. The Texan's frustration shows visibly after each disastrous attempt.

"You need some help, Private?"

"I'll never get the hang of throwing this thing," Moss says. "I'm afraid I'll blow my arm off."

"Son, if that thing explodes in your hand, you'll be missing more than jus' an arm.

"Wait here. I'll be right back," Stewart says, walking toward his barracks. When he returns, he carries a worn baseball.

"Throwing a grenade is a lot like throwing a baseball," he says. "You can't point a grenade at a target like you do a rifle. Grenades have a blast radius. You've got to identify your enemy before you pull the pin. When you've got your target, take the grenade with your throwing hand, like this."

Sergeant Stewart demonstrates the grip as Moss watches closely.

"Put it in the palm of your hand with the pull ring pointing up. Use your thumb to put steady pressure on the safety lever, and don't let up till you're ready to throw it. Use your other hand to pull the ring. Then throw it overhand."

Stewart places the baseball in Moss's right hand. "Here, try it.

"Plant your feet about shoulder-width apart," he says. "Bend your knees slightly, then cock your arm back and hurl the grenade over your head jus' as you take a strong step forward."

The young private looks at the field ahead as if targeting the enemy. He holds the baseball tightly in his right hand, using his thumb to put pressure on the side as if it were the safety lever. Keeping the pressure applied, he pretends to pull the pin with his other hand and positions his arm high as if ready to throw it.

"Good," Stewart says. "Now plant your feet, bend your knees, and throw it, just like I said. Your arm should pass next to your ear, and you should twist slightly at the hips. Then jus' let it roll out of your fingertips as it leaves your hand."

With an overhand motion, Moss throws the ball, letting it roll gracefully off his fingers.

"Good job!" Stewart says, slapping Moss's back. "Now, after the grenade leaves your hand, let your arm continue its natural path downward. Then hit the deck. Shrapnel will kill you jus' like a Kraut."

Moss practices hurling the baseball over his head, hitting the ground, and burying his face in dirt.

They spend the afternoon throwing the baseball, standing and kneeling, pulling pretend pins, and blowing up imaginary enemies. By chow time, Moss has become an expert.[4]

During supper, Moss sits down beside Stewart.

"I reckon you're wanting to get back to pitching that baseball again, aren't you, Sergeant?" Moss asks. "I hear you're a pretty good pitcher."

"Yeah, I miss the game. Wonder how the Piedmont Giants are doing without me. That is, if they have enough men left to make a team."

Moss smiles. "You'll be back on the team soon. And one of these days, I'll bet you and ol' Jackie Robinson'll be in the big leagues. Probably giving that lefty Hal Newhouser a run for his money!"

Stewart grins, closes his eyes, and shakes his head. "Won't be holding my breath waiting for that to happen!"

When Sergeant Forte walks by, the men pull out a chair for him.

"Join us, Sergeant," Moss says. "Sergeant Stewart and I are talking about baseball. I told him he's got the stuff to be up there pitching with Newhouser."

Forte smirks. "You dreamin'! Coloreds and whites on the same field?"

"One day, maybe," Moss says. "Who knows?"

Stewart takes a long sip of coffee. "Heard Newhouser tried to enlist but was four-F."

"Now, why would anybody want to enlist?" Forte asks.

"Jus' maybe he wants to serve our country," Stewart says. "Can't see you or me learning German or Japanese if we lose this war."

Forte ignores his remark. "Not everyone's like you, Sergeant. You're just a plain fool enlistin' when you were too old to get drafted. You coulda stayed home."

"Thirty-eight's not that old," Stewart says. He turns his head and looks squarely at Forte. "And no, Sergeant, I'm no fool. Not by a long shot."

Forte stays silent, looking down at his tray.

"I hear the doc said Newhouser's got a bum heart," Moss says, as if trying to calm things between the two men. "Gather Newhouser's pretty disappointed."

"I know Detroit's glad he'll be back on the mound," Stewart says.

Sergeant Forte drops his fork into the half-eaten food and pushes his tray away.

"If you ask me, his heart doesn't hurt his pitchin' none!" Forte snaps. "How can he throw a ball like a killer-diller with a broke ticker?"[5]

"Don't know," Stewart says. "But ease up, son. Don't need to blow a fuse."

CHAPTER 32

THE VISITOR

Mager Bradley, twenty-six, a Mississippian, arrived at Gruber back in the summer of 1942, joining the 333rd in August when the battalion was activated. At home in Bolivar County, his eighteen-year-old fiancée, Eva Mae James, stitches her wedding dress, anxiously anticipating their December wedding.

Along with her regular "sugar reports," Eva Mae sends Bradley boxes of homemade goodies and toiletries, including a bar of his favorite Woodbury soap. She knows Bradley loathes the army-issue soap he calls "bear grease."

Corporal Bradley shares most of the presents with others, but not the Woodbury. It's special, and he keeps it hidden.

He has the small bar of soap tucked in his pocket on Sunday, April 18, 1943, when President Roosevelt visits the camp. Bradley thinks about giving the bar of soap to Roosevelt but decides the soap's too precious to him to give away, even to the president of the United States.

Bradley and the others stand at attention as the president's light-colored convertible rolls slowly down the narrow road. Photographers swarm around him, snapping pictures of the smiling president.

Bradley's eyes gleam when the president's car passes the line of 155mm howitzers. At lunchtime, Bradley watches Roosevelt eat chili with GIs in the mess hall. Bradley hears that FDR has never reviewed a full division, and he's pleased the commander in chief seems impressed.

At day's end, Bradley listens to Roosevelt's remarks to the troops, complimenting them on their fine appearance. They laugh when Roosevelt brags about the camp's cooks, confessing he doesn't eat that well at the White House. He congratulates the men who've just completed training and will soon be heading for overseas service.

That night, Bradley unwraps the new bar of Woodbury, sniffs its familiar fragrance, and heads for a hot shower. It's been a splendid day, he concludes.[1]

On the first day of Passover, April 20, 1943, Sergeant George E. Shomo, twenty-one, reflects as he sits on the barrack steps reading a comic book. Leaning back, enjoying the warm weather, he spots a group of Jewish trainees sitting nearby, eating matzos. In the distance, he watches trainers teach sentry dogs to leap five-foot hurdles.

Shomo recalls his graduation from high school in Red Bank, New Jersey. It was just two months before Hitler invaded Poland.[2]

As a boy, Shomo never thought about separating blacks from whites. Growing up where minorities of both races lived peacefully together, he never experienced racism. His best friends, "Butch" Marx, Mitty DeFazio, and Tony Vaccarelli, were white. Shomo and the three white boys proudly called themselves "Four Friends Forever." Skin color was no factor. They just wanted to have a good time.

George had lived his whole life in Red Bank with his parents, Irving and Mabel, sisters Helen and Mabel, and brothers Irving, James, and William. When the president declared war on Japan, George's mother was visibly upset.

"Our boys . . . ," Mabel cried. "They'll be drafted."

"They won't put coloreds in combat," Irving assured his wife. "They'll be driving trucks, on KP duty, or something else. They won't be fighting."

"Well, that's a relief," she said, wiping her eyes. "But I still hate them being so far away."

When the draft notices arrived at the Shomo home, George and his brothers, along with a childhood friend, Wesley Forehand, packed their bags and left for the army.

Shomo recalls the day he went on active service, December 1, 1942, nearly a year after Pearl Harbor. Posted first to Fort Dix, New Jersey, he was then sent to Camp Gruber, Oklahoma. Originally the thirty-one-thousand-acre camp had been one of eighty-four hastily built training facilities during 1941 and 1942. To enlarge the camp, the War Department took several thousand acres from the Cherokee Nation. The Native Americans weren't happy, but the war took precedence.

Entering training, Shomo got his first glimpse at Southern racism. Whites in nearby Tulsa still talked about the race riot that had happened there two decades earlier as if it had occurred the week before. They shook their fists at African-Americans arriving at Gruber, complaining loudly when black GIs spent their liberty weekends in Tulsa.

The tension between Tulsa's whites and the camp's black GIs nearly rivaled that in 1921, when a large group of whites, aided by hooded Klansmen, burned and destroyed thirty-five blocks of the black-owned Greenwood District.[3]

After the Great War, Greenwood had been industrious and extremely prosperous, while the city's white areas suffered an economic slump and high unemployment. Dubbed the "Negro Wall Street," blacks built thriving businesses, published two newspapers, and erected large churches, movie houses, and nightclubs. The district boasted a number of professionals, including doctors, dentists, lawyers, and clergy. It elected its own community leaders. Some believed the unrest stemmed from nothing but envy. Lasting sixteen hours, the Tulsa Race Riot caused hundreds of deaths and injuries, leaving ten thousand Greenwood residents homeless and unemployed.

Shomo and the rest of the 333rd know nothing about the 1921 Tulsa Race Riot. Tulsa officials have kept a lid on the outrage for two decades.[4]

White Oklahomans' prejudices have shocked Shomo, but he's stunned when black troops are assigned to segregated barracks.

He stares at the ground and shakes his head. "Don't understand it," he says aloud. "Never will."

As Shomo sits on the steps, reading and deep in thought, he is suddenly interrupted.

"Boy!" a white stateside officer shouts to him. "Get up and cut that grass!"

Shomo jumps to his feet and smartly salutes.

"Sir," Shomo says, "with all due respect, as a noncommissioned officer I'm not required to do manual labor. You can put me in charge of a detail, but I'm not going to cut that grass."

"MPs!" the officer hollers, and begins to curse. "Jail that—"

"You don't need to call the Snowdrops!" Shomo interrupts. But he is shortly flanked by two hefty MPs, each taking an arm. The young artilleryman is whisked to the camp brig.

A few hours later, Captain McLeod shows up to rescue Shomo.

"Sergeant Shomo is correct," the captain says. "He does not have to perform manual labor. The sergeant is part of the 333rd Field Artillery Battalion training with the 155mm howitzer. He is *far too important* to this war effort to be sidetracked from his primary duties to mow grass!"

Amid apologies, the prisoner is released, and Sergeant Shomo quickly departs, head held high and sporting a wide smile.[5]

CHAPTER 33

THE NEW POW COMPOUND

—CAMP GRUBER, OKLAHOMA—
MAY 1943

One month after FDR's visit, the camp adds a prisoner of war compound with well-heated green and white barracks built to comfortably hold four thousand prisoners.

In May, Private George Moten and some men from the 333rd watch the arrival of the first load of German prisoners, veterans of Erwin Rommel's elite Afrika Korps. Ordered to trash their desert uniforms, the POWs are issued new khaki uniforms with a white *PW* printed on the back. A guard tells Moten that some of the Germans posted pictures of Adolf Hitler above their bunks upon entering their barracks.[1]

Moten and his buddies know the POWs will be well treated, as required by the Geneva Convention. But they are shocked to see how well the POWs are respected and catered to by some of the white officers and GIs.

"They're getting treated better than us coloreds are," he tells Sergeant Pritchett. "Don't they know they're the enemy?"

"Yep," Pritchett says. "But nothing we can do about it."

One day, while the Germans are working at the rock quarry, they start a loud ruckus. Moten hears the noise, including a pistol being fired. Moten can't believe it when he hears that the guard, who fired his pistol in the air to get the prisoners' attention, received a harsh reprimand and was busted in rank.[2]

Moten also discovers that the camp's cooks are preparing traditional German dishes for the POWs—roast beef, potatoes and vegetables, puddings, and tea.

"Those Krauts are getting fat from all that good German chow!" Moten tells Pritchett. "I hear they've gained ten pounds each since they got here."

"That ain't fair," Pritchett replies. "I've lost weight since I got to this place. I miss Mama's good 'Bama cooking. We need to do something about it."

"You go talk to Captain McLeod," Moten says. "Maybe he'll help us."

"I may just do that very thing, Private."

A few days later, Sergeant Pritchett works up the nerve to tell Captain McLeod about the white troops' over-the-top hospitality to the German POWs. "Sir, I don't mean to be bothering you. And I ain't complaining. And I don't wanna cause trouble—"

"What's the problem, Sergeant?" McLeod asks.

"Sir, I see those Krauts getting more respect from the whites and being treated better than our colored troops," Pritchett says, his eyes lowered and his hands visibly shaking. "They're eating better, too, sir. We're eating swamp seed while the enemy's eating good sauerkraut."

McLeod winces. "I didn't know this, Sergeant Pritchett. Thanks for telling me. I'll check into it."

Pritchett later hears that when Captain McLeod broaches the matter with his superior, Kelsey glares at him, then waves him off, snapping: "We have bigger problems here than sauerkraut, Captain. For crying out loud, there's a war going on!"

CHAPTER 34

OPERATION CITADEL

Hitler is frustrated with his army's recent defeats. He decides to assume the role of supreme commander of the German Armed Forces as well as commander in chief of the German Army. He stops listening to his advisers and, without wise counsel, makes all the intricate battle decisions himself.

When Hitler launches his attack—Operation Citadel—he learns the Soviets, having broken German signals and knowing German plans, are well entrenched in multiple lines of defense. The two armies fight savagely around Kursk, waging one of the largest tank battles in history.

The German panzers are relentlessly bombed by Soviet planes. Hulks of German armor soon litter the battlefields. Hordes of new Russian T34s outgun the smaller and lighter-armored German tanks. The twenty-six-ton Soviet tank is the perfect balance of speed, firepower, and armor protection. It proves to be the best tank of the war.[1]

The airborne element of the German Blitzkrieg has always been the screaming Ju 87 Stuka dive bomber, used successfully in previous lightning attacks. But the Stuka proves too slow when faced with the Russian Shturmovik fighters, the plane Germans call *Der Schwarze Tod* (the Black Death). Armed with thick steel plating, the Shturmovik is a low-altitude tank buster, flying at 250 miles per hour. It feasts on the Germans' Stukas and tanks.[2]

Things move from bad to worse for Hitler at Kursk. Exasperated by the continuing reports of disastrous events, and having lost seventy thousand men, three thousand tanks, and fourteen hundred planes, Hitler calls off Operation Citadel on July 13.

As German soldiers are pushed westward by the Red Army, liberating their captured Soviet cities one by one, Hitler's soldiers retreat. In their withdrawal, they massacre Soviet civilians and destroy bridges, railways, crops, livestock, homes, and businesses. They leave few civilians alive, and no standing structure intact.

Hitler's dreams of Lebensraum in Russia are seriously failing, and his troubles are just beginning.[3]

For years, Gustav Knittel has faithfully followed Hitler, certain that Germany will prevail. Although wounded in Kursk in July 1943, he remains with his troops. He isn't ready to quit, but now, after some of the catastrophic defeats in Russia, Knittel's former enthusiasm begins to fade.[4]

"The Allies are strong," he confides to a friend. "I must admit that I am no longer certain Germany can win this war."

"Don't let anyone else hear you say that," his confidant whispers. "The Führer has ears everywhere!"

Hitler has sent his trusted Sepp Dietrich to Russia and, despite losses, heaps praise on the proud Dietrich, awarding him the Swords to the Knight's Cross after his impressive and brutal performance there. In

July 1943, Hitler selects Dietrich to command the First SS Panzer Corps, promoting him to the rank of SS-Obergruppenführer and Generaloberst der Waffen-SS.[5]

The Führer has big plans for Dietrich, the stern-faced old Nazi. He eventually gives him command of the Sixth SS Panzer Army.

CHAPTER 35

DISILLUSIONED

—GERMANY—
SPRING/SUMMER 1943

By the summer of 1943, Hitler's generals and military advisers worry about the Führer's wisdom and war strategy. One of his most trusted leaders, Claus von Stauffenberg, a devoted Christian and family man, has supported Hitler with unusual loyalty throughout the war, having served with the Sixth Panzer Division since November 1939. He knows the German Reich trusts him, and he has served faithfully even though severely wounded.

But while fighting in the Soviet Union during Hitler's Operation Barbarossa, and watching German soldiers slaughter scores of Soviet Jews and other innocent citizens, Stauffenberg finds his loyalties undergoing a sea change.

"I am nauseated and appalled by the atrocities committed by the German army against Soviet prisoners of war," he confides to Major Joachim Kuhn in August 1942, after his military stint in the Soviet Union.

"The Schutzstaffel [SS] and the German Army slaughtered masses of Jews in Russia," he says. "I can no longer support and serve Hitler. We must move against him and overthrow Hitler's regime. I am personally prepared to kill the Führer."

But Stauffenberg struggles with his decision.

"Is it right to sacrifice the salvation of one's own soul if one might thereby save thousands of lives?" he asks a trusted relative. "If I oppose Hitler, I will be committing high treason."

"Are the consequences of such an action worth what they will cost you?" his relative asks.

"Faced with such an evil regime," he continues, "I have to choose between action and inaction. For an active Christian, there can only be one decision."[1]

G eneral Ludwig Beck, like Stauffenberg, has also been growing more and more horrified by the civilian slaughters ordered by Hitler in the Soviet Union.

Beck entered the German Army in 1898 as a cadet. A gifted German officer, dedicated and loyal, he served on the Western Front in World War I as a staff officer. In 1930, Beck met Adolf Hitler, and the men have enjoyed a lasting friendship based on mutual respect.

Beck supported Hitler's rise to power in 1933.

"I have wished for years for the political revolution," he stated at the time. "Now my wishes have come true. It is the first ray of hope since 1918."[2]

Working with Hitler to rebuild a strong German military, Beck wanted to see Germany fight a major war, or a series of wars, to restore its lost power in Europe. He was delighted when Hitler broke the Versailles Treaty agreement and sent German troops into the Rhineland in 1936, an active declaration of war that the rest of Europe ignored. But he believed this was not the time to start a war, knowing that Germany couldn't compete against the military powers of the United Kingdom and France.

"We are not prepared to go to war in Europe," Beck had told Hitler. "We cannot win a war before 1940."

But Hitler disagreed. "You are still imprisoned in the idea of the one hundred thousand–man army imposed by the Treaty of Versailles," he shouted to Beck. "My advisers are recommending we go to war *now*."

As time went on, and as Beck began to lose faith in Hitler, he openly challenged the Führer on many issues. His opposing views and unsolicited advice created problems that began to slow down Hitler's war plan. No longer supportive of Hitler, Beck knew he should resign his position as colonel general.

"Resign quietly," Hitler suggested, "and I will give you a major field command."

General Beck resigned in secret on August 18, 1938. Hitler, however, failed to keep his promise, instead placing Beck on the retired list.

Now, angry and disillusioned, the "retired" Beck begins to work behind the scenes to overthrow the Führer. He teams up with Colonel Claus von Stauffenberg and others in their secret quest to kill Hitler.[3, 4]

CHAPTER 36

THE SONG

Throughout the cold winter months of early 1943, the men of the 333rd study, work, hone their skills, and practice the 155's complicated firing sequence. They soon discover that moving, loading, targeting, and firing the "Long Toms" prove slow, exhausting, and complex tasks. During the long days of training, Captain McLeod stands beside his men, timing the operation.

One afternoon, Captain McLeod and Lieutenant Colonel Kelsey stare out Kelsey's office window, watching the trainees' clumsiness. "What a disaster!" Kelsey snorts. "We'll be in Berlin before these coloreds get the hang of this weapon!"

"The men are determined to learn and master it, Colonel."

"Well, Captain, make sure they do or your fitness report will show it."

The massive six-ton howitzer is difficult to transport, requiring trucks to tow it and a skilled team to position it. Its large wheels groan under its weight, and it often gets stuck in mud.

It takes two to three men to lift and load the hundred-pound shells. The powder propellant charge, fuse, and primer must be loaded separately. From start to finish, it requires a dozen skilled men to operate it.

On one occasion, Private Davis, while handling the powder charge, lets it slip from his hands and fall to the ground. McLeod hears a sudden collective gasp among the men. The Alabama trainee smacks his forehead and exclaims, "I may blow us all up before I get this right!"

"Yes, soldier, but in time and with practice, you'll get it right," the captain says, smiling. "Now, men, let's have another go at it."

The men start over, moving, positioning, targeting, and loading. "Stand back!" a GI shouts, grasping the lanyard to fire it.

"Wait!" McLeod shouts. "Using those coordinates, you'll take out Tulsa! Double-check all your settings. We need to get together on the whole procedure."

All afternoon the men of the 333rd work on the firing sequence. The captain carefully times each effort.

"Twelve minutes is too long," McLeod tells his men, shaking his head. "We must get it down to five. If a German tank is coming at our troops, it won't wait for us to reload."

"Five minutes!" several mutter.

"We'll work at it until we do," McLeod responds. "Once you master all the steps and figure out how to work together better, the time will come down. It'll become second nature."

"Trust us, Captain," Sergeant Stewart shouts from the back. "We'll master this beast."

"I'm certain you will," McLeod says. "Let's do it again, from the start."

Despite several sighs, the men try again. The shell is fired, the barrel recoils violently. A loud explosion splits the air, shaking the ground. The men cover their ears, disregard the large swirling cloud of white phosphorus, and hustle to repeat the process.

"Still too much time," McLeod says, checking his stopwatch.

For weeks, McLeod pushes his trainees. Some days they make a little progress; other days, hardly any. He is relentless but respectful in every detail.

"Just admit it, Captain," Colonel Kelsey says, smirking. "Ten minutes to reload, position, and fire won't cut it. Their movements are unco-ordinated and slow. They're not working together as a team."

During a brief break, Georgie Davis plops on the ground beside the 155, exhausted and discouraged. "It's not working. We're never gonna learn to load and fire this thing in five minutes." He takes a deep breath and begins to quietly hum the tune his mother sang when she became disheartened.

"What are you humming, son?" Sergeant Stewart asks Georgie, sitting down beside him.

"Something my mother sings when she gets down."

"You know the words?"

With little enthusiasm, Georgie begins to sing, "'Roll, Jordan, roll. . . . I wanter go to heav'n when I die, to hear ol' Jordan roll.' Don't know the rest of the words, 'cause Mama always made up different words every time she sang it."

"Got a a nice rhythm, George." After a long silence, Sergeant Stewart smiles. "What if . . ."

When the break ends, the GIs stand and face the howitzer. The captain picks up the stopwatch, ready to time the next loading and firing practice. Like before, the men's movements are clumsy, slow, lacking interest and energy.

Sergeant Stewart turns to George. "Sing that tune, son," he tells him. "Sing it loud."

"Roll, Jordan, roll," Lil' Georgie sings as he does his part in the loading process. "Roll, Jordan, roll," the rest of the men, one by one, join in singing, following George's lead.

"Song's too slow," Stewart calls. "Pick up the tempo."

Georgie and the men shift the song into high gear, singing the words over and over, and faster and faster, as they work. They begin to sway, getting in step with the rhythm, coming together with the beat, the rich, deep voices of the GIs growing louder, faster, stronger with each movement. Before long, as they sing they become a synchronized body moving, aiming, and securing the gun barrel. Georgie bellows out the words he heard at his mother's feet. "Roll, Jordan, roll. . . ." The heavy shell loads into place and is rammed forward. "Roll, Jordan, roll. . . . Oh, brothers, you oughter been dere. . . ." Soon the rest of the GIs are singing the lyrics. The charge, fuse, and primer are inserted, the coordinates called, the chamber secured. To the rhythm, someone shouts, "Stand back!" The men turn their heads away, covering their ears as the barrel lurches back, launching the shell and belching clouds of white smoke. Still singing, smiles covering their faces, they rush to repeat the process.

Georgie's excitement is contagious as the men move together as one, again and again beating their time, reducing the minutes to load, aim, and fire the howitzer.

Captain McLeod cheers, "Good job! Two verses of 'Roll, Jordan, Roll' and, men, you're down to eight minutes! Let's do it again!"

"I vote we sing Glenn Miller tunes," Sergeant Forte says, "maybe 'In the Mood'—you know, 'Don't you keep me a-waitin', darlin', when I'm in the mooooooood.'"

"I vote for 'The Caissons Go Rolling Along,'" someone else says. "My dad told me he sang it back in the Great War.

"Over hill, over dale, as we hit the dusty trail," he sings loudly, "and those caissons go rolling along. . . ." Some of the men join in: "Then it's hi! Hi! Hee! In the field artillery, shout out your numbers loud and strong—!"

"I think we need to stay with Georgie's 'Roll, Jordan, Roll.'" McLeod grins, interrupting the loud singing. "We'll sing others, too, but right now this one seems to be working."

Day after day, and week after week, with Captain McLeod standing by his men's side, timing and encouraging them, the GIs sing "Roll, Jordan, Roll" at the top of their voices, taking turns making up the words and loading and firing the 155. With practice, as in a dance, each becomes more focused and precise, accomplishing his part of the process in step with the song. Before the white smoke clears, "Roll, Jordan, Roll" fills the air and another shell is successfully launched.

By autumn's end, the men of the 333rd have mastered the 155.

"I'm proud of you men," Captain McLeod says, smiling.

Before the Oklahoma winter arrives, Captain McLeod invites Colonel Kelsey to evaluate the men's progress. When he joins them on the field, the men get into position, competently and confidently, and, led by Georgie, they begin singing loudly.

"We got a message for ol' Hitler / We are a-comin' after him / Gonna blast his Krauts clear back to Berlin / And end this war! / *Amen!* I say / Roll, Jordan, roll / Roll, Jordan, roll / My soul arise in heaven, Lord / Gonna hear ol' Jordan roll / Hallelujah!"

Before the final hallelujah, they have fired a sustained rate of forty rounds per minute.

"You will notice, Colonel," McLeod says loudly, "that our troops have bettered the instructor's team's time by a full minute!"

Kelsey looks at the beaming GIs as they stand proudly beside the smoking howitzer.

"Frankly, men, I am shocked," Kelsey says, his face deadpan. "Are you planning to serenade the Krauts while you kill them? Let's see how you do in combat."

With that the colonel turns and leaves.

McLeod stands in the training field with his men, feeling pride in their accomplishments, elated that the 333rd has just demonstrated firsthand to the doubting Kelsey their intelligence, skill, hard work, and discipline.

McLeod smiles, whispering under his breath, "Not half bad, Colonel, huh? Oh yeah, 'I told you so.'"[1]

CHAPTER 37

LATE-NIGHT REFLECTIONS

— CAMP GRUBER —
FEBRUARY 1, 1944

Late one night, Sergeant Stewart sits on his bunk listening to the snores of sleeping GIs around him. The battalion will ship out the next morning. They have finished training, mastered the mighty howitzer, and proven that black troops can operate the 155 with record-setting speed and accuracy. Anxious about what might lie ahead for them in Europe, Stewart can't sleep.

"What's wrong, Sergeant?" Private Turner whispers from the next bunk. "Looks like you lost your last friend."

"Jus' thinking," Stewart whispers. "Jus' thinking about the terrible mess we've got in this world."

"Yep. Shipping out tomorrow. We'll take our Long Toms. Drop a few rounds on old Adolf."

Sergeant Stewart shakes his head. "Not jus' Germany who's got problems," he says. "We've got them right here at home. Blacks and whites killing each other in Missouri, Japanese-American citizens locked up in U.S. internment camps, white soldiers and Mexicans fighting in Los Angeles, riots and strikes in Detroit where they're supposed to be making our weapons. No, son, we're not only fighting the Jew-killing Nazis, we're fighting each other right here at home."[1]

Stewart reaches into his footlocker, pulling out a handful of newspaper clippings. Shining his flashlight on the articles and photographs, he shows them to Turner.

"Look at this," Stewart says, holding a page torn from a Missouri paper. "A mob of whites stormed the city jail in Sikeston, Missouri, taking a colored man, Cleo Wright, who was accused of assaulting a white woman. They dragged him through a black neighborhood, made his wife look at his bloody body, and then burned him at a church in front of Sunday worshippers. Nobody was ever convicted of the crime."[2]

"Yep. But nothing new," Turner says. "Been going on for years, at least back in Arkansas. I was born right in the middle of riots—the Elaine Riots, after the Great War. Problems between Elaine's black sharecroppers and white cotton plantation owners. Labor unions got into it, too."

"Anybody killed?"

"Yep. Hundreds of Negroes. Only a handful of whites."

"I remember hearing about that," Stewart says. "Had jus' turned thirteen years old."[3]

"Same thing's happening in Detroit, Sergeant. Blacks from the South are going to Detroit looking for work. Whites and blacks are fighting over jobs. They're rioting and killing when they ought to be making our ammo. It's terrible," Turner says. "Think there'll ever be peace between whites and blacks?"[4]

"Don't know, son. But it's not jus' the coloreds having trouble with the whites. Look at this." Sergeant Stewart places another clipping under his flashlight. "Like I said before, there's trouble between whites and Mexicans out West."

"You mean the Mexicans brought to California to work? The ones with funny clothes?"

"Yeah. The zoot-suiters. Whites there hate them. Claim they're un-American 'cause they're making fancy suits when everybody else is wearing old clothes till the war ends."[5, 6]

"Japs here in America don't have it easy," Stewart says. "Locked up in internment camps on the West Coast."

"That's okay. They're the enemy!" Turner says. "Should be locked up. Maybe shipped back to Japan!"

"Nope. Those people are American citizens jus' like us. I hear they've been rounded up and sent to camps with barbed-wire fences. That's jus' not fair."[7]

"Life's not fair, Sergeant Stewart."

"You said it there, son. Wonder if the world will ever start treating each other like the Good Book says. Sure would solve lots of problems."

"What are you guys talking about when you should be sleeping?" Private Adams asks, rubbing his eyes, looking at them from a nearby bunk.

"Go back to sleep, Private," Stewart whispers. "We're jus' talking about how we've got no business fighting Hitler halfway around the world when we can't even fix our own problems here at home."

"Well, maybe things'll be different after we win this war and we can get back to our families," Private Adams says. "Columbia, South Carolina, is already beginning to try to get rid of Jim Crow laws, starting with the public schools. For my little boy's sake, I sure hope they do. Don't want him growing up like I had to."

Sergeant Stewart stays awake throughout the night, waiting for daylight, when the 333rd Field Artillery Battalion will ship out for Europe.

CHAPTER 38

THE WEAKENING REICH

Even though the Reich is hemorrhaging men and resources, Hitler still believes Germany can win the war. He is concerned, however, about the declining postwar population with so many of Germany's finest young men dying in battle.

Who will be left to father Germany's children? Who will lead the Reich into future generations?

Concerned, Hitler confers with Martin Bormann, his loyal deputy.

"We are losing far too many men to ensure the future of the Reich," he tells Bormann. "We must begin planning now on how to safeguard Germany's future."

"I will study the problem, my Führer," Bormann says, "and find a solution."

On January 29, 1944, meeting with the Führer, Bormann delivers a memorandum to Hitler titled "Safeguarding the Future of the German People." It details how Germany is experiencing the second enormous bloodletting within three decades, and expresses deep concern for the Reich's future once the war is won.

"Yes," Hitler agrees. "After this war, three to four million German women will have no husbands. Just think of how many Wehrmacht divisions we will be lacking in twenty to forty-five years."

"Precisely," Bormann says. "The greater the number of births in our nation, the more secure its future will be. We must somehow convince our women to have as many children as possible, and our healthy men to increase their procreation."

"But we must wait until war ends before starting this mass breeding program. It will, no doubt, take some time to educate the people to think and accept this way," Hitler says. "Not every soldier will necessarily want his wife or fiancée to have children by another man after he has been killed in battle."

"Of course, my Führer," Bormann agrees.

"But now we must remove all undesirable barriers to our goal," Hitler says. "We must change our society's ideas about marriage and adultery and rid our land of all books and plays that treat illegitimate children as inferior. And we must hope that German widows, as well as all single girls, will have relationships with men in order to produce as many children as possible for the Vaterland.

"And," he continues, "insulting a woman who has children without a husband must be harshly punished. And childless marriages and bachelors must be taxed much more heavily than married men with children."[1]

Such is the state of war in Europe when at Camp Gruber, on the early morning of Wednesday, February 2, 1944, the men of the 333rd Field Artillery Battalion prepare to sail to the United Kingdom.

Early that morning, Sergeant Stewart writes his parents, promising them that after the war he'll return to Piedmont, West Virginia, find a good woman, and give them a whole baseball team of grandkids. He tells his mother not to worry about him, and to spend the money he sends home any way she sees fit.

Private Adams scribbles a quick note to his bride, Catherine, with his new Sheaffer fountain pen, assuring her he'll be home soon to help with baby Jesse.

Sergeant Forte writes several brief letters: one to his father, Jack, and his mother, Florence, in Alexandria, Louisiana; another to sister Maggie in Jackson, Mississippi; and to sister Juanita in Chicago, Illinois. He pens a long letter to his wife, Angelina, promising her he'll return safely and join her in the "Double V Campaign."

Private Georgie Davis tells his parents in Bessemer, Alabama, about his part in firing the mighty howitzer. He brags that army training has helped him. "It was tough training," he writes. "But it was sure worth it. In fact, I think I've grown an inch or two taller since I got here."

Others in the 333rd write letters to family, friends, and loved ones: Jimmie Leatherwood, William Pritchett, Mager Bradley, Nathaniel Moss, George Moten, Due Turner, Robert Green, Robert Hudson, and George Shomo. No one knows what the next year might hold. Few will admit that death is a possibility. They are tough, confident, and ready for the next challenge, fully aware that, like generations before them, war is often the price one must pay to protect a country's freedom. On that morning of departure, both excitement and fear knot the stomachs of the 333rd Field Artillery Battalion as they prepare to join a bloody battle already in progress.

The 333rd FAB, believed to be Battery A, in France.
National Archives

General Eisenhower addresses paratroopers before D-day, 1944.
National Archives

Knocked out Tiger tank in France, 1944.

National Archives

Black artillery unit in Belgium, 1944.

National Archives

Soldiers stack shells, 1944.
National Archives

A soldier unloading shells in Belgium.
National Archives

On Easter morning, 1945, Tech Sergeant William E. Thomas and
Private First Class Joseph Jackson will roll specially prepared eggs on Hitler's lawn.

National Archives

Members of Battery A, 4520 AA, stand by and check their equipment while the convoy takes a break on November 9, 1944.

National Archives

George Shomo, member of the 333rd captured in Belgium.

US Signal Corps, National Archives

Entrance to the town of Wereth, Belgium.
Robert Child

The Langer home in Wereth, Belgium, where the Wereth 11 took shelter.
Patrick Langer, on behalf of the Langer Family

The kitchen in the Langer home,
where the Wereth 11 stayed before they were captured.

Patrick Langer, on behalf of the Langer Family

PART 3

LEAVING CAMP GRUBER

"*There can be no democracy in the United States that [does]
not include democracy for blacks. . . . Americans [want to talk]
only about the good features of American life and to hide
our problems like skeletons in the closet.*"

ELEANOR ROOSEVELT[1]

CHAPTER 39

TRAINING IN THE U.K.

—CAMP GRUBER, OKLAHOMA—
FEBRUARY 2, 1944

On February 2, 1944, George Davis, Curtis Adams, Thomas Forte, Aubrey Stewart, Mager Bradley—with a new bar of Woodbury in his pocket—and the rest of the 333rd begin their long journey from Oklahoma to England by way of train and troop transport ship, singing all the way: "Over hill, over dale, as we hit the dusty trail, and those caissons go rolling along . . ." Their training is over, and they are ready to put it and their 155s to the ultimate test.

After the long, exhausting trip, made by many soldiers before them, they arrive in the United Kingdom on February 19, part of 1.6 million GIs transported to England early that year to receive additional training before deployment to Europe.

From March through May, the 333rd and 969th Field Artillery Battalions take part in continuous combat and field exercises with the VIII Corps.[1]

Day after day, instructors help them to hone skills they will need to fight and survive in combat.

The GIs are all ears during a morning class on map reading.

"To keep from getting lost," the instructor begins, "a soldier must know how to read a map. A combat area has no street addresses," he says, and smiles. "A military map will help you identify a location accurately."

He points to a large map mounted on the wall. "Notice the vertical and horizontal lines. They form small squares—a thousand meters on each side—called grid squares. They're numbered along the outside edge, and no two grid squares have the same number."

He pauses, looking away from the map and directly at the men. "Just remember: Read right up. Horizontal first, then vertical. Any other way and you are in the world of hurt."

"I had no idea reading a military map is so hard," Private Moten whispers to Sergeant Stewart. "Grids, coordinate scales, digits—"

"You'll learn it, Private," Stewart says. "After learning to fire the 155, you can learn anything!"[2]

Classes on the .50-caliber machine gun prove a cinch after mastering the howitzer.

"The Browning M2 is an air-cooled, belt-fed machine gun," a trainer tells them. "It fires from a closed bolt, operated on the short recoil principle."

For the rest of the afternoon, the 333rd learns about cyclic rates of fire, round bursts, butterfly triggers, spade handles, bolt switches, and various types of machine-gun ammunition.

"I can do that with my eyes closed," Georgie Davis says, smiling.

"I'm sure you can," Stewart says.[3]

Instruction in bomb reconnaissance proves one of the most interesting exercises.

"The Germans are producing land mines that bring lethality to a new level," the instructor says. "In the past, when they employed Teller mines with a sheet metal casing, or the S-mine—the 'Bouncing Betty'—we could detect their land mines with standard minesweepers."

He pauses. "But we can't detect their new nonmagnetic wooden and glass mines. Especially dangerous is the Schu-mine 42, an antipersonnel blast land mine, and the Glasmine 43, a land mine made entirely of glass, both undetectable by regular minesweepers. We guess they have already produced millions of these land mines.[4]

"Handling unexploded bombs is one of the most challenging problems you'll face," the instructor continues. "Bombs are becoming more complicated these days, especially with delay and antitamper fusing designed to detonate hours later. Bomb disposal is dangerous work, and the casualty rate is high."

"Don't wanna run into one of those," Georgie says.

"Me, neither, son," Stewart agrees.

"I'll teach you how to stop clockwork times, remove fuses, and steam explosives out of bombs," the instructor tells them. "You'll also learn how to use disposal equipment, excavation, and rigging, as well as recognize different explosives."

He frowns. "Men, explosive devices don't always look like bombs. Sometimes the devices are disguised to look like common everyday things, like soap, or shoes, or even rats."

"Rats?" Private Adams asks.

"Exactly! Rats. A rat is skinned, and the skin is sewn up and filled with plastic explosives to assume the shape of a dead rat. The 'explosive rat' is placed in areas where rats normally live, and causes no suspicion until it's too late."

"Cruel to the rat, and deadly to the Allies," Stewart mumbles.

"The Germans have recently developed radio-controlled bombs, some with wings," the instructor says. "You can't be too careful, men, when it comes to explosives."[5]

"Think we'll ever get back alive?" Adams asks Sergeant Stewart.

"Yes, son. Jus' need to avoid them. You're gonna get back to your bride and baby."

During training, the men learn how to waterproof vehicles with a newly invented asbestos fiber-based material called Compound 219.

"Compound 219 is waterproof, has good electrical insulation properties, and resists heat," the instructor explains. "It protects vehicle engines, allowing them to run underwater during beach operations. So simple to use that any soldier can plaster it on like jam. Removes easily after it's done the job."

The men spend an afternoon coating jeep engines with the compound, singing about caissons rolling along, and driving the vehicles into the sea to test them.[6]

The 333rd engages in 155 howitzer refresher courses, singing "Roll, Jordan, Roll," as they load, position, and fire. Soon other howitzer teams are singing along.

CHAPTER 40

A STIR IN BRITAIN

Most of the 333rd have never traveled to another state, much less to a foreign country. When they land in the U.K., they expect the same Jim Crow treatment from English people they experience in America. When white English girls first see African-American men, they are curious and immediately infatuated. Most Brits have never seen an African-American, and the sight of their ebony skin captivates them. Many girls begin choosing to date black instead of white GIs. Britain's residents aren't sure what to make of the phenomenon. Some white GIs grow furious, having never before competed with a black man for a white girl's affection.

Georgie Davis can't believe the attention he's receiving from the British girls.

"Daddy always told me to stay away from white girls," he tells Stewart and Forte. "Now they're throwing themselves at me."

"Your daddy gave you good advice," Forte says. "Better stay away from those fool girls."

"Jus' do your job, son," Stewart advises. "We won't be here long. If you date the white girls, you'll jus' stir up a heap of trouble with the white GIs here."

"Those guys hate us," Forte says. "They don't wanna see the races mix. If you fool around with those girls, we'll all end up dead."

"These white girls have never seen blacks before," Sergeant Stewart says.

"They're asking me if I'm 'Native American,' you know, an 'Injun'! Or they think I'm a *tanned* American," Georgie laughs. "And they're real impressed when I show them my granddaddy's pocket watch. They say they've never seen one like it before."

"An 'Injun'?" Sergeant Forte asks with a straight face. "Most of them are treatin' us a whole lot better than whites back home treat us. Guessin' they've never heard about ol' Jim Crow."

"Some jus' don't know what to make of us," Stewart says. "Some Brits treat us nice. Others act like white GIs."

"Maybe things'll be different when we get home," Davis says. "After we help the white boys win the war, maybe they'll treat us better."

"Don't count on it, Lil' Georgie," Sergeant Forte says. "Just keep your nose to the ground, like Sergeant Stewart says, and mind your own business."

"Better listen to him," Stewart says. "It's one thing getting shot by a Kraut, but you don't want to get killed by another GI."

The race dilemma in Britain doesn't end. Some Brits take to the black GIs, treating them with kindness. Their actions irritate other civilians, however, who suggest that the British "be educated out of their hospitableness towards black Americans."

Others, like one outspoken British vicar's wife, voice harsh instructions to young women, ordering them, "Have no social relationship with colored troops, and don't invite them into your homes. If one sits down by you in a cinema, get up and move. Cross the road to avoid meeting blacks."

To the shopkeepers, she advises, "If blacks come into your shop, you may serve them. But tell them not to come again."

When American newspaper reporters learn of the growing race problem among American troops in Britain, Chicago's *Daily Herald* advises Brits how to relate to black American soldiers:

"Although the black soldiers are a very useful addition to our war effort," the reporter writes, "their presence certainly raises a problem. So that there can be no friction in the manner of dealing with them, I want your standards to conform as near as possible to those of our American allies. In the States, they are separated from white men. The American regards a Negro as a child and not the equal of the white races. Please conform to that idea."

Some Brits confess they like the black GIs better than the white GIs. One West Country farmer quips, "I love the Americans, but I don't like these white ones they've brought with them."[1]

CHAPTER 41

PLANNING AN ASSAULT

— SUPREME HEADQUARTERS —
ALLIED EXPEDITIONARY FORCE (SHAEF), BRITAIN
SPRING 1944

By the spring of 1944, after having driven the British Army to the sea at Dunkirk in 1940, the Germans have occupied France. As Hitler watches the growing military buildup of American, Canadian, and British forces in England and Scotland, he calculates that the Allies will invade France from England, most likely by a surprise coastal assault.

"Everything indicates the enemy will launch an offensive against the Western Front of Europe," Hitler predicted in November 1943. "At the latest in the spring," he added. "Perhaps even earlier. . . ."[1]

To prepare for the probable invasion, the Führer ramps up work on the Atlantic Wall, a 1,670-mile defensive barrier running from Norway, across the coastlines of Belgium and France, to the Spanish border. Along the wall, Germans build additional artillery emplacements with machine-gun posts, place gigantic antitank and antivehicle obstacles, and pepper the northern France beach with six million mines. Constructing the concrete and steel wall, purchasing weapons and ammunition, and paying the French workers a fair wage to build it eat up much of Germany's resources.

"We must stop the Allies at the beach," Hitler insists, figuring the most logical place for the Allies to strike is the port of Calais, across the Channel from Dover, the narrowest point between Britain and France.[2]

Plans for a secret invasion onto the beaches at Normandy now occupy General Eisenhower's every waking hour. Like many Allied generals and advisers, Eisenhower believes "there [will] have to be a massive invasion of Northwest Europe aimed at the heart of the Axis empire," trapping Germany "between the Soviets in the east and the Americans and British in the west."[3]

Eisenhower arrived in Britain the previous January, setting up Supreme Headquarters of the Allied Expeditionary Force (SHAEF), and working with the British chief of staff, Lieutenant General Frederick E. Morgan, on the invasion strategy.

The plan is to invade Normandy, seize Cherbourg's port, and then push Allied troops into Germany, driving the German army out of Europe.

As supreme commander of SHAEF, Eisenhower is selected to plan and carry out the largest amphibious invasion force in history. He makes it clear to everyone that he "will accept nothing less than full victory.

"The operation is not being planned with any alternatives," he states. "The operation is planned as a victory, and that's the way it's going to be. We're going down there, and we're throwing everything we have into it, and we're going to make it a success."[4]

The United States and United Kingdom work around the clock, training soldiers in attack exercises and holding rehearsals to prepare them for the top secret invasion. The plan proves monumental, involving landing nine divisions of sea and airborne troops on the beaches of Normandy within twenty-four hours, dropping three airborne divisions behind the landing beaches on D-day, seizing the beaches, taking over primary transportation and communication points, and blocking the inevitable German counterattacks. Six divisions will attack the five chosen beaches: the U.S. Fourth Division at Utah Beach, the U.S. Twenty-ninth and First Divisions at Omaha Beach, the British Fiftieth Division at Gold Beach, the Canadian Third Division at Juno Beach, and the British Third Division at Sword Beach.

The epic operation will include more than 160,000 Allied troops, 5,000 ships of every type, and 13,000 aircraft. It will require at least 16,000,000 tons of supplies; 137,000 jeeps, trucks, and half-tracks; 4,200 tanks and fully tracked vehicles; and 3,500 pieces of artillery. The first week of June, the Allies plan to launch a surprise air and ground assault along a sixty-mile stretch of heavily fortified French coastline. For several months, Allies have been bombing Germany and France, destroying German warplanes and pilots, as well as demolishing French bridges, roads, and railroads in an effort to hinder or stop any German counterattack. They are also working with the French Resistance, disrupting transportation and sabotaging trains and railroad junctions.

Since the Allies predict the German armies will be waiting for the invasion at Pas de Calais, Eisenhower appoints General George Patton to stage a mock military buildup in East Anglia and southeast England.

"German aerial observation will report it," he states.

Allied builders and artists design inflatable vehicles and tanks, place a fleet of rubber landing craft in the Thames River Estuary, and conduct massive false military maneuvers near the phantom force. They set up make-believe hospitals, mess halls, tents, and fuel depots, and around them park ambulances, jeeps, tanks, and trucks. Crowding the area with real and straw soldiers, and recording bogus radio transmissions, they use the clever deception to trick the Germans into believing they will attack at Pas de Calais.[5]

During the first week of May, Eisenhower moves almost two million troops to southern England by boat, train, bus, and on foot from Allied bases all over Great Britain. He schedules the D-day attack for the morning of June 5, instructing GIs to pack and wait for orders.

Troops pack everything they will need for the invasion: orders, matches, vomit bags, antiseasickness pills, French currency, French language guides, life belts, ration heating units, stove fuel tablets, paperback books, pocket guides to France, condoms (to keep sand and water out of rifle barrels), raincoats, insecticide powder, water purification tablets, extra socks, candy bars, razor blades, waterproof rifle cover bags, and cigarettes.

Everything comes together perfectly for the June 5 attack. Everything, that is, except the weather. On June 4, the eve of the planned invasion, a huge storm brews in the English Channel. Eisenhower must postpone the assault until the morning of June 6.[6]

As the men ready for D-day, Eisenhower tells them, "You are about to embark upon the Great Crusade, toward which we have striven these many months. The eyes of the world are upon you."[7]

CHAPTER 42

D-DAY

The eyes of the world are, indeed, upon Allied troops when they invade the five Normandy beaches at dawn on June 6, 1944, with nine battleships, twenty-three cruisers, a hundred and four destroyers, seventy-one large landing craft, troop transports, minesweepers, merchantmen, and more than a hundred thousand fighting men.[1]

The paratroopers and glider troops come first, landing behind enemy lines and capturing roads and bridges. Invasion from the sea begins at 0630 (H hour), with troops quickly loading into Landing Craft Vehicle & Personnels and Landing Craft Assaults from mother ships, a process made difficult by strong winds and six-foot-high, choppy waves. Rough seas hammer the small craft filled with men and equipment, veering them off course, snagging them on sandbars, and filling them with water. The pumps overwhelmed and the vessels threatening to sink, the men use their helmets to bail water from boat bottoms. Some vessels sink, sending equipment-laden soldiers to their deaths at the bottom of the sea. Others spend hours in the sea trying to stay afloat, waiting, hoping, praying for rescue.

Troops landing on Gold, Juno, Sword, and Utah Beaches find medium to light resistance. But Omaha Beach, stretching the length of six miles and overlooked by high cliffs, proves a different story. Some of the twenty-nine amphibious Sherman tanks sink into the sea. Strong winds and tidal currents push landing craft off course. American troops are battered with German artillery fire before they come ashore. Boats are shelled, many breaking apart and sinking, taking a number of soldiers down with them.

When, one by one, the boats' ramps drop, wet, chilled, and seasick GIs jump into the water, dodging machine-gun fire and mortars bombarding them from the cliffs. The first men, wading through waist-high water, are torn apart by German fire. Some, only somewhat wounded, drown, pulled underwater by their heavy equipment, unable to swim to the surface while strapped to waterlogged packs. Some cling to the boat trying to keep their heads above water, while others are swept away by powerful tides. Bodies float on the surface, staining the sea red with blood. Many who make it to shore are cut down by machine-gun fire or consumed by sheets of flame. The victims of German artillery fire lie facedown and motionless, bleeding onto the sand. Others encounter land mines planted on the beach and are blown apart in fiery explosions. Some become tangled in coastal obstacles and are shot trying to escape them. Omaha Beach is no longer an aggressive invasion. In a short time, it becomes a rescue operation, each man trying to help himself and others. A few survivors crawl to a space beneath the shadow of the cliff, exhausted, wounded, and shocked, without rifles, food, or water. They simply hang on to life and hope for rescue.

General Eisenhower interrupts the morning's radio broadcasts, announcing the first D-day landings to the people of Western Europe.

"All patriots, young and old," he states, "will have a part to play in the liberation."[2]

After the first landings, additional small craft, filled with men and equipment, drop their ramps, sending more soldiers into strong sea currents, storms of machine-gun fire, and mortar blasts. Weighed down with burdensome packs, they struggle among the bobbing corpses to come ashore, trying to stay alive. Some reach and climb the bluff, making it through deadly chaos, blanketing smoke, and artillery fire.

When U.S. Navy destroyers come close to shore, they set off German mines planted in the sand. There are terrific explosions, but the "tin cans" don't back off. They hug the coastline, pouring fire into German positions.

Later shipments, containing trucks, jeeps, and half-tracks, have problems getting close enough to shore to unload their heavy equipment. When numerous vehicles land too close together, they produce a bottleneck traffic jam, becoming easy targets for enemy artillery. Much-needed matériel is sunk or damaged.[3]

By nightfall, Americans have landed thirty-four thousand troops at Omaha Beach, suffering twenty-four hundred casualties.[4]

During the next week, the Allies continue to move more troops, equipment, and supplies to Normandy. In spite of delays, rough seas, overcast skies, off-course landings, heavy enemy artillery fire, shore obstacles and mines, beachfront traffic jams, and loss of men and equipment, Eisenhower's D-day operation proves a success. The Allies have a foothold in France, but it is purchased at a high price: nine thousand dead, wounded, or missing. Now they must begin the long, bloody trek across occupied Europe and into the heart of Hitler's Reich.[5]

CHAPTER 43

AN INVASION FROM THE WEST

—ENGLAND—
JUNE 7, 1944

The world's newspapers and radios have a field day covering the D-day drama.

Prime Minister Winston Churchill announces that the landing of airborne troops is "on a scale far larger than anything there has been so far in the world."

King George VI calls on radio audiences to pray for the liberation of Europe.

Admiral Sir Bertram Ramsay, the Allied naval commander, states the landings have taken the Germans completely by surprise.

Berlin radio claims the German troops are "nowhere taken by surprise" and have wiped out many Allied parachute units, taking prisoners.

President Roosevelt tells reporters, "The invasion doesn't mean the war is over. You don't just walk to Berlin, and the sooner this country realizes that, the better."[1]

New Yorkers wake to a special edition of the *New York Times* claiming: "Allied Armies Land in France in the Havre-Cherbourg Area. Great Invasion Is Under Way."[2]

Londoners, commuting to work, are surprised to hear of the attack on the BBC's seven a.m. broadcast.[3]

The men of the 333rd are disappointed they missed the Normandy invasion. Still in training in England, they soak up every scrap of news.

"The howitzers didn't do so well," Sergeant Forte tells Adams, Davis, and Stewart. "They brought in the 105s, not the 155s. Guess it's because the 105s are lighter, easier to transport."

"I hear crews were inexperienced and probably didn't know much about operating them," Private Adams says. He grins. "And they didn't have Lil' Georgie to teach them to sing 'Roll, Jordan, Roll.'"

"Yeah," Davis says. "Heard some fell in the water about half a mile from shore."

"Considering all the ammo, sandbags, and heavy stuff the how' needs, they probably went straight to the bottom," Adams says.

"Heard several more got lost in the rendezvous area," Davis says. "And one got buried deep in the sand after they got it ashore."

"Too bad," Forte says. "Kinda surprised any of 'em got to shore."

"Another almost made it but had engine trouble in the water," Adams says. "German artillery took it out. And others blew up when they hit land mines on the shore."

"Heard they jettisoned one how' overboard because its weight was sinking the boat," Davis adds. "We shoulda been there. We'd gotten all those how's ashore."[4]

"Did they have any black GIs participatin' in the invasion?" Sergeant Forte asks. "Maybe we got left out because we're—"

"No, Forte," Stewart interrupts. "Not because we're *black*. We're still trainees. Probably felt we jus' weren't combat ready without more training."[5]

"Did *anybody* represent us on those beaches?" Davis asks.

"Yes, son," Stewart says. "Every American GI on those beaches represented us. Don't need to be a *black* soldier to represent us. Jus' an *American* soldier."

"Heard the black Balloon Battalion landed on Omaha and Utah," Adams says. "Dangerous job that battalion has. Most of them got shot down."

"Well, at least they had somebody of color there," Forte says. "Wish it could've been us."

"We're gonna miss all the action now," Davis says. "They say the war'll be over by Christmas."

"I sure hope so," Stewart tells him. "Anyway, son, be glad if it is. You've gotta get back home to Bessemer. And I've got some nephews in the service that wanna go home, too."[6]

"Yeah," Davis says. "But I wanna see some action and go back home a hero."

"Just get yourself home alive," Stewart says. "You're *our* hero. Be proud of yourself and what you're doing. We're gonna be the best crew in the 333rd."[7]

A t their home in Wereth, Mathias and Maria Langer are horrified when they hear on the radio about the unprovoked massacre on June 10 in the village of Oradour-sur-Glane, France. They speak in whispers late at night in the privacy of their bedroom, not wanting to frighten their children should they overhear.

They learn that on a warm summer day, 180 or more German soldiers enter and seal off the tiny farming village located in the Haut-Vienne Department of France, some fifteen miles northwest of Limoges.[8]

The residents of the sleepy little community are together with their families, eating their noonday meal. The soldiers rush in, searching homes, farms, barns, and outbuildings, rounding up the village's residents, and setting fire to their property. They gather 190 men into barns, shooting them with machine guns. They round up 245 women and 207 children, lock them inside the village church, set it ablaze, and burn them alive. On that day, more than 600 townspeople die in Oradour-sur-Glane.

Maria wipes tears from her eyes. "Why, Mathias, why did the Germans kill all those innocent people?"

"There is no explanation for their brutality, Maria."

"Oh, Mathias, do you think that could happen here in Wereth? Soldiers coming into our house and killing us and our children for no reason?"

Mathias takes his wife's hand in his, closes his eyes, and says nothing.

God and history will one day judge their cruelty to Europe's people, especially to the little ones, he thinks. *They will not get away with all their senseless savagery, their slaughter of the innocents.*[9, 10, 11]

CHAPTER 44

ARRIVING AT UTAH BEACH

In mid-June, the VIII Corps becomes operational in Normandy, teaming up with the U.S. First Army. The Allies now control Normandy.[1]

On June 29, 1944, as part of Major General Troy Middleton's VIII Corps, Sergeants Stewart and Forte, Privates Davis and Adams, and the rest of the 333rd Field Artillery Battalion board a ship in England, cross the English Channel, and land on Normandy's quiet, battle-scarred Utah Beach.[2]

As they trudge along the sand-duned beach, they are careful to step around remaining pieces of twisted metal, helmets, broken weapons, and abandoned backpacks—sad, silent eyewitnesses to the tragedy of war.

"Three hundred men, out of twenty thousand, were killed here three weeks ago," Sergeant Stewart tells Private Adams. Stewart pauses to reflect. "You know, Private, every man's death changes all of history."

"What do you mean, Sergeant?"

"Well, son, think on this. When one man is killed, he loses not only his own life but the lives of all the children and grandchildren he'll never father, and who'll never be born."

Stewart stops, focusing his eyes on a helmet on the sand, a single bullet hole in the center. "Think about all the men who've been killed in this war already." He shakes his head, exhaling loudly. "All because of greed—wanting land that isn't theirs."

"Glad I already have a son," Adams says. "Just in case I . . ."

Adams takes a deep breath, not finishing his sentence. He reaches into his pocket and wraps his hand around the small Bible Catherine gave him at Camp Gruber.

"Our Father," he whispers, "which art in heaven . . ." He blinks several times and then falls silent.

"Forgive us our debts," Stewart says softly, "as we forgive our debtors."

"And deliver us from evil . . . ," Adams whispers, his voice trembling.[3] "Death. Evil. When will it ever end?"

Sergeant Stewart lowers his head as he and the men walk silently across the sand.

"Lots of folks gonna be receiving telegrams this month," Stewart mutters. "I feel bad tromping on the places our men bled and died. It seems disrespectful."

Georgie spots an abandoned boot and stops to pick it up.

"This guy had a *big* foot!" he says, grinning. "Biggest shoe I ever saw."

"Put it back, son," Stewart says softly. "That shoe belonged to some GI, jus' like you, who gave his life for our country. We've got to be reverent. There are layers of blood and sacrifice on this shore. We're walking through a graveyard."

"Yes, sir," Georgie says, kneeling and gently placing the shoe back on the sand.[4]

"Lil' Georgie," Adams says as they leave Utah Beach, "from what I hear, looks like we're going to see some action soon. You ready for it?"

"More than ready," Georgie says. "We're gonna drive Hitler all the way back to Germany and end this war."

"I suspect we're in for some heavy fighting," Stewart says. "The Germans are tough, never forget that."

"But we've got the 155s," Georgie says.

"Jus' the same, son, we're up against a well-trained, well-equipped, and experienced army. Many of these birds have been fighting for years while many of us were down South shooting pool."[5]

CHAPTER 45

"READY! FIRE!"

On July 1, 1944, Colonel Kelsey briefs the 333rd on their assignment when they enter Pont-l'Abbé, a small South Breton seaport dating back to Roman times. Founded by a monk in the fourteenth century, Pont-l'Abbé has known a long, violent history of wars, sieges, and deaths.[1]

"Men," Kelsey says, "let me introduce you to Sergeant Bill Davidson from *Yank* magazine. He'll be with us a few days. You might want to be on your best behavior."

The men laugh. Kelsey continues. "We will be supporting the Eighty-second Airborne Infantry Division in Pont-l'Abbé. Settle in, men. We have some waiting time. Waterproof your vehicles and get set up.

"And, men," he adds, "for heaven's sake, don't drink the water. Boil it first. It'll make you sick as a dog."

Georgie's wish for combat is granted sooner than anyone expects. Suddenly the men see a Piper Cub circle overhead. The pilot radios a code word to Kelsey and gives him firing coordinates. "There's a tall church steeple in the center of town," he says. "The Germans are using it as an observation point and a sniper's nest."

Kelsey looks at a map and finds the target.

"Fire mission," Kelsey says into the phone.

"Battery adjust shell HE, fuse quick compass five thousand, elevation three hundred."

The men quickly prepare the howitzers, positioning and loading them. "Rommel—count your men!" they yell.

"Stand back!"

"Ready!" a gunner calls. A GI raises his right arm vertically.

"Fire!" The GI drops his right arm sharply to his side.

"Rommel—how many men you got now?" They laugh.

Within ninety seconds, the 155 crews fire four rounds toward Pont-l'Abbé, using the coordinates they have received. Three heavy shells crash into the church steeple, destroying it and allowing the infantry to move through the town unhindered.

"Direct hit!" Kelsey calls. The men cheer, slapping each other on the back.

At the end of the day, as if baptized by fire, after almost nonstop firing in Pont-l'Abbé, the men collapse from exhaustion.

"So, Lil' Georgie," Sergeant Forte spits, his eyes narrowed, "is this what you were in such a big hurry to—"

"Leave him be, Sergeant," Stewart interrupts, his voice slightly raised. "No one knew it'd be like this."

Georgie lowers his head, offering no response.

Sergeant Forte continues, his hands balled into fists. "Heard Captain Workizer got hit in the gut and leg by 'friendly fire.' If Krauts don't shoot us, our own guys will."

"No use griping about it," Stewart says. "We've gotta keep our minds on our job, putting out those rounds."

"I hear they'll be no letup tomorrow, either," Forte says.

"So let's cut the chatter and get some sleep," Stewart says, standing up and patting Forte's back. "The Krauts start bright and early."

The next morning, July 2, the GIs reinforce the Ninetieth Infantry Division, as well as provide direct support to the airborne troops of the Eighty-second. In record-setting time and with remarkable accuracy, they spend a frantic day loading, targeting, and firing the 155s.

They rest little that night, intermittent enemy fire interrupting their sleep. The 333rd Field Artillery Group wakes on a rainy morning, July 3, with new attack orders.[2]

"Is this what we'll be doin' till the end of the war?" Forte asks as he makes coffee for Stewart, Adams, Davis, and Private James Erves.

"Let's hope not," Adams says. "None of us can take this kind of beating every day."

Private Davis frowns, rubbing his head. "My head hurts. My back hurts. My bones hurt. I've never felt so bad. My whole body hurts."

"All of us are hurting," Stewart says. "Maybe today will be easier."

"Don't count on it, Lil' Georgie," Forte says.

The men sit quietly, sipping the hot liquid, trying to shield their faces and maps from the rain.

"Maybe we'll take some prisoners today," Erves says.

The GIs barely finish their coffee before the attack begins. They meet stiff German resistance but are able to penetrate numerous German positions, surround the enemy, and take prisoners.

During combat, some of the 333rd are wounded and killed. Private Adams and the other medics race from one fallen GI to the next. Some injuries are superficial, allowing them to quickly remove gravel, splinters, or other foreign objects buried in the skin. Some slight lacerations just need bandaging. Other wounds, however, are far more serious, requiring medics to inject the injured men with pain-easing morphine and transport them to a medical facility.

That night Adams sits against a rock wall and tries to rest, his uniform covered with blood and bits of human flesh.

"I've seen as much blood and guts and war as I ever want to," he tells Green, Davis, Leatherwood, and the other GIs sitting around him.

"Me, too," Private Robert Scott says. Scott, a white GI from another division, slumps against the wall beside Adams. "Heard you lost a howitzer today."

"Yeah. It ran over a Teller mine," Green says. "The fragments from the blast damaged the how' and hit one of the commanders in the leg."

"Will he be okay?" Scott asks Adams.

"I think so. I dressed and cravatted it, then transported him out."

Private Scott smiles. "You know, you guys are really good with that how'. Sure saved our tails today."

"Thanks, Private," Stewart says. "This is jus' the beginning. We're gonna drive Jerry all the way back to Germany! Won't be easy, though. They're tough."

CHAPTER 46

THE SYMPHONY SERENADE

— PONT-L'ABBÉ, FRANCE —
JULY 4, 1944

On July 4, in the midst of an ongoing attack, the GIs receive an unusual request from the Ninetieth Division Artillery: "Request for group to participate in the 'Fourth of July Symphony Serenade.' Every artillery piece in the corps is to loosen its lanyard upon the firing pin—cannoneers' choice of ammunition—at 1200. Americans must celebrate."[1]

At noon, after a loud harmonizing chorus of "Stand back! Ready! Fire!" comes the celebratory explosion of fire, with GIs all over the Cotentin Peninsula shooting artillery and cheering in remembrance of Independence Day. Late that afternoon, the 333rd and 174th are released from fire missions.

On July 5, artillery fire is unusually heavy. At midnight, Private Robert Scott walks around the dark camp, trying to clear his head.

"Identify yourself!" a voice commands. "Password!"

Scott turns toward the challenges. Dumbfounded, he's hesitant to answer.

When the young sentry receives no reply, he panics, firing an M1 at Scott and severely wounding him.

Adams hears shouts for a medic and rushes to stop Scott's bleeding.

But it's too late. Private Scott is dead. On that same day, Sergeant William Pritchett is injured, hit by shell fragments.

"Pritchett's going to get a nice long rest," Adams says. "Not hurt bad, but out of action for a while."

A few days later, a black soldier in Charley Battery is killed from a shell burst. An officer and a black and a white soldier are injured in the blast and taken away by ambulance. One M4 tractor and some powder charges are destroyed.

On July 9, to the relief of the group, the 969th Field Artillery Battalion arrives from England to give them general support. Owing to a heavy bombardment the night before, headquarters orders all artillery units to make a thorough check of camouflage, personnel, matériel, and ammunition.

The 333rd Group, supporting the Ninetieth Infantry Division, leaves Pont-l'Abbé and heads toward La Haye-du-Puits, a town located in the Manche Department of lower Normandy, important to advancing Americans because of its vital road junction. They struggle through thick hedgerows as they travel mountain trails and wade through marshes on their way to the town once assaulted by Scandinavian Vikings and claimed by William the Conqueror. As they travel, they dodge sporadic enemy fire. The hedgerows, dense walls of vegetation French farmers use to protect property boundaries and keep livestock enclosed, make good hiding places for armed German snipers, causing a number of Allied casualties.[2]

When the 333rd arrives on the outskirts of La Haye-du-Puits, they are fired upon by enemy artillery and strafed and bombed by German planes. GIs in foxholes are blown to pieces, as well as men on observation post hills. The fighting is brutal. The 333rd's Able, Baker, and Charley Batteries receive fire coordinates one after another, loading, positioning, and firing the 155s almost without ceasing.

A German Me 109 flies overhead. A gunner hits the plane with an

M2 .50-caliber machine gun, knocking it out of the sky. GIs cheer, shouting, "That's *some* shooting!"

On Hill 95, north of La Haye-du-Puits, a three-man reconnaissance patrol stringing telephone line back to the battalion spots a Tiger tank, camouflaged and hiding behind a hedgerow along the road. The Germans open up on them with 88s. A shell bursts five feet behind them, knocking them to the ground.

"Let's get out of here!" one man yells as they stand and run. At that second, another shell bursts right in front of them, knocking them backward and covering them with dirt. They plug in the telephone wire and quickly telephone the 333rd Group.

"We need help!" they shout. They give the coordinates of the tank's location and then run up the hill to watch the action.

Charley Battery receives the coordinates and loads the 155 with delayed-fuse shells that are timed to penetrate first and then burst.

"Stand back! Ready! Fire!" The first round falls short of the target.

"Fire!" The second round drops through the turret and explodes inside the tank. "Fire!" The third round hits the rear end, destroying the tank, splitting it in half.

"Fire!" The fourth round misses.

Colonel Kelsey receives the message "Bull's-eye!"

"Do you know what you just did?" Kelsey asks Charley Battery, a look of both surprise and delight on his face. "You destroyed an enemy tank with just four rounds, at a distance of sixteen thousand yards! That's nine miles! Congratulations! You're setting new records!"

The men cheer, thrilled to hear the news of the direct hit as well as Colonel Kelsey's first and only praise.

"You men are gaining quite a reputation for your remarkable accuracy," Kelsey says.

When Colonel Kelsey turns around to leave, he sees Captain Mc-Leod standing at a short distance behind him, watching and smiling.

The artillerymen enter the town of La Haye-du-Puits on July 12, finding shops closed, windows smashed, homes empty, trash and rubble piled high in the vacant streets.

"It's a ghost town here," Shomo says. "Where is everybody?"

"Hiding in the countryside," someone replies. "They'll be back when we liberate this place."[3]

"Must have been a pretty place once," Shomo says, "before Jerry came."

"Glad we can help give it back to them," Private Moss says.[4]

On July 16, the Field Artillery Group learns that Captain John G. Workizer has died from his wounds received earlier.

"That's too bad," Stewart says. "He'll be missed. Heard he has a big family."

"Yep. And Captain McLeod says Workizer's got two brothers in this war," Moten says, "and that his daddy was a major in the Great War. Died at the end of the war."[5]

Night after night, Germans shell the Americans. Despite constant bombardment and drenching rain, engineers work around the clock trying to clear mines, repair roads, build bridges, and keep main supply routes open. They are wounded again and again by the enemy, who fires at them from hilltops surrounding La Haye-du-Puits.[6]

On the evening of July 24, Sergeant Stewart reports some bad news.

"Sorry having to tell you boys, but I jus' heard Private Erves is dead. He didn't get out of the way fast enough when his 155 gun barrel recoiled."

The sergeant shakes his head, frowning. "Such a needless death. The instructors hammered that fact into our heads at Gruber. When the gunner shouts 'Stand back!' you gotta move! No lollygagging. Move!"

During their time in La Haye-du-Puits, Private Adams treats several cases of dysentery.

"Must've drunk impure water," he says, adding salt tablets to their canteens. "Need to drink only purified liquids." He hands out Halazone tablets. "Stay as still and quiet as possible until you're well. I can give you sulfaguanadine tablets every four hours until your bowel movements are normal."

He also treats victims of heat exhaustion with canteens of salt water. On especially hot days, the men complain of muscle cramps, dizziness, and vomiting.

When the Americans liberate La Haye-du-Puits, residents suddenly reappear in town like chirping birds returning home in springtime. They gather to thank the Americans, draping their storefronts with French flags, holding signs proclaiming *Vive la France*. People too old or sick to stand sit on curbsides to greet the troops. Most are weary and dirty, but everyone is all smiles and cheers for the Amis.

Corporal Mager Bradley waves at an elderly couple sitting on the side of the street, their fingers raised in the "V" sign for victory.

"They sure act grateful," Forte says. "Doesn't seem to matter that our skin's black. They're just glad the Krauts are gone."

"Looks like engineers will be here awhile, digging up mines and repairing streets. This place is a mess. Not many homes fit to live in. But the people are happy anyway," Green says.

"Wish we could stay and help them," Bradley says, and smiles. "But, as they say, there's no rest for the weary!"[7]

CHAPTER 47

THE PLOT

On July 18, 1944, Colonel Stauffenberg, thirty-seven, kisses his pregnant wife, Nina, hugs his four children, and says good-bye to his beloved family as he moves them from their home in Barnberg to the safety of Schloss Lautlingen, the family's country house nestled among the Swabian Hills. The previous month, Colonel Stauffenberg had been promoted to chief of staff to Commander General Friedrich Fromm, giving him direct access to the Führer's briefing sessions.

On July 20, Stauffenberg carefully places two plastic high explosives in his briefcase and dresses for the meeting with Hitler, to take place on the Eastern Front at Wolfschanze. He covers his missing left eye with a black patch, and with the remaining three fingers on his only hand he buttons his shirt.

He and his aide, Lieutenant Werner von Haeften, also a veteran of Operation Barbarossa, fly to the Führer's "Wolf's Lair" headquarters. His plan? To personally kill Adolf Hitler.

In an effort to overthrow Hitler, Stauffenberg, along with members of the anti-Nazi German Resistance, including his brother, Berthold, General Friedrich Fromm, and others, plans to take control of the German Army, seizing most government buildings, as well as telephone/radio communication services. Upon Hitler's death, Stauffenberg has been promised the position of state secretary of the War Ministry in the new government.

"I must do this for my wife and children," he tells his brother. "And I must do this for the future of our Fatherland."

Stauffenberg thinks long and deep about the consequences for his family if he is caught. His wife, Nina, understands the risk, agreeing with his feelings about Hitler and his evil regime. But his children, especially his oldest son, ten-year-old Berthold, do not. Berthold knows about the harshness of war. A Catholic altar boy, he has participated in numerous memorial services for German soldiers killed on the battlefields. Already a young Nazi, Berthold was devastated when told he was three days too young to join the year's intake of the Hitler Youth's junior branch.

"I so wanted to march through Barnberg," he told his father, "and carry a Nazi banner at the youth parade."

Stauffenberg has seen his eldest son only three times in the past year: for two days during Christmas, at the funeral of his wife's father in January, and for a week in June. He knows that, even at his young age, Berthold places his youthful faith in Germany's victorious success, wishing one day to become part of Germany's military.

Stauffenberg and other members of the German Resistance hope this new plot will succeed in killing Hitler, overthrowing the Nazi Party, releasing German soldiers from their loyalty oath to Hitler, and making peace with the Allies, thus ending the war. They name the assassination attempt *Unternehmen Walküre* (Operation Valkyrie).

Arriving at the Wolf's Lair on July 20, 1944, with Lieutenant Werner von Haeften, Stauffenberg carries the armed bomb in a briefcase, placing it on the floor beneath the massive briefing room table under the place where Hitler stands.[1]

Adolf Hitler leans over the table, his elbow resting on the side as he studies a map in the briefing room. Twenty German officers and staff members stand around him at the thick oak table. He thinks nothing of the large black briefcase beneath the table on the floor right beside him.

Colonel Heinz Brandt, a dedicated officer who joined the German military in 1925, stands beside the Führer. He strains his eyes to see the map Hitler is explaining, but the briefcase is in his way, blocking him from moving in closer. He bends down and moves the briefcase about six feet away to the other side of the table leg and then steps closer to Hitler.

An excellent equestrian, Brandt, with his horse, Alchemy, won the Olympic gold medal at the 1936 Berlin Summer Olympics. One year ago, he was promoted to Oberst.

Brandt feels grateful the Führer is alive and well. The year before, on March 13, 1943, Brandt was asked by General Major Henning von Tresckow to carry a package of Cointreau, a French liqueur, onto Hitler's plane to be delivered to Oberst Helmuth Stieff in Rastenburg. Brandt cheerfully obliged, placing the box of two bottles on the plane, not knowing they contained bombs timed to explode in midair, killing Hitler somewhere north of Minsk.

Fortunately, Brandt thinks, remembering the incident and exhaling a deep breath, *the bombs failed to detonate.*[2, 3]

After depositing the briefcase under the table, Stauffenberg quickly excuses himself to the next room pretending to make a telephone call. Once out of the briefing room, he rushes from the building, not wanting to be caught in the blast or to be associated with the briefcase.

Seconds before the explosion, as Hitler looks at the map on the table, he listens to General Heusinger make a presentation.

"The situation in the East Prussian sector is increasingly critical,"

Heusinger says. "The Russians are drawing closer. A major Russian striking force to the west of the Duna is wheeling around toward the north."

He pauses, takes a deep breath, and continues. "If we don't withdraw our army groups around Lake Peipus, a catastrophe—"[4]

At 1242, the bomb explodes with an ear-deafening noise, rips through the room, destroys the ceiling, and blows a large hole in the floor. Some officers are thrown across the room by the sheer force of the blast. Others are tossed through open windows to the ground outside. A large splinter of wood from the table breaks off, impaling one of the men. Dazed, Hitler feels an intensely sharp pain in his arm, looks down, and sees that his coat has been shredded. Through the thick smoke, Hitler sees Brandt lying near him, his leg blown completely off.

He watches the room burst into chaos and feels strong arms lift him to a safe place. He soon learns that one man is dead and three others are seriously injured. Hitler has long trusted his loyal associates who have his personal permission to join him in the briefing room. A shudder of fear passes through him as he wonders which of them tried to murder him.

From outside the building, Stauffenberg hears the blast.

Hitler is dead. Finally we can end this war and save Germany from total destruction.

With a sense of relief, Stauffenberg boards a plane and flies to Berlin, ready to take his part in initiating Operation Valkyrie. Not knowing what the Nazi regime might do when they hear the Führer has been murdered, the German Reserve Army waits in Berlin to put down a possible uprising.

CHAPTER 48

THE TERRIFYING NEWS

When Stauffenberg's conspirators hear the news that Hitler is alive after having survived the assassination attempt, one after another withdraws from his commitment, fearing Hitler's wrath and concerned about the welfare of his family.

Hitler sustains minor injuries to his arm and ear, but much greater damage to his confidence in his trusted colleagues. His arm is doctored and bandaged, and his ear treated and stuffed with cotton balls. Later that afternoon, he welcomes Italian dictator Benito Mussolini to the Wolf's Lair, giving him a personal tour of the bomb site. When Hitler learns that Brandt has died, he posthumously promotes him to the rank of brigadier general.[1, 2]

General Friedrich Fromm, the commander of the reserve army, and a silent conspirator in the assassination attempt, shows pretended outrage when he hears of the explosion planned to kill Hitler. Fromm supported Hitler in the early years of his leadership, but after a while he, too, became disillusioned. In 1942, wanting to negotiate a peace agreement with the Soviet Union, Fromm secretly stopped supporting Hitler.

He immediately telephones the Wolf's Lair, seeking a report on

Hitler's condition. Field Marshal Wilhelm Keitel tells him the Führer has been only slightly injured.

"Arrest the conspirators!" Fromm shouts, cursing. But officers suspecting his participation in the plot overpower him, confining him to a room under guard at the Bendlerstrasse Headquarters.

Fromm is freed by loyal regime officers around midnight. He bursts into Stauffenberg's office and orders an armed escort to arrest the conspirators of treason, including Colonel Stauffenberg, General Friedrich Olbricht, Albrecht Mertz von Quirnheim, General Ludwig Beck, and Lieutenant Werner von Haeften.

"Are you not also a conspirator?" one of the men asks Fromm.

Fromm is silent.

Close to midnight, General Fromm has a private talk with accused general Ludwig Beck.

"In just a little while," Fromm tells Beck, "I will have you executed, as well as Stauffenberg and the other men responsible for the attack on Hitler's life."

Beck looks at the floor and says nothing.

"I am giving you the opportunity to die with dignity," Fromm says. "If you wish to kill yourself rather than face the firing squad, I will allow it."

"Are you not just seeking to protect *yourself* from the firing squad, Fromm?" Beck asks. "With my death, you can better keep your conspiracy involvement a secret."

Fromm frowns. Noticing the officer's tired, sad face, he hands Beck a pistol. "Yes," Beck says. "I do prefer to die with dignity by my own hand."

Beck puts the pistol to his head, takes a deep breath, and closes his eyes. He pulls the trigger, firing the bullet deep into his skull. But it does not kill him. He lies on the floor in pain, blood pouring from the wound caused by the bullet lodged in his brain.

Fromm calls for a nearby army sergeant.

"Beck has failed in his attempt to kill himself." Fromm smirks. "Kill him, Sergeant."

The sergeant puts his pistol close to Beck's head, pulling the trigger and fatally wounding the lifelong devoted German officer.

At half past midnight, in the Matthäus Churchyard in Berlin's Schöneberg District, Fromm lines up the remaining group of men in front of a firing squad. He orders them swiftly executed and buried. Later Fromm orders their bodies exhumed, burning them and scattering their ashes.

After the murders of Stauffenberg, Olbricht, Quirnheim, and Haeften, Fromm is approached by Joseph Goebbels, who has heard rumors about what happened. Upon learning that Fromm has already executed the four conspirators, Goebbels sneers, looking Fromm in the eye and accusing him of being in a big hurry "to get your witnesses belowground."[3]

Under the policy of Sippenhaft, Hitler orders the Gestapo to find and arrest Stauffenberg's entire family, as well as Quirnheim's parents and one of his sisters. He has Quirnheim's brother-in-law, Wilhelm Dieckmann, arrested and executed. He inwardly questions the loyalty of his commander of the reserve army, General Friedrich Fromm, and wonders if he has in some way participated in the assassination plot.[4, 5]

Nina, Stauffenberg's wife, staying at Schloss Lautlingen with her children and extended family, learns of her husband's failed assassination plot and of his hurried execution. She instinctively places her hand on her belly as if to somehow shield her unborn baby from the horrors she knows she and her family will face.

When she sees her oldest son, Berthold, and his eight-year-old brother, Heimaren, listening to the radio newscast late that afternoon, she turns it off and shoos her children out of the room. She decides not to try to answer their questions about the assassination plot at that moment, and wonders how she can possibly protect them from the consequences of their father's actions.

"Please, Uncle Nux, take the children for a long walk," she asks her uncle Nikolaus, also a member of the conspiracy. Alone in the quiet, Nina thinks about how she will tell her children the dreadful news.

The next day, Nina has a talk with her two eldest sons.

"Berthold, Heimaren," she says, "I have two things to tell you."

After a few seconds of silence, she tells the boys, "It is your father who carried out the attack on Hitler. He is the one who planted the bomb meant to kill the Führer."

She watches her sons' mouths drop open.

"Father? *Our* father!" Berthold gasps, his eyes wide and wild. "He tried to kill our beloved Führer?"

"Yes, Berthold," she says softly. "Your father has been executed for his part in the plot. I'm so sorry to have to tell you this terrible news."

The boys start to cry.

"Why, *Mutter*?" Heimaren asks, his voice quivering. "Why would Father do such an awful thing?"

"He did it for us, Heimaren," she says. "And he did it for all of Germany. One day, son, you will understand the reasons."

The next day, Nina and Uncle Nux, as well as Nina's mother and aunt, are arrested by the Gestapo and taken to Berlin. The children are left behind in a housekeeper's care, guarded by two Gestapo officials.

"They will forever be outcasts here in the Vaterland," Nina cries. "All alone. No friends, no parents, no one to love and protect them."

Hitler feels satisfaction after arresting Stauffenberg's family members. He thinks his policy of Sippenhaft[6] will keep his officers from committing actions against him and they will remain loyal to him.

"If anyone else commits treason," he threatens, "not only will *they* suffer the consequences of their actions, but *their family* will be arrested and punished."

Hitler decrees that the name "Stauffenberg" be wiped out, erased from all German records, and no longer spoken in the Fatherland.

"Change the children's name from Stauffenberg to Meister," he orders. "And put them on a train to Buchenwald."

The men of the 333rd Field Artillery Battalion are fighting in La Haye-du-Puits when they hear about the attempt on Hitler's life, Stauffenberg's execution, and the arrest of his family. They are sickened.

"Too bad Stauffenberg didn't kill Hitler!" Sergeant Forte says. "Might've stopped this war."

"I'm sorry for Stauffenberg's family—his wife and children," Private Adams says. "They don't deserve to be . . ."

"Arrested and probably killed?" Sergeant Forte says.

"Loyalty to Hitler ends up costing them their lives and the lives of their children," Private Adams says. "I could never do that to Catherine and Jesse."

"The Nazis aren't thinkin'—just obeyin' orders blind," Sergeant Forte says. "They're fools."

CHAPTER 49

THE PUSH OUT OF NORMANDY

— LA HAYE-DU-PUITS, FRANCE —
JULY 25–26, 1944

The fighting in Normandy during July has been unremitting and violent. U.S. First Army commander Lieutenant General Omar N. Bradley argues for a massive Allied assault to break out of Normandy and move into Brittany. While the 333rd Group fights in La Haye-du-Puits, the First Army, Second British, and First Canadian armies burst through German lines and advance into Brittany. The move, named Operation Cobra, is supported with bombardment by thousands of Allied aircraft. The Germans' lock on the Cotentin Peninsula is sprung at last.[1]

On July 28, the 333rd Field Artillery Group moves with the Ninetieth Division a few miles south to the vicinity of Saint Sauveur-Lendelin, a commune in the Manche Department in Normandy. Americans are in hot pursuit of the enemy, but subjected to heavy strafing by Luftwaffe fighters. They return fire, downing several German aircraft. They soon move into Brittany's Saint Aubin-d'Aubigné, an old Roman city replete with ancient castles, churches, mansions, and statues.[2]

Bombed and strafed by more than fifty low-flying planes while assisting the Fourth Armored Division, the 333rd captures twenty prisoners. They are then attached to the Eighth Division Artillery, moving to secure Rennes.

A Roman-era city located at the junction of the Vilaine and Ille rivers, Rennes has been ravaged by the Norsemen, the Hundred Years' War, and a 1720 fire in which much of it was destroyed. Rennes was heavily damaged when Nazi forces seized it in 1940. In the spring of 1943, U.S. and RAF bombers leveled much of the city.

During their time in Rennes, a symphony rises steadily into the sky: "Stand back! Ready! Rommel—count your men! Fire! Rommel—how many men you got now?" The sound of 155 blasts can be heard for miles, belches of white phosphorus smoke hanging heavy in the air. After many direct target hits, Able, Baker, and Charley Batteries receive accolades from the troops for their accuracy.

The enemy withdraws on August 12, 1944, and the grateful citizens return home.

For a few hours the GIs rest, strolling through the now-quiet city, savoring the rare chance to catch their breath.

"Hard to see the beauty of the city under all these piles of rubble," Corporal Green says. "Hard to imagine what it used to look like."

"What a way to see the world," Moten exclaims. "Always wanted to see Europe. And now I'm seeing it at Uncle Sam's expense."

"Besides," Green laughs, "you are learning some valuable trades."

"Yeah," Moten smirks. "I hear there are plenty of jobs back in Texas to fire a 155."

"Aw, stuff it, you guys," Forte says. "The chow truck's pulling up. We're dining alfresco tonight, boys."

"What did he say?" Green asks.

"He means we're dining on the good ol' black dirt of France," Moten says. "And there's no waiting to be seated."[3, 4, 5]

CHAPTER 50

ONWARD INTO BATTLE

— SAINT MALO/DINARD, BRITTANY —
AUGUST 13, 1944

The GIs cannot rest long. While most of General Patton's Third Army turns east toward Paris, a part of Third Army—the Eighty-third Division—turns west into Brittany, moving through Coutances and Avranches toward the coastal towns of Saint Malo and Dinard. The VIII Corps, led by General Troy Middleton, begins its westward drive to capture Brittany's ports. Brest is their major target, the ancient city of Saint Malo their first objective.

"Okay, men, listen up. The word is that the Germans are holed up in a fortified citadel. They're well-armed, tough fighters who have plenty of battle experience in Normandy. They're commanded by a Stalingrad vet, Colonel von Aulock. The troops call him 'the Mad Colonel'—not to his face, I'll wager. He's sworn never to surrender, defending the port to his death."

"Maybe we can help him on that score," someone says.[1]

The quick dash across Brittany creates logistical problems for the VIII Corps. Communications prove difficult, as well as keeping a rapidly moving army supplied with food, equipment, and ammunition.

On August 13, the 333rd Group is attached to the Eighty-third Division and heads north to the Brittany coast, part of Germany's Atlantic Wall defense system. Their assignment is to consolidate Saint Malo and mop up Dinard.

"Word has it," Stewart tells Adams, Forte, and Davis, "they've got thousands of Germans in Saint Malo."

"Yeah, I hear hundreds of civilians are being held hostage behind the city's gates with little food or water," Adams says.[2]

"This will be a slugfest," Captain McLeod tells the men. "So hitch 'em up. The Germans are dug in and ready. How about it, Charley Battery—are you ready?"

On the fringe of Saint Malo, within ten thousand yards of the fortified citadel, the troops settle in, digging straddle trench latrines, readying their equipment, and preparing for an intense fight. The day before, an infantry battalion battled the Germans, suffering heavy casualties. The 333rd finds the orchards and foxholes filled with dead bodies, strewn with body parts, and littered with bloody helmets, boots, and debris. The summer wheatfields are pockmarked with deep black craters from a steady storm of exploding bombs.

Signalmen string telephone lines, stepping cautiously around undefused German mines. "Communication established," they report when finished. The ammunition sergeant unpacks, sorts, and stores ammunition by lot, placing it on and covering it with tarpaulins to protect it from moisture and sun. In a notebook he records all ammunition at the site, tabulating receipts and issues and reporting on ammunition expenditures. The fuses and primers are stored in dry places, a short distance away from components of the ammunition. Powder charges, kept in moisture-proof containers, are placed in a dry and ventilated area. Circulation sentinels inspect the area, ordering individuals, animals, and vehicles away from howitzer positions.

Charley Battery begins weapon emplacement, leveling the ground for the 155s, building wheel platforms and firing-base supports. With massive camouflage nets, they conceal the howitzers from enemy ground and air observation. Chief mechanics inspect the howitzers and matériel, testing the machinery and, if necessary, making repairs. Sentinels stand by, ready to guard and protect the weapons when gun crews take scheduled breaks.

The chief of Piece Sections, holding a notebook, prepares to keep current information on each gun, listing calibration corrections, base deflections, range of elevation, and data for defensive fires. Each gun book is required to show the number of rounds fired, as well as the weapon's defects and repairs. The recorder prepares a journal to list all fire commands, reports, and messages.

The 333rd Field Artillery Group is a well-oiled machine, camouflaged, set up, and ready to load, position, and fire at a moment's notice.[3]

Colonel von Aulock had been very specific when assuming his command, making a devoted vow to Hitler: "I was placed in command of this fortress. I did not request it. I will execute the orders I have received and, doing my duty as a soldier, I will fight to the last stone. I will defend Saint Malo to the last man even if the last man has to be myself."[4]

He is now holding, to the death, the walled seaward fortress of Saint Malo. The impressive sharp spire of the twelfth-century Cathedral of Saint Vincent towers over the city. The Citadel, an ancient fortification heavily reinforced with concrete by the Germans, is set up with underground tunnels, storage areas, power plants, ammunition dumps, living quarters, and a hospital. The Citadel's thick granite walls, designed in the Middle Ages to withstand surprise sieges, are impenetrable. The four hundred German troops inside are well supplied, comfortable, and safe.

From the beginning, the fighting is fierce. Allied and German troops shower the city with incendiary shells, damaging, burning, and destroying hundreds of stately granite houses built on winding cobblestone roads. Steady clouds of smoke rise from the gentle pasturelands as planes drop bombs that explode and dig up the ground. GIs enter Saint Malo with tanks and trucks pulling heavy howitzers through the mud, driving past crumbling stone buildings and dodging villagers riding bicycles on narrow roads. The two sides exchange hours of deadly artillery fire. In the midst of the chaos, confused old women and children hurry through the city in wooden wagons drawn by worn-out horses. Adams and other medics treat injured soldiers, bandaging their wounds, splinting broken limbs, and loading them into dusty brown ambulances.

Able, Baker, and Charley Batteries' gunners are hit by stray bullets. The slightly wounded walk to battalion aid stations. Others are treated by medics on the site. Some are seriously wounded and removed by litter. Others are killed.

Firing, however, is never stopped when one of the gun crew is hurt or killed. The man is quickly replaced, the firing too important to interrupt.

After the troops breach the walled old city, the VIII Corps bombards the thick-walled Citadel. A group of GIs and French Resistance volunteers scale the side of the fort, being careful not to alert the enemy inside. They crawl to the top, preparing to invade. But just as they begin to move inside, they are blasted by machine-gun and mortar fire from the enemy within the fortress, as well as artillery fire from an off-coast island.

"The Citadel is well built and heavily fortified," McLeod tells Kelsey. He runs his hands through his thick dark hair. "I don't think we can penetrate it."

"Let's give the howitzers a go at it," Kelsey advises. "At close range."

The Americans move the 105mm and 155mm howitzers within fifteen hundred yards of the fortress, firing at the concrete-fortified walls at point-blank range.

"Fuse impact . . . three rounds . . . fire!"

The ground quakes as four barrels from each battery spout tongues of flame at the fortress. But when the smoke clears, the bulwark is solid, the hundred-pound shells hitting the wall again and again and simply bouncing off.

For two long days without ceasing, the howitzer crews pummel the Citadel. They fire directly into the fortress's portholes and vents. But it has no effect. The Citadel stands strong, intact, and undamaged, still harboring the well-armed enemy within its bowels.

"Suspend firing!" an executive finally shouts. The howitzers grow quiet. Gunners wipe their foreheads and rub their eyes. Thick white smoke fills the air.

CHAPTER 51

THE SURRENDER

—FESTUNG SAINT MALO, FRANCE—
AUGUST 17, 1944

On the afternoon of August 17, from within the Citadel, Colonel von Aulock leans against the fortress wall, his shoulders slumped, his expression blank. He hasn't washed his hair and face in days; his clothes are so dirty they stink. He feels tired, defeated, and ashamed.

"Men," he says, trying to swallow the knot lodged in his throat, "I am convinced that, at this point, we are unable to counterattack the enemy. Our only choice is to . . . to surrender."

He looks at his men. Their heads are lowered, their arms hanging loosely at their sides. No further words are spoken. Von Aulock leaves them, washes his body, puts on a clean uniform, and slumps into a chair.

How has this happened? How will the Führer respond to my failing him?

He picks up the pistol on the table beside him, pointing it at his temple. *It is my duty. An officer of my rank and standing doesn't surrender. He takes his own life. Hitler will expect it.*

He puts his index finger on the trigger, holding it there for a full minute. But he doesn't fire. Instead he takes a deep breath, stands up straight, pulls on a long black coat, and puts the monocle to his eye. With his four hundred men behind him, Colonel von Aulock leaves the protection of his hiding place, the fortified sixty-foot-deep underground shelter, and surrenders Festung Saint Malo to the Allies. When, on the outside, he makes eye contact with Colonel Kelsey, the old "Mad Colonel von Aulock" raises his hands above his head and smirks.

"I have demolished the harbor's quays, locks, breakwaters, and machinery," he says. "You will find them unusable."

French townspeople shake their fists, spit, and hurl insults and curses at the Germans as they watch them loaded into trucks. Von Aulock steps into a jeep and is driven toward Division Headquarters. He refuses to say a word.

When the trucks, troops, and prisoners leave, the residents stand quietly and look at their city. Saint Malo lies in ruins, its buildings destroyed, its fields torn up, friends and family members buried somewhere in the rubble. But, in spite of the horror, the townspeople cheer, hug each other again and again, and sing together their national anthem. With the enemy gone, even in their sadness, they celebrate their newfound freedom.[1, 2]

Two days later, on August 19, the 333rd Field Artillery Battalion begins the long journey to Lesneven, a town fifteen miles northeast of Brest. Moving through Dinan and into the small valley of Jugon-les-Lacs, they have little time to admire the area's lakes, rivers, and countryside.[3]

"I could do some serious fishing here," Due Turner says as they pass Jugon and Arguenon lakes.

"War's gotta be won first," Stewart says. "Fishing comes later."

The convoy moves to Lamballe and passes through Saint Brieuc, Guingamp, and Morlaix, the town built around an impressive port. Entering Lesneven, they join with the 969th Field Artillery Battalion to provide fire support for the Twenty-ninth Division. Their orders are straightforward: "Attack and capture Brest."

"Seems to me we're moving in the wrong direction," Georgie Davis tells Sergeant Forte. "We're going west. Shouldn't we be heading east to Germany? Has anybody told the brass we're moving west, not east?"

"Shut up, Georgie! That's the army for you," Forte says. "Dumb white brass don't know east from west."

Private Adams walks forward and places his hand on Georgie's shoulder. "Georgie," he says. "We're not going in the wrong direction. VIII Corps wants us to liberate Brest. They probably don't want to leave occupying Krauts behind us while our troops push into Germany."

"That's right, George," Stewart says. "And the army wants Brest's port so the U.S. can ship supplies straight to us without going to England first. That way, we'll get supplies much quicker."

"What's more," Adams says, "we need to capture the Germans' submarine bases there, where they keep their U-boats under concrete roofs twenty feet thick."

CHAPTER 52

BREST

The army's opening attack on Brest is scheduled to launch on August 25, although preliminary assaults begin earlier. Once a major deep harbor base of the French Navy, the German-occupied city is home to eighty thousand residents. General Middleton aims to eliminate the German naval base and seize the submarine pens.

For centuries, Brest has been a key naval port, heavily fortified by the French and used to guard its naval base from sea and land attacks. When Germans captured the port and submarine pens several years before, they constructed new fortifications around the city and shoreline.

"Brest will not fall quickly," McLeod tells the men. "Even with thirty-four battalions taking part in this operation, the surrounding countryside with its hills, low ridges, and deep-cut valleys will provide the enemy a definite defensive advantage."

McLeod continues. "We think the Krauts have thirty thousand troops in Brest. Their defense is built around the veteran Second Paratroop Division. Their CO, General Hermann Ramcke, is one tough bird, a splendid leader according to the brass. The city's old forts, concrete pillboxes, and gun emplacements will defend it, not to mention all the barbed wire, minefields, and antitank ditches. They've even sunk ships at the mouth of the harbor to block our invasion route.

These guys are here for the long haul. Don't expect another Saint Malo. This one will be far worse.[1]

"Let's set up camp," McLeod says. "You know the routine: Dismount the howitzers' breechblocks for cleaning and oiling. Examine all the safety features to make sure they're in order and the bores are clear. Also, wipe down the ammo with an oiled rag in case it's been exposed to gas."

The captain addresses the crew designated to dig the latrines. "Dig deep pit latrines and urinal troughs. Remember to locate the deep pit latrines at least a hundred yards away from the kitchens—in an area enclosed with brush, and a hundred feet away from any well or spring. I don't need to remind you to drain the ditches away from fresh water supplies. Fill some cans with water—both clear and soapy water—for hand-washing."

The men groan. "Yes, sir."

"Until the deep pit latrines are finished, set up some temporary straddle trenches. You know the standards: a foot wide, two and a half feet deep, and four feet long. That'll give each man two feet of length. Be sure to place the boards securely along both sides of the trench for sure footing. And don't forget the toilet paper, fly traps, and powdered borax."[2]

Sergeant Forte, the mess sergeant, checks field rations C. "Three cans of meat and vegetable components; three cans of crackers, sugar, and soluble coffee. Hardly Thanksgivin' dinner, but it'll keep us from starvin'. No wonder the men complain about the chow." He examines field rations D, making sure each nonperishable ration contains three four-ounce concentrated chocolate bars.

Sergeant Forte, with pen and checklist, inspects the kitchen facilities and food handlers' reports. He also makes sure screen doors and windows fit tightly, outside doors open outward and close automatically, food containers are insect-proof, mess hall tabletops are thoroughly scrubbed with soap and water, permanent food handlers have all had physical examinations, and all are physically fit to handle food.

Don't want sick food handlers spreading disease, and certainly don't need infected or contaminated food causing intestinal disease. Can't fight a war with the "runs."[3]

The medic, Private Adams, examines and replenishes individual first-aid kits each soldier is required to carry in a web pouch attached to his cartridge belt.

"One sterile wound dressing, five grams of sulfanilamide in a double-wrapped envelope, eight sulfadiazine tablets—point-five grams each—or twelve sulfanilamide tablets, point-five grams each." He also restocks supplies in the first-aid kits and packets placed in vehicles.

That afternoon he meets with Colonel Kelsey to determine the troops' potential daily medical needs. Kelsey scratches out a list of supplies based on army experience tables, the size and composition of the army, the character of the operations, the nature of the enemy, and the climate. Most of all, troops will need supplies to treat wounds caused by bullets and shell fragments—provisions to stop bleeding, overcome shock, relieve pain, and prevent infection. High on the lengthy list is the opiate morphine, its collapsible tube and attached needle ready for immediate injection.

Bandages, splints, slings, tourniquets, iodine, ointments! How can we possibly pack enough medical supplies to deal with every type of battlefield injury and situation?[4]

CHAPTER 53

THE BATTLE, FIERCE AND DEADLY

—BREST, BRITTANY—
AUGUST 25, 1944

General Troy Middleton's VIII Corps plans to attack Festung Brest with three infantry divisions.

"We'll go in with the Twenty-ninth, Eighth, and Second divisions," he explains. "The Air Corps will bring in heavy and medium bombers. The French Resistance will be available as needed. We plan to employ heavy shelling, air strikes, ground troops, building-to-building searches, and, if necessary, hand-to-hand combat."

The Allies attack on August 25. From the air, planes bomb and strafe enemies on the ground while British warships fire from the coast. Infantry and artillery employ heavy continuous fire.

General Middleton receives an early report from the field. "The Brest defenses are unyielding. The infantry has been unable to make much progress. Enemy strongpoints are camouflaged and well protected."

He also learns the army's flamethrowers are proving ineffective in destroying German pillboxes, fortifications, and weapons. The fuel unit holds a limited ten gallons, permitting only six two-second bursts. The twenty-six-gallon unit delivers only fifteen brief bursts. The unthickened fuel produces a dispersed, short-range flame. Under ideal conditions, the maximum range is only eighty yards. The heavy winds and severe weather make ignition unreliable and drastically decrease the flamethrower's range.[1]

The 333rd's howitzers blaze continuously through heavy rain and thick fog. The men have no time to sing, no time to shout Rommel-inspired insults, and no time to eat C rations or chocolate bars.

On the left side of the howitzer, the gunner corporal works the scope, setting its horizontal deflection after receiving the firing officer's orders. Turning the number wheel, he moves the tube right or left until he perfectly levels the scope's alcohol bubble.

"Command left ten!" He lines up the scope's vertical crosshair and shouts, "Ready!" He struggles to keep the gun aligned until firing, especially when firing multiple times.

The assistant gunner stands on the right side of the breech, using a hand wheel to set the elevation. "Up fifteen!" He spins the wheel to the correct angle while operating the breechblock and setting the primer. When he hears the order "Fire!" he pulls the lanyard.

After a bright flash and deafening roar, the breech is quickly opened, allowing the shell casing to drop out. A loader picks up the casing, throwing it to the side. Without taking a breath, the whole process starts anew.

Trajectory accuracy—putting the shell on the right path to hit the target—is no simple matter. The howitzer crew must allow for air density and temperature, wind, projectile weight, powder temperature, erosion and wear of howitzer pieces, the amount of copper deposits on the surface of the bore, cleanliness, correct ramming, and the proper action of fuse and booster that causes the bursting charge to detonate. Some shells prove duds, failing to burst.

In spite of everything that can go wrong, Charley Battery fires with accuracy and speed.[2]

The men load and fire howizers until exhausted, but the German garrisons are strong, showing few signs of weakening.

CHAPTER 54

THE CAPTURE OF BREST

The battle for Brest continues, bloody and violent. The high number of casualties overwhelms Private Adams and the other medics. With so many injuries, medical supplies run low.

A GI is hit in the belly. Adams discovers the bullet has passed through the abdomen. He checks to see where the bullet has exited. Then he sprinkles sulfanilamide over the wound, dresses it with a large sterile bandage, and orders the man transported out.

Shell fragments rip open a soldier's abdomen, causing his intestines to spill out. When Adams sees the gaping gut, he turns his head and vomits. *I'll never get used to seeing this.*

He treats the open wound and displaced organs with sulfanilamide, dresses it, and calls for an ambulance.

"You're going home, soldier," he says, leaning down to the man's ear and whispering a brief prayer.

"You shouldn't tell him he's going *home*, Private, when you know he's dying," a medic nearby tells Adams.

"Not *that* home," Adams says.

Day after day, Adams treats wounds on the battlefield. Most common are broken bones caused by bullets, high-explosive shell fragments, bombs, and grenades.

"Medic!"

Adams kneels beside a wounded GI.

"Where does it hurt?" he asks.

"Right here," the GI groans, touching his lower arm.

Adams presses the area lightly, checking for pain and tenderness. *Possible fracture.*

"Can you move your arm?"

"No, sir."

Adams looks for deformity, swelling, and discoloration.

"Can't be sure," Adams says, "but you might have fractured your fibula."

He pulls the arm gently to straighten it, splinting it securely on both sides, and watches for signs of blueness.

Bindings too tight. He loosens the bindings until the blueness disappears. Grabbing a triangular bandage, he makes a sling to support the arm.

Adams finds simple bone fractures easy to treat. But compound fractures are a different story.

"Medic!" someone screams. Adams rushes to a bleeding soldier. The flesh on his muscular thigh is torn and hanging, the ragged sharp end of the broken bone piercing the skin, jutting out above the knee.

Compound fracture. Femur.

The patient screams from pain. Adams injects him with morphine.

"The pain'll stop in twenty minutes. Hang on."

Adams stops the bleeding and straightens the leg, pulling it gently from the knee, careful not to push the exposed bone back into place. But the pain is too much, and the soldier goes into shock. Adams covers him with a blanket. To prevent infection, he sprinkles sulfanilamide into the wound. With lightweight blankets, he pads two poles, splinting first the outside of the leg all the way from the armpit to beyond the foot. He uses a shorter pole for the inside of the leg, splinting it from crotch to foot. He binds both poles around the leg, securing them with cloth strips. Placing the unconscious GI on a litter, Adams calls for transport help.

All day long, screams for medics are constant, overwhelming the exhausted private. Late at night, long after the battlefield screams stop, Adams cups trembling hands around his ears, relives the day's horrors each time he closes his eyes, and struggles to sleep.

In early September, after weeks of heavy shelling, air strikes, ground troops, building-to-building searches, and hand-to-hand combat, things began to change for the Allies in the battle for Brest.

On September 13, General Middleton sends a message to General Ramcke, demanding his surrender. The grizzled old veteran of Crete and countless other campaigns gives a quick "*Nein!* A German soldier does not surrender!"

"Well, then," General Middleton says, giving a new order to his men, "let's take the Germans apart."[1]

For the following five days, the Americans attack with everything they have—artillery, explosives, tank destroyers, and howitzers. Several garrisons raise white flags, but not the center of resistance, Fort Montbarey, an old fortress enclosed with walls thirty feet high and fifteen feet wide. One by one, GIs attack the Germans' seventy-five defensive strongholds, often using thousand-pound armor-piercing bombs to blow craters through walls. They finally capture Brest's old city. The railroad systems are destroyed, the buildings lie in rubble on the streets, and the entire city is almost demolished.

On September 18, the defeated General Ramcke surrenders. Escorted by American troops, Ramcke raises his head high, arrogantly displaying at his neck the Oak Leaves to his Knight's Cross of the Iron Cross, presented to him by Hitler himself. The price for seizing Brest is high: ten thousand VIII Corps casualties.

"Brest's port is so damaged," General Middleton confirms, "it will take months to repair it."

General Bradley calls off any further attacks on the fortified Atlantic ports.[2]

———

The 333rd FAB is glad to leave Brest. They fill the deep pit latrines with dirt, remove the boxes, spray the pits with oil, and cover them with burlap. On top of the dirt-filled pits, they place heavy stones, logs, and brush to keep animals from unearthing the waste. They mark the site with a sign: CLOSED LATRINE. They march out of Brest, their job done.[3]

CHAPTER 55

THE LIBERATION OF PARIS

— PARIS, FRANCE —
AUGUST 25–29, 1944

The Germans have occupied Paris for four years before the Allies finally liberate the city on August 25. For the next week, most of the world celebrates Paris's new freedom.

The BBC announces with jubilee, "Paris is now free . . . at 1900 local time, General Charles de Gaulle, leader of the Free French, who has been living in exile in London since the Fall of France in 1940, entered the city."[1]

General de Gaulle leads a parade of ecstatic Parisians down the Champs-Élysées all the way to Notre Dame. Generals Eisenhower, Bradley, Gerow, and others on the platform watch the Twenty-eighth Infantry Division march triumphantly through the city. Even sporadic German sniper fire doesn't dampen the citizens' joy and sense of celebration.[2]

Back in Berlin, Hitler slams his fist down on his desk, scattering papers to the floor, and swearing long and loud. He has just learned that General Dietrich von Choltitz has purposely disobeyed his orders. He has repeatedly told his general of infantry to have his troops defend Paris to the very last man.

"Mine the city's bridges and blow them up, demolish them if the city falls into enemy hands," Hitler had ordered.

On hearing of the city's liberation, Hitler asks a messenger, "Is Paris burning?"

"Paris is not burning, my Führer, but is safely in the hands of the Allies!"

Furious, Hitler orders artillery and bombers to destroy the beautiful City of Light.

He soon learns, however, that the general has also ignored these orders.[3]

Adolf Hitler, alone in his room, is furious that Paris is free and undamaged. He opens a copy of *Mein Kampf*, his book first published in 1925, and begins to read the words he wrote about Nazi racial philosophy.

". . . [It] by no means believes in an equality of races . . . and feels itself obligated to promote the victory of the better and stronger, and demand the subordination of the inferior and weaker."[4]

He drops the book on the floor. He has eliminated millions of the "inferior and weak" through unrestricted slaughter, widespread massacres, and death camps. But what he has gained after years of war he is now losing, his past victories turning into major defeats. His plan for Lebensraum is in decay. Stalin's Red Army is gaining ground, heading west to Berlin to destroy him. Allies have liberated Paris and are quickly liberating all of France, making their way east to Belgium. In recent months, the Führer has made one bad decision after another, pushing his few remaining soldiers to exhaustion, ordering them to stand to the last man and to the last bullet. In declining health, Hitler feels tired and discouraged.

He thinks about recent betrayals by his once closest, most trusted officers.

"I can no longer trust anyone," he whines.

Although he has survived six assassination attempts since the Munich Beer Hall melee of 1921, he feels especially grieved by the most recent attempt that summer by Colonel Claus von Stauffenberg at his Wolf's Lair in Prussia.

"Traitors, all of them, especially—" He doesn't finish his sentence, hurt too deeply to even say Stauffenberg's name.

During his one dozen years of Nazi rule, Hitler has watched many of his supporters become less loyal and more disillusioned with him. The explosion on July 20 proved the last straw, adding insult to injury, the blast injuring his arm as well as his hearing and vision on his right side.

He remembers the days of his Wolf Pack glories, the mighty U-boats that prowled the Atlantic, torpedoing and sinking great Allied ships carrying desperately needed supplies. It saddens him to know those days are gone, that he and his powerful forces, once the mighty hunters, have now become the hunted.

"But the war is not over yet," he says. "I have one last trick up my sleeve."

He recalls telling his subordinates the month before that he intends "to carry on the fight until there is a prospect of peace that is reasonable, of a peace tolerable for Germany which will safeguard its existence of . . . future generations."[5]

He hurries his scientists to develop new and powerful weapons in secret underground facilities.

No, the war is not over yet.

CHAPTER 56

THE BIVOUAC

After weeks in fierce battle to capture Brest, the 333rd returns to Lesneven, where they bivouac and rest before heading south to capture the German-held ports of Lorient and Saint Nazaire. They set up a temporary camp, boiling vats of water for drinking and digging simple straddle trench latrines.

Captain McLeod welcomes Sergeant William Pritchett, wounded earlier and now healed. The men of the 333rd greet him warmly, telling him all about the long, intense battle for Brest.

"Too bad they destroyed the seaport," Pritchett says, "but I bet some general will be coming through with a fistful of medals."

"For the white troops maybe, but not for us," Forte replies. "You just wait 'n' see if we blacks get medals like the whites."

"Can't be this way forever, Sergeant," Stewart says. "Things are a-changing."

"I doubt anything's gonna change, Sergeant," Forte says. "People will always have prejudices."

"Yeah, I know. People'll probably be the same way when we get home—Jim Crow 'n' all. But, Sergeant Forte, *we* won't be the same. No, sir. We've changed."

"What do you mean?" Georgie asks.

"Well," Stewart says, looking first at Forte and then at Davis, "let's jus' say that the next man who calls you *Lil' Georgie* is gonna get his nose busted. After what we've been through, people are gonna call you by your *right* name: *Private First Class George Davis*. Lil' Georgie's gone, son, and he ain't coming back."

For the next few days, the 333rd cleans and maintains its 155s as well as other equipment.

While they rest and recuperate, they sing, making up new words for their battle songs "Roll, Jordan, Roll" and "Low-down Babe."

"Got a a new verse for 'Jordan,'" George says, and starts to sing.

"I saw those Krauts a-running / From Brest clear back to Berlin / I'm gonna march right home to 'Bama / This war we're gonna win! win! win!"

The men laugh, joining George in the chorus: "I say / Roll, Jordan, roll / Roll, Jordan, roll / My soul arise in heaven, Lord / Gonna hear ol' Jordan roll / Hallelujah!"

When the men stop singing and laughing and calm down, Sergeant Pritchett says, "I heard our GIs are in Paris."

"Think we're gonna get to Paris?" Davis asks.

"Could be, son," Stewart responds. "We'll soon see."[1]

The artillerymen enjoy their first USO show on September 23. The next day, SHAEF tells the VIII Corps, including the 333rd and 969th, to prepare for a five hundred–mile trip to Houffalize, Belgium.

"Our earlier plans to seize the ports of Lorient and Saint Nazaire have been scrapped," SHAEF explains. "Men, you have four days to prepare. We leave on September 28."

"Glad our 155s are finally heading in the right direction," Davis says.

"Guess they're gonna let the Krauts in Lorient and Saint Nazaire wither on the vine," Forte says.

"Okay by me," Stewart says. "It's a crying shame what we had to do to Brest." He frowns, shaking his head. "But we aren't paid to make decisions. We jus' obey them."

"When are we getting new winter uniforms, boots, and camouflage?" Corporal Bradley asks. "The weather's getting right nippy. These old summer rags and boots are worn-out. And with the snow, this old camouflage won't do."

"Haven't heard anything about it," Moss says. "Still hot summertime in Texas."

"I'm gonna miss this warm Texas winter," Moten says.

"Rumor has it we'll be home soon," Stewart tells them. "We probably won't be getting winter gear if the army thinks we'll be leaving by Christmas."

"I'll be home for Christmas," Leatherwood croons in his best Bing Crosby voice.

The others laugh, joining in the song. "You can count on me . . . snow and mistletoe, and presents under the tree. . . ."[2]

"Boys, do you remember how that song ends?" Turner interrupts. "We might be home for Christmas 'only in our dreams.'"

"If we get stuck here for Christmas," Leatherwood says, "that's no dream. That's a nightmare."

"If this war's not over by Christmas," Forte says, "we're sunk. The guys in Supply say we don't have enough shells to last more than a few weeks."

"Why the shortage?" Turner asks.

"Plants back home can't make ammo fast enough," Forte says. "And once they're shipped to Cherbourg, they've gotta be hauled eight hundred miles to where our guns are. Those Red Ball Express drivers are bustin' their tails to get us shells, wearin' out trucks right and left."

"Mail call! Mail call!"

The chatter suddenly stops as troops race to the jeep where battalion mail clerks are handing out something more important than shells—letters from home.[3]

CHAPTER 57

THE YOUNG, THE OLD, AND THE WOUNDED

— WOLF'S LAIR, EAST PRUSSIA —
FALL 1944

Adolf Hitler paces the floor at his Wolf's Lair bunker. He has received urgent reports of continuing massive losses of manpower on the Eastern Front. To win the war, he knows he must somehow build up troops.

He orders Heinrich Himmler, leader of the Waffen-SS, to beef up the number of infantry troops under the command of the Wehrmacht.

"Organize a new army infantry division," he orders. "Recruit men from broken or destroyed infantry divisions, convalescent soldiers recently discharged from hospitals, Luftwaffe and Kriegsmarine personnel, workers from industry and railways, and every available male from sixteen to sixty years of age. Replace male industry and railway workers with civilian women."

He pauses, rubs his chin, and continues. "Train them quickly. Give them powerful automatic weapons to compensate for their lack of training and their physical and age shortcomings."

"What shall we name this new division?" Himmler asks. "And with what weapons shall I equip them?"

"Name it the Volksgrenadier Division—the Peoples Infantry Divi-

sion. Equip them with new StG44 storm rifles—the Sturmgewehr 44—
as well as MG42 machine guns, and Panzerfaust antitank weapons."[1]

"Good choice, my Führer. What shall I do if these men refuse to
join and fight?"

"Shoot them or hang them on the spot, of course. And station SS
executioners on the streets to hunt down deserters."

"Heil, Hitler!" Himmler salutes, leaving to carry out Hitler's orders.

Under the Nazi Party, and also commanded by Himmler, Hitler
orders the conscription of Hitler's Youth members, the Volkssturm.
Some boys and girls are as young as eight years old.[2]

"Outfit the children with uniforms and weapons, and train them
for combat," Himmler tells Hitlerjugend leader Artur Axmann.

Facing the group of excited youngsters, their uniforms hanging from
their tiny frames and adult-sized helmets covering their eyes, Axmann
appeals to their devotion to Hitler and Germany, telling them:

"You must decide whether you want to be the last of an unworthy
race despised by future generations, or whether you want to be part of
a new time, marvelous beyond all imagination."

"We want to be part of the new time!" the children cheer, jumping
up and down with enthusiasm as they try to pick up the heavy weapons.[3]

When Mathias and Maria Langer learn about Hitler's new re-
cruitment laws, they panic. Two of their three teenage sons
still live at home in Wereth: Heinrich, sixteen, and Paul, fifteen. Walter, nineteen, is already in hiding in Brussels.

"We must make arrangements to hide Heinrich and Paul," Mathias
says. "The Germans will conscript them into their boy-soldier army."

"I see why we must send away Heinrich," Maria says. "But Paul is
just fifteen and too young for the German Army. We must keep Paul
with us at home."

"No, Maria," Mathias tells her. "The Germans are recruiting boys—and even girls—much younger than Paul. We just cannot risk it. I also worry about Tina and Hermann."

Mathias makes immediate plans to send Heinrich and Paul away from Wereth. Friends of the Langers, Johann Mertes and his son, Vincenz, as well as German deserter Leo Hennes, offer to take the two Langer boys to a safe place of hiding.

Seven of the Langer children stay at home in Wereth: Tina, seventeen, Hermann, twelve, Hans, ten, Gertrud, eight, Leo, seven, Resi, five, and the new baby, Anneliese, only six months old.

Mathias and Maria wrap their arms around their two sons, hugging them, and praying for their survival. The boys pick up small suitcases, each filled with clothes, food, and a tiny crucifix, and leave their home and family.

"We will return," they call to their parents and siblings, struggling to hold back tears.

"We will pray for you every day until you are safely home again," Mathias and Maria tell them.

After they walk away, Maria grips the hand of her friend Maria Mertes, Johann's wife, and cries.

"I worry I will never see my sons again," she says.[4]

CHAPTER 58

THE REPORTS

—BERLIN, GERMANY—
SEPTEMBER 1944

Adolf Hitler reads with disgust one of the first battle reports of the new Volksgrenadier Division, formed earlier that month, its commander the newly promoted Generalleutnant Wolfgang Lange, a veteran from 1915.[1, 2]

The report describes the 183rd Volksgrenadier Division replacements as "battle-inexperienced, and showing great caution, [with] a measure of noticeable uncertainty in all battles."

The Führer flattens his lips, looking to the ceiling in frustration.

"A spirit of bravado and daring enterprise was practically always lacking," the report continues. "Although clear numerical and material superiority existed, favorable conditions leading to quick successes were not utilized."[3, 4]

In October, SHAEF receives documents from a captured German officer, the confidential "Kempfgruppe Stoessel Report." On October 12, its contents are presented to members of SHAEF.

"The captured document tells us several interesting things about German soldiers."[5]

"Give it to us in a nutshell," an officer requests, checking his wrist-watch.

"The enemy is fighting fanatically to hold his territorial gains, attacking vigorously, even in the face of losses."

"How is troop morale?" another asks.

"Morale is good. The report reveals, however, that the soldiers are extremely suspicious and cautious when fighting in wooded areas, and bring in additional heavy infantry weapons. But the report says they are also cunning and know how to move about the woods."

"And in fortress fighting?"

"They have also proven their worth, quickly adjusting to each new situation."

"Reconnaissance?"

"Except for small reconnaissance squads of three or four men, the enemy does not carry out active reconnaissance. That's left to the Luftwaffe."

"So our type of 'Indian' scouting, where the patrol remains in contact with the enemy for twenty-four hours or more, isn't employed?"

"That is correct, sir."[6]

Back in Alabama, the home of Davis and Pritchett, the new governor, Chauncey Sparks, has succeeded former governor Frank M. Dixon, an open advocate of white supremacy. Governor Sparks's jaw muscles tense when he hears about the extraordinary combat and leadership roles being carried out by the Ninety-ninth Fighter Squadron at Alabama's Maxwell Air Force Base in Montgomery. The all-black Tuskegee Airmen are participating in campaigns in Europe, accomplishing difficult feats and winning Distinguished Unit Citations.

He bites the inside of his cheek, fearing rumors the military might be abolishing segregation at Maxwell and other Alabama bases. He writes a letter to the War Department, complaining that white and black soldiers are intermingling too much at Alabama bases.[7]

At the same time, NAACP civil rights activist Walter White is touring the ETO, making keen observations about racism in the U.S. military. He reports that black servicemen face harsher penalties for lesser crimes than whites, and that white prejudice often causes violence for black soldiers.

"Black soldiers are kept in service positions when they are needed in combat," he claims. "Changes must take place. We must increase training for black officers and use our black troops in combat."[8]

Only the year before did the War Manpower Commission and Selective Service System force the navy and Marine Corps to accept black draftees.

W hen former Alabama governor Frank Dixon hears that his friend Governor Sparks is taking a strong stand against de-segregation in the military, he writes the governor, delighted with his action.

August 31, 1944

My dear Chauncey:

I noted with very great interest your immediate reaction to the order of the War Department abolishing segregation at Maxwell Field and at other Army Posts.

It is a heartbreaking thing for those of us in the South who realize what the destruction of segregation would mean, and yet are determined to give the negro a better break, to have all our plans wrecked by the type of very dangerous thinking which produced this order.

Of course, the President and Mrs. Roosevelt are directly responsible for it and regard it as a very great victory. They see eye-to-eye with the Political Action Committee and regard this fool order as a great step forward. The net result of it is, and will be, a tremendous increase in tension, because it opens a festering sore at exactly the point which is most sensitive to the Southern people. Our situation as Southern Democrats is rapidly becoming absolutely intolerable.

This letter does not call for an answer. I simply want you to know how greatly I approve of your courageous stand, and how deeply I sympathize with you in your efforts to do the job to which the people of Alabama elected you, in a sane and intelligent way, and with justice to all of the elements among our people.

Good luck and best wishes. I am looking forward to the fishing trip.

Regards: Frank (Frank M. Dixon)[9]

CHAPTER 59

THE LONG MARCH TO BELGIUM

—LESNEVEN, FRANCE—
SEPTEMBER 28, 1944

The 333rd moves through France with the VIII Corps, headed by the brilliant, soft-spoken Southerner general Troy Middleton. The men respect Middleton, who led troops in the Saint Mihiel and Meuse-Argonne offensives during World War I, becoming one of the army's youngest colonels. After the war, he left the army for civilian life and for many years served as Louisiana State University's president. After Pearl Harbor, Middleton, fifty-two, returned to active duty. Promoted to major general in 1944, he assumed command of the VIII Corps, arriving in Normandy on June 13, one week after D-day.

On September 28, with Middleton's VIII Corps, the 333rd and 969th Field Artillery Battalion begin their long trek to Belgium.[1]

The troops travel almost 165 miles, bivouacking in Saint Aubin-d'Aubigné, revisiting the small commune 11 miles north of Rennes. Residents welcome the troops with flowers, wine, and kisses, expressing gratitude for earlier liberating their city.

"I feel like a hero," Davis says after a young French woman tosses flowers to him.

"You *are* a hero," Stewart says. "These people know we ran the Krauts outta their country."

"They've been put through it," Turner says. "Think about it: four years of arrests, deportation, mistreatment, executions, and bombings."

"I'd like to come back here one day," Adams says, "and bring Catherine and Jesse with me—when the city's rebuilt and beautiful again."

"Catherine and Jesse's lucky to have you, Private," Stewart says. "When I get back, I'm gonna settle down and start a family, too."

"You'd make a good daddy, Sergeant," Adams says, smiling. "But you're getting on up there in years. Best get busy and do it quick when you get back home."

Stewart laughs. "When I find jus' the right woman, son, I'll bring her down to South Carolina and introduce her to you. And I'll teach Jesse how to throw a baseball."

"You guys are dreamin'," Forte says, sneering. "Last time I checked, the Germans hadn't quit. Lots a fightin' still ahead."

"Sure hope you're wrong, Sergeant!" Moten blurts out.

"Don't be so gloomy, son," Stewart tells Forte. "And you might try smiling once in a while. Haven't seen you smile since you got here. You've gotta believe good things are gonna happen. We're already pushing Hitler and his boys back to Berlin. Then it's back to the old U.S. of A. and civvie life."

"Like I said, Sergeant, you're dreamin'. You're just hopin' and wishin' things'll turn out hunky-dory. Life ain't like that. And I don't have anything to smile about."

"Have faith, Sergeant," Green says. "We've gotta believe in each other and why we're in this mess together."

"And don't forget," Stewart says, and smiles. "We are the best artillery battalion—black or white—in this man's army. Right, boys?"

"Right!" all cheer, except Forte.

The next day, September 29, the troops cover 170 miles before stopping in Chartres. For centuries, Chartres has known a turbulent past, as far back as the year 858, when it was burned down by the Normans. Chartres had fallen into English hands until recovered by France in 1432. The Germans seized Chartres in 1870, occupying it for one year during the Franco-Prussian War.

As they drive eastward through the wheatfields of Beauce, the troops spot the impressive spires of the magnificient twelfth-century Gothic cathedral from fifteen miles away.

A woman, her head shaved and her scalp nicked, walks beside the road. In her arms, she cradles a baby.

The men watch the forlorn figure in silence.

"Looks sad. Scared, too," Davis says. "Why's she bald?"

"That's what happens to French gals when they have sexual relations with German soldiers," Shomo says. "Sometimes they get beat up or even killed. The townsfolk treat them bad. Jeer at them. Humiliate them."

"Kinda feel sorry for her," Adams says. "Poor kid with Kraut blood!"

"They deserve it," Forte says. "They know better than takin' up with the enemy."

"No, son," Stewart says, frowning. "It's a crying shame treating another human being like that. 'Specially one with a baby. That child can't help who's its daddy."

The men say little as they watch people walk through narrow streets, past half-timbered buildings.

"Compared to the damage of Normandy and Brittany," Stewart says, "Chartres looks relatively undamaged."

"Glad to see the church wasn't hurt," Moss says. "I saw a picture of it in a magazine once. I was afraid it wouldn't be here anymore."

"Did you hear how it got spared?" Stewart asks. "It was saved last month by a Texan, a Colonel Griffith with the XX Corps. Seems he got orders to shell it. The brass thought Kraut snipers were in one of its towers. The colonel went inside by himself and searched the whole cathedral and bell tower. Found no Germans."

"That's great," Shomo says, pointing to the northern tower. "Too beautiful to destroy on the chance a sniper might be up there."[2]

"So the colonel saved it, just for us," Davis says, grinning.

"I reckon so," Moss says.

"I heard the colonel was killed in a tank attack just after leaving here," Leatherwood says.[3]

The troops stare silently at the cathedral's two strangely dissimilar towers. The large round window is boarded over to protect it. Three ground-level doors are topped with arches, crammed with carved figures.

"Wow! Look at those!" Moss says. "Who are they?"

"I believe they're from the Bible—the apostles, maybe. I'm pretty sure that's Jesus at the top," Stewart says.

"Check out the row of statues between the towers," Moss says. "They should've left a space for that Texas guy who saved the church. If it weren't for him, we'd be looking at a rock quarry."

"Amen to that!" Shomo says. "Hey, I hear we're going through Paris tomorrow."

"Another place the Krauts didn't destroy," Stewart says.

"They say you ain't seen nothing till you've seen Paris," Moss says.

"Probably off-limits to us GIs," Forte says. "At least all of us below the rank of general."

CHAPTER 60

THE CITY OF LIGHT

—PARIS, FRANCE—
SEPTEMBER 30, 1944

For the men of the 333rd Field Artillery Battalion, seeing Paris is like stepping into another world. Buildings, streets, and monuments are undamaged. The trees have leaves. The streets and sidewalks are clear.

"Never thought I'd get here," Davis exclaims as they pass through the beautiful City of Light. "Can't wait to tell my folks about this place. Maybe I'll bring them here one day."

"Soon these days will be jus' memories for us," Stewart says. "We'll be telling our children and grandchildren about strolling through Paris during the war."

"I'm surprised Hitler didn't level this place," Pritchett says. "Can't believe it's all still in one piece."

"We can thank the FFI [French Forces of the Interior], the Second French Armored Division, and our boys for pushing the Germans outta Paris," Bradley tells them.

"Lots of resistance fighters were killed trying to free French civilians," Stewart says.[1]

"I hear we're gonna get some free time here in Paris," Forte says. "I'm plannin' to buy Angelina a weddin' ring. Maybe one with a *real* diamond."

Stewart smiles. "I'd like to invest in that purchase," he says, emptying change from his pockets. "I'd give you more, Forte, but this is all I've got."

Davis, Green, Pritchett, and Bradley reach into their pockets, too, pulling out change and some crumpled bills. They hand them to Forte.

Forte blinks several times and bites his bottom lip. "Thanks. The ring'll mean a lot to Angelina," he says without smiling.

After leaving Paris, the 333rd moves with General Middleton's VIII Corps a hundred miles or so northeast to Saint Quentin, a town liberated by General Patton's troops a week earlier. During a brief bivouac in Saint Quentin, they prepare to begin their long journey to Bastogne, Belgium.[2, 3]

On the last day of September, Kelsey calls together the members of the 333rd Field Artillery Battalion. They gather, standing at attention, waiting for Kelsey to address them. Around them in the fields stand hundreds of GIs from other battalions, both black and white.

"What's going on?" Private Davis whispers to Stewart, without moving his head or lips.

"I have no idea, Davis. Looks like we might be in trouble," he says, looking straight ahead.

Colonel Kelsey, with Captain McLeod beside him, stares at the men with a deadpan expression. Then both men break into laughter.

"At ease! And congratulations!" they shout. The GIs in the fields cheer at the top of their voices and clap their hands. "Good job!" they shout again and again.

Someone in the back calls out, "How many men you got, Rommel?" A group of white GIs in front responds loudly, "Boom! How many men you got now, Rommel?"

"These men have lost their minds," Forte says. "Anybod' know what's goin' on?"

Colonel Kelsey steps forward, still laughing, and motions for the men in the fields to be quiet.

"Men," Kelsey shouts so that everyone can hear, "it is my special honor here today to congratulate the men of the 333rd FAB!"

Everyone cheers. Colonel Kelsey waves a magazine high above his head. McLeod grins.

"Men, do you remember the journalist Sergeant Bill Davidson, who came from the States to visit us here at the end of June?" Kelsey asks. "Well, yesterday, *Yank* magazine published the article he wrote about the 333rd FAB. And, boys, it's a doozy!"

Davis's mouth drops open. "He wrote an article in *Yank* about *us*?"

Kelsey continues. "After you boys first arrived in France, fired four rounds in ninety seconds, and knocked down a church steeple more than nine miles away, this is what Davidson wrote."

He opens the magazine and reads from the article: "'That's the kind of shooting the battalion has done ever since. It was the first Negro combat outfit to face the enemy in France. Today it is greatly respected.'"

Kelsey pauses, giving the troops another opportunity to cheer. After loud and long applause, Kelsey continues reading:

"'It [the 333rd FAB] is rated by the Corps to which it is attached as one of the best artillery units under the Corps' control. And I've heard doughboys of five divisions watch men of the battalion rumble past in four-ton prime movers and say: *Thank God those guys are behind us!*'"[4]

"We're extremely proud of you, guys!" Kelsey shouts. "You make us all look good!"

Captain McLeod steps forward and salutes his men, beaming like a proud father, his dark brown eyes moist. For the next few minutes, white and black GIs stand side by side, waving their arms and cheering loudly, their united voices sending hundreds of shouts of congratulations high into the Saint Quentin sky.

CHAPTER 61

THE PLAN

Hitler sits at his desk, thumbing through his twenty-year-old personal dog-eared copy of *Mein Kampf.* He feels exhausted, sick, and defeated. He worries his empire will soon lie in ruins. The Allies have liberated France and are now moving into Belgium. Not even his mistress, Eva Braun, can cheer him today. He knows he must do something drastic if he is to save the Fatherland. He stops and reads aloud:

"'Strength lies not in defense but in attack.'"[1]

He wrote those words many years before.

His eyes widen, and his expression suddenly changes, a rush of adrenaline racing through his veins.

My words are as true today as they were then.

"Counterattack!" he shouts. "Germany's final attempt to turn this war around in our favor."

Quickly spreading a Belgian map out in front of him, he strains his eyes to find Antwerp.

What if . . .

He traces the Eifel region with his finger.

Our staging area!

He takes a pen, circling the port of Antwerp.

Our objective!

A battle plan begins to take shape in his mind. "Yes! Yes! Yes!" he says aloud.

We will strike through the Ardennes Forest area of southern Belgium and Luxembourg, break through American lines, cross the Meuse River into the open countryside, and capture the port of Antwerp.

He thinks about his success in 1940 when he surprised the Allies by crossing through the dense Ardennes Forest.

We will split Allied armies, just like in 1940, severing Allied supply lines and separating the British from the American forces. Then we'll finish off the Brits.

He envisions his massive new Tiger II tanks and Panthers armed with the latest deadly weapons. "We are much better equipped now than we were in 1940! We shall destroy them!" he shouts, his face lighting up.

Then I will turn my attention to the east, astound them with my new weapons, and negotiate peace with the Soviets.

"A perfect plan! A surprise attack!" he says aloud. "Those fools didn't expect an attack through the Ardennes in 1940, and they won't expect one now. We will confuse, cripple, and defeat them!"

He licks his lips and spends the next few minutes in deep thought.

If we attack in mid-December, the inclement weather will give us the cover of heavy fog. It will also ground Allied planes, making it impossible for aerial observation and attack. The ground will be frozen, making it less difficult to move our tanks and troops through the forests. I will order strict radio silence as we amass our equipment to strike. The enemy will have no idea what we are doing until it is too late.

His plan set in stone, he contacts Hasso von Manteuffel, confiding the attack idea, but not the scheduled date.

"Hasso," he says, "I am putting you in charge of a military buildup at the West Wall. Begin amassing troops, equipment, and weapons."

"But, my Führer, soldiers and supplies are scarce. Where shall I find them?" Manteuffel asks.

"You speak as if you doubt me!" Hitler tells him. "We will begin immediately to produce a large volume of war materials in our underground factories. Himmler is already putting together a new Volksgrenadier Division of soldiers."

The Führer ends the conversation and takes a pad of paper, writing the names of Field Marshal Gerd von Rundstedt and Field Marshal Walter Model, as well as others in his inner circle.

In the North: General Sepp Dietrich, Sixth SS Panzer Army; Colonel Joachim Peiper, First SS Panzer Division.

In the Center: General Hasso von Manteuffel, Fifth Panzer Army; Field Marshal Walter Model, Army Group B; SS Major Gustav Knittel, First SS Panzer Recon Battalion.

In the South: General Erich Brandenberger, Seventh Army.

If needed: Fifteenth Army.

Hitler pauses to reflect, reading back over his list.

"Gustav Knittel will be the one to lead his 'fast group' reconnaissance battalion to the Meuse River."

A captured bridge on the Meuse will enable SS-Leibstandarte to move toward Antwerp.

He reflects upon Gustav Knittel's devotion to him, and his extraordinary service record. *Knittel was a veteran of campaigns in France, Yugoslavia, Greece, and Russia. I greatly admire his fire brigade. He has certainly distinguished himself on the Eastern Front even though wounded four times in battle. For his courage and dedication to the Vaterland, he more than deserves the German Cross in Gold and the Knight's Cross I gave him.*

With renewed and enthusiastic determination, Hitler begins planning his Ardennes Offensive.

Yes! "Attack—not defense!" I shall show the world that I am still the man in charge! We haven't lost the war yet!

He makes detailed notes as he finalizes the details:

Attack the positions along the 60- to 80-mile Belgian-German-Luxembourg border, cutting off Canada's First Army, America's First and Ninth Armies, and Britain's Second Army. To accomplish this, we will need:

> *Two hundred thousand men or more.*
> *Thirteen Infantry Divisions.*
> *Seven Panzer Divisions.*
> *One thousand tanks.*
> *Two thousand guns.*
> *Fuel. Much, much fuel.*

When shall I tell my generals and officers about my plan?

He draws a deep breath, holding it for a long time, and exhaling it slowly. He is still reeling from the unsuccessful assassination attempt on his life that summer by Stauffenberg. "Can anyone be trusted?" he asks aloud.

Not now. Except for Manteuffel, I will keep the matter a secret, telling them when I am ready to.

Hitler makes one last note:

> *Contact SS Commando Otto Skorzeny to carry out a sabotage spy mission.*
> *Name it "Operation Greif."*[2, 3]

CHAPTER 62

BIVOUACKING IN BELGIUM

—HOUFFALIZE, BELGIUM—
OCTOBER 1, 1944

The weather turns wet and nasty as the troops enter Belgium, bivouacking in Houffalize, a village several miles northeast of Bastogne. Houffalize is no stranger to wars. Throughout its long history, vicious battles have destroyed most of its ancient buildings and landmarks.[1]

Heavy rains deluge the small town in the dense Ardennes Forest, turning dirt roads and fields into knee-deep mud pits. The men struggle to wade through the sludge, to hike, or to move equipment. The fog is thick, requiring the men to strain their eyes to see a few feet ahead of them. The autumn air is cooling as temperatures drop with each new day. The troops, still clad in summer uniforms, shiver constantly trying to stay warm.

"With all this rain, looks like we're not gonna get to Saint Vith today or tomorrow," Stewart tells the men.

"Okay by me," Turner says. "We need some rest."

For the next two days, the men bivouac in Houffalize while storms drench the area. It proves impossible for them to keep their socks dry, a necessity to protect their feet from the dreaded trench foot. Instead of digging straddle trenches, they use simple pail latrines, emptying and disinfecting them daily and burning the waste.

"Hard to believe we got written up in *Yank*," Davis says, smiling and shaking his head.

"It's quite an honor," Stewart says as he wrings the water out of his socks and massages his numbing feet. "Not jus' for us, but for all blacks in the U.S. military. Makes all this hard work, and these wet socks, worth it."

"Slap some Compound 219 on those holes in your boots, Sergeant," Turner says, watching Stewart pull on dry socks.

"Glad some of us black GIs are finally gettin' some *good* recognition," Forte says. "We'll show 'em what we can do if we're just given the chance."

"You said it there, brother," Pritchett says.

On October 3, the rains let up and the troops move into Saint Vith, a town located on a vital road junction into the Ardennes Forest, a dozen miles from German front lines. Their sister battalion, the 969th, heads in another direction.[2]

From Saint Vith, the 333rd Field Artillery Battallion, with the VIII Corps, marches six miles east into the Schönberg area, located on the Our River, west of the forested hills and ridges known as the Schnee Eifel—the "Snow Mountains." They will provide general support and reinforcing fire for the veteran Second Division, stationed dangerously close to the Siegfried Line. Headquarters, along with Colonel Kelsey and Captain McLeod and most of the 333rd Service Battery, set up camp along the Schönberg–Andler road on the west side of Our River. The 333rd's Able, Baker, Charley, and the remaining part of Service Battery cross the old stone bridge and make camp on the east side of the river. They dig deep pit latrines at the front in the Ardennes. They are planning to stay here awhile.

On a hilltop in the area around Bleialf, a small German farming village just over the Belgian frontier, southwest of the Schnee Eifel and less than ten miles from Schönberg, four men of the 333rd set up one of two observation posts. One GI, Second Lieutenant Reginald W. Gibson, is white. The other three men—Tech Sergeant J. C. Colemen, Private Earnest Williams, and Private Samuel Harris—are black. They will keep a close eye out for any unusual and unexpected Axis movement in the dense Ardennes Forest.[3]

The Siegfried Line—or, as the Germans call it, the West Wall—is a four-hundred-mile-long, well-built, and heavily fortified German defense system. Hitler had built the West Wall in stages, between 1938 and 1940, to protect Germany's western border. The wall stretches from Kleve, near the Dutch border, to Weil am Rhein near the Swiss border, and is equipped with eighteen thousand machine-gun bunkers (pillboxes), tunnels, and rows of tank trap barriers called dragon's teeth. Barbed wire and mines have been placed between the "teeth," the three-to-four-feet-tall concrete pyramids designed to stop tanks from crossing.[4, 5]

When General George Patton hears that General Omar Bradley intends to keep the area around the Siegfried Line thinly guarded, using only six U.S. divisions with about sixty thousand men, he balks. "That was the major German invasion route through the Ardennes in 1940," he says. "First Army is making a terrible mistake by leaving VIII Corps static. It is highly probable that the Germans are building up east of them."

But General Bradley disagrees. "I know it's a calculated risk, but the weather's too bad in the Ardennes. They won't attack in these conditions. Not with winter coming. It's a Ghost Front—a quiet front. Nothing is happening there. Anyway, there is simply no way the Germans can secretly pull off such an operation in the Ardennes."

"Intelligence is aware that the Germans have assembled the Sixth Panzer Army in the area east of Aachen," Patton says.

"Yes, I know. But SHAEF defines the buildup as defensive, readying their troops to defend the Reich," Bradley says. "They think the Germans are waiting for the final showdown, when your Third Army pushes forward, cracks the Siegfried Line, and drives to the Rhine."[6]

CHAPTER 63

OPERATION GREIF

Devoting all his energy to the upcoming surprise attack, Hitler amasses tanks, equipment, weapons, ammunition, and troops at the West Wall. Military production is drastically increased. He orders all German radio communications shut down.

"We want to make the Allies think nothing is happening here, that all is quiet."

He contacts SS commando Otto Skorzeny, a Vienna-born, six-foot-four-inch artillery officer who joined the Nazi Party in 1930 and saw action in the Low Countries and France, fought on the Eastern Front, and took part in the invasions of Yugoslavia and the Soviet Union.

Hitler had called on Skorzeny's help the year before.

"Go to the Abruzzi Apennines and rescue Benito Mussolini, who is a prisoner there," Hitler had told Skorzeny.

On September 13, a skilled pilot, "Scarface" Skorzeny, led a force of glider-borne commandos, freeing Mussolini in a dramatic rescue and flying him to safety. He quickly earned the title of "the most dangerous man in Europe," and became highly admired for his military prowess.[1]

The Führer had also asked the loyal Skorzeny to round up and torture members of the German Resistance who participated the previous summer in Stauffenberg's assassination attempt on him. Hitler admires and trusts the brutal Austrian Nazi.

Hitler meets with Skorzeny at Rastenburg, promoting him to Obersturmbannführer (lieutenant colonel) and asking him to devise a scheme to sow confusion and fear among Allied troops.

"Assemble a special brigade of German soldiers, each one able to speak good English with a distinctive American accent and a knowledge of Yank slang. Dress them in American uniforms, infiltrate the Allies, and cause terror and havoc," Hitler tells him. "I also want you and your men to capture one or more of the bridges over the Meuse River."

Skorzeny agrees.

"You know that if I am caught, my Führer," Skorzeny says, "I will face execution."

"I trust you not to be caught, Obersturmbannführer," Hitler says. "You will have my full support."

To prepare for the special mission, Skorzeny's unit, named the Panzer Brigade 150, scours Germany, collecting captured American uniforms, jeeps, tanks, weapons, and equipment. Finding soldiers who can speak passable English and American slang is a bigger challenge. When assembled, Skorzeny orders the spies to "make the Amis believe you are one of them and then cut their lines of communication. Switch road signs. Give them misleading directions. Undermine their morale. Confuse them every way you can."

Skorzeny's unit plans to slip behind U.S. lines during the early stages of the surprise attack, blending in with unsuspecting GIs, eating, conversing, traveling in captured jeeps among them, and committing acts of sabotage whenever possible. They also plan to report tactical information back to their panzer units.[2]

Hitler knows the spies will be targets for both the Germans and the Americans—most likely shot by Germans, thinking them to be Americans, and/or by Americans, finding out they are German spies.

The Langer family *(back row, left to right)*: Heinz, Tina, Trauchen, Hans; *(middle row, left to right)* Hermann, Anneliese, Joseph, Resi, Walter; *(front row, left to right)* Paul, Mathias, Maria, Leo.

Patrick Langer, on behalf of the Langer Family

Hermann Langer.

Patrick Langer, on behalf of the Langer Family

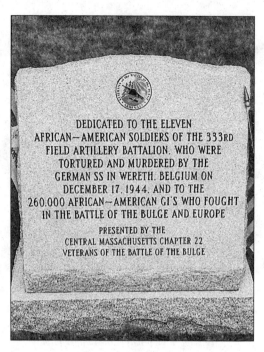

The memorial to the Wereth 11 in Winchendon, Massachusetts.

Patrick Langer, on behalf of the Langer Family

The Wereth memorial that Hermann erected in 1994.

Patrick Langer, on behalf of the Langer Family

Veteran George Shomo of the 333rd.

Mabel L. Mendes

George Shomo and Norman Lichtenfeld.

Mabel L. Mendes

Color guard at the Wereth Annual Ceremony, May 2016.
US Memorial Wereth V.O.G. Paul Mckelvie, Photographer

The Langer family at the Wereth ceremony, May 2016.
US Belgian Embassy

Former U.S. Surgeon General Regina Benjamin
and U.S. Belgian Ambassador Denise Bauer.

US Memorial Wereth V.O.G. Paul Mckelvie, Photographer

Spectators at the Wereth ceremony.

US Memorial Wereth V.O.G Paul Mckelvie, Photographer

(left to right): Tina Langer *(seated)*, Patrick Langer,
U.S. Belgian Ambassador Denise Bauer, Unidentified, Unidentified,
Unidentified, Former U.S. Surgeon General Regina Benjamin,
Former U.S. Surgeon General and Brigadier General (Ret.) Arnold Gordon-Bray.

US Memorial Wereth V.O.G. Paul Mckelvie, Photographer

ADAMS, Curtis
BRADLEY, Mager
DAVIS, George
FORTE, Thomas J.
GREEN, Robert L.
LEATHERWOOD, Jimmie L.
MOSS, Nathaniel
MOTEN, George W.
PRITCHETT, William E.
STEWART, James A.
TURNER, Due W.

Engraved names of the Wereth 11.

US Memorial Wereth V.O.G Paul Mckelvie, Photographer

The Wereth 11 Memorial Cross, Wereth, Belgium.

US Memorial Wereth V.O.G. Paul Mckelvie, Photographer

American flags representing the Wereth 11.
US Memorial Wereth V.O.G. Paul Mckelvie, Photographer

PART 4

THE BATTLE
OF THE BULGE

*"Never in the field of human conflict was so much
owed by so many to so few."*

WINSTON CHURCHILL[1]

CHAPTER 64

LIFE AT THE WEST WALL

— SCHÖNBERG, BELGIUM —
OCTOBER 1944

The month of October is relatively quiet for the 333rd Field Artillery Battalion. They settle into daily work schedules on the quiet "Ghost Front," experiencing little, if any, action. As fire support for the highly competent and combat-experienced Second Division Artillery, they participate in a few fire missions almost daily, most light, some heavy. But mostly the men, including Stewart, Forte, Davis, Adams, Moten, Turner, Green, Moss, Pritchett, Leatherwood, Bradley, Hudson, and Shomo, practice maneuvers, maintain their equipment, and, with weekend passes, rest and party in Paris.[1]

The days are boringly long. Temperatures are dropping steadily, and in late October the men see snowflakes swirling in the skies.

"You boys ever seen snow?" Shomo asks, sipping coffee. "We get lots of it in New Jersey."

"It's snowed a few times in 'Bama," Davis says. "Doesn't stick to the ground, though."

"We don't see much snow in Texas, 'cept in the Panhandle," Moten says. "Certainly would like to, though. Looks pretty in pictures I've seen."

"Boys," Shomo laughs, "you don't wanna see Belgian snow! From what I hear, it's worse than New Jersey."

"Only good thing about snow is it'll freeze all this mud hard as rock," Pritchett says. "I just wanna make sure I'm not standing in it when it freezes up."

"Not so worried about us getting frozen in ice," Shomo says. "But I don't want to be digging out 155s if it freezes."

"Better hope we're outta here before snow starts piling up," Pritchett says. "If we're still wearing these flimsy summer rags and worn-out boots, we're all dead. The cold'll get us before the German bullets do."

"War can't last much longer," Stewart tells the men. "Krauts are getting hit hard on two fronts."

"Hope it ends soon," Hudson says. "I'm sick of all this."

"You gonna go back home to St. Louis, Corporal?" Stewart asks.

"No. Not many jobs there. Anyway, I don't have good memories of St. Louis. Think I'd like to live in Chicago one day."

"You might be in Chicago sooner than you think," Adams says. "General Eisenhower thinks the war'll be over by Christmas. Hope so. I'm tired of patching up wounded GIs."

"You mean you're not thinking of becoming a real doctor when you get home?" Stewart asks, smiling.

Sergeant Forte grunts, standing and tossing his last drops of coffee on the ground.

"You think Adams has a ghost's chance of gettin' into med school?" Forte says. "If you're thinkin' he's goin' to med school with the white boys, you're a plain fool. It'll never happen."

"You've gotta get rid of all that hatred bottled up inside you, Forte," Shomo says. "If you don't, it's gonna eat you up. And, for our sakes, smile once in a while. Your face always looks like you just ate a lemon!"

Forte makes a fist, shaking it in Shomo's face. "You grew up in the North, Shomo," Forte spits, his voice loud and angry. "Things are different in Louis'ana. Blacks get beat up and hanged from trees. Whites there think blacks aren't even full humans. You oughta try livin' in the South and see for yourself. They act like we're still their slaves."

Shomo stands up and faces Forte. "Get your fist out of my face, Forte. You think hate and prejudice are just in the South? Study your history books, Sergeant. Monmouth County, New Jersey, where my family's from, was built on the bloody backs of black slaves. White masters owned my own kin, beating them up and burning them at the stake when they tried to run away. Louisiana ain't got nothing on Monmouth County!"[2]

"Men!" Stewart says, standing up quickly and placing himself between Forte and Shomo. "We're supposed to be fighting the Germans, not each other. Jus' stand down. This war's gonna be done soon enough, and we'll all be going home."

When things calm, the men sit down, Shomo's nostrils still flaring, Forte clenching his jaw and staring at the ground. Stewart takes a deep breath and turns to Davis, eager to change the conversation.

"What time's it getting to be, Davis?"

George pulls out his granddaddy's prized pocket watch, smiles, and announces loudly, "It's time to eat!"

"And what's your mama gonna cook you and your family for Christmas this year?" Stewart asks.

"Good 'Bama chow!" George says, laughing. "Ham hocks, turnip greens, creamed taters, corn bread . . . pecan pie—"

"You're just gettin' his hopes built up for nothin', Sergeant," Forte snaps, glaring at Stewart. "Nobody's goin' home for Christmas. War's not even over yet."

"Brass says it'll be over by then, son," Stewart responds calmly.

"Even if it is," Forte spews, "the brass'll make us blacks stay back and clean up the mess. Whites might get home for the holidays, but you are all fools if you're thinkin' we're gonna get outta here by Christmas."

Stewart and Shomo glance at each other, both wrinkling their brows and shaking their heads.

CHAPTER 65

THE ROCKETS

On October 21, the men of the 333rd Field Artillery Battalion spot three German V-1 rockets flying over their camp near Schönberg on the east side of Our River.

"I hear those rockets are new and can do some heavy damage," Stewart tells the men as they ready the 155s to try to bring the rockets down. "When those things buzz overhead, we need to either shell 'em or run."

When the small, pilotless aircraft first appear, Captain McLeod tells the troops about the enemy's newest weapons.

"The Germans have the V-1 cruise missile, the V-2 ballistic missile, and the armor-piercing FX 1400 'Fritz' glide bomb, used primarily to destroy battleships," he explains. "The V rockets are robots, designed for aerial launch and destruction. They use gasoline and compressed air as fuel, fly about three hundred and fifty miles per hour, and have a range of up to two hundred and fifty miles. They are proving deadly."

"Are these the bombs that hit London last summer?" Hudson asks. "I heard they did a lot of damage there."

"Yes, Corporal," McLeod responds. "One of those rockets killed fifty-eight civilians and sixty-three service personnel. These missiles aren't preprogrammed but are remotely piloted. The Germans drop them from a bomber at high altitude, and a bombardier steers the missile by radio link to the target. We believe the Germans have built thousands of them."

"What size warheads do they carry?" Hudson asks.

"Well, the 'Fritz' is the monster, a three thousand–pound glide bomb that carries a seven hundred–pound warhead. Last year, the Krauts dropped two 'Fritz' bombs from a Dornier Do 217 on the Italian battleship *Roma*. Broke it in half. Sank in mere minutes. Killed more than twelve hundred crewmen."[1]

"Those Krauts are building some mighty scary weapons," Leatherwood says.

"That's for sure," Hudson agrees.

By the end of October, the men observe numerous flying bombs passing over the Schönberg area, sometimes three or four a day, and on other days as many as twenty.

November proves cold, wet, and miserable. The men of the 333rd are restless. Captain McLeod receives word that the Second Division is pulling out of the Schnee Eifel area the following month and will be replaced by the 106th Division—the "Golden Lions." He is not happy about the change.

"Colonel," McLeod tells Kelsey, "the 106th has just been recently activated. They have no combat experience and are as green as gourds. I'm upset that my men will be providing fire support for them and that their lives will be in the hands of such an inexperienced division."

"I'm with you, Captain. But those are the orders. The commander, Major General Alan W. Jones, and the 106th are arriving on December 11."

"I understand the 106th will be responsible for holding twenty-two miles of front lines," McLeod says. "That's three times the distance normally allocated to a division."

"Well, don't let it worry you, Captain. Absolutely nothing has happened since we got here. The boys upstairs must not think the 'Ghost Front' needs a combat-experienced veteran division like the Second."[2, 3]

During November, as firing decreases, the 333rd builds some sturdy log huts and winterizes some of the older cabin facilities located near the camp. Seeing little action, officers and men rotate on a generous pass schedule, some traveling to camps in Arlon, Belgium, and Longwy, France, to rest, while others head to parties in Paris.

Colonel Kelsey keeps the men informed about both the American and the Red armies' progress, telling them the Soviet Red Army breached the borders of East Prussia months before, invading Poland and Romania.

"They have now reached Budapest," he tells them, "and are preparing to invade Germany. As you already know, the Americans reached Aachen in late October."[4]

On November 7, Lieutenant Colonel Harmon S. Kelsey is awarded the Bronze Star Medal for meritorious service. The 333rd congratulates him, clapping and cheering. Two days later, the first heavy snowfall blankets the Ardennes, reducing visibility to zero and grounding all Allied planes. The men struggle to stay warm as they work in knee-deep snow and blowing sleet and try to keep their feet dry and blood circulating, lest they become victims of frostbite. When outside, the 333rd hover around portable gas stoves, warming their hands and stomping their feet, trying to keep them from freezing. They still have heard no word about receiving winter scarves, gloves, overcoats, winter uniforms, or boots.

On December 11, as predicted, the Second Division departs the Schnee Eifel, and the inexperienced Golden Lions replace them, moving into their new positions—the 422nd, 423rd, and 424th regiments patrolling and guarding the Siegfried Line at the German Front.

CHAPTER 66

THE SECRET REVEALED

Adolf Hitler has managed to keep his Ardennes counterattack plan a secret, telling only Hasso von Manteuffel, who is coordinating the West Wall buildup of arsensal and troops. On December 11, Hitler invites fifty officers, including field marshals Rundstedt and Model and generals Dietrich and Manteuffel, to the Adlerhorst in Ziegenberg, where he intends to announce his secret Ardennes Offensive plans.

Remembering the most recent assassination attempt, Hitler orders his guards to confiscate the officers' weapons and briefcases, load the men into buses, and take them to the Eagle's Nest. Field Marshal Gustav Keitel; the chief of the Operations Staff of the Armed Forces High Command, Alfred Jodl; and the Führer arrive later in separate cars.

Once everyone is assembled, Hitler greets the group, giving them a brief overview of his attack plan. "It is only proper we should meet here today, for it is here that I orchestrated the 1940 Ardennes Offensive, capturing Belgium, the Netherlands, and France. Let us hope that history will repeat itself."

Before he explains the plan in detail, however, he insists that each commander take a pledge of absolute secrecy, signing the dreaded Sippenhaft document in order to silence those tempted to tell.

"Since the Stauffenberg bombing, I must not trust anyone anymore, not even the officers in my own army!" Hitler whispers under his breath as he watches each officer sign the document, agreeing to his instant execution, as well as the arrest and imprisonment of his family, should he betray the Führer.

"I begin our meeting today by honoring Major Generals Baron Harald von Elverfeldt, commander of the Ninth Panzer Division, and Siegfried von Waldenburg, commander of the 116th Panzer Division," the Führer says, decorating both honorees for battlefield bravery.

"I invite you to express your opinions," Hitler says, extending to them the special honor of speaking to him and the group.

"My Führer," von Elverfeldt states, "I have great reservations about—"

With a wave of his hand, Hitler motions for Elverfeldt to stop talking.

"I will permit no change to my campaign's design," he shouts, immediately silencing him.

Waldenburg looks at the floor and remains silent.

For the next two hours, Hitler speaks with great animation about his plan.

"We will attack the Allies at the West Wall," he tells them, his face lighting up with excitement. "We will destroy the Allied coalition, dividing them with a surprise attack that will cause them great confusion."

Before he ends the meeting, he announces, "We will meet and discuss this again tomorrow."

The meeting resumes the next morning, Tuesday, December 12. Hitler catches General Dietrich's eye and nods to the old Nazi. He knows Dietrich is one of his best generals, a much-admired part of his inner circle of advisers, a protective bodyguard, and a loyal

SS soldier. Hitler also knows that the Wehrmacht's Prussian elite officer corps despises Dietrich, but that he is adored by his Waffen-SS soldiers. Hitler admires Dietrich's ways of identifying with his men—inspiring them with his own example at the front lines, sharing their hardships, and refusing to live better than they must live.

I feel closer to Sepp than to any other Waffen-SS general.

Hitler smiles as he notices the Swords to the Knight's Cross with Oak Leaves that the SS-Oberstgruppenführer wears so proudly.

"General Dietrich," Hitler says, "you have been with me, supporting me from the beginning. As the commander of the Sixth Panzer Army, I entrust this campaign—this offensive in the Ardennes—to you. Your army will spearhead the attack and seize Antwerp. Is your army ready?"

The stern-faced fifty-two-year-old soldier clears his throat, answering reluctantly, "Ah . . . no, my Führer. We are not yet ready for this type of offensive."

His answer takes Hitler by surprise.

"You are never satisfied, General Dietrich," Hitler says, frowning. "Do you not understand my brilliant plan? You can count on twenty-four divisions, ten of them armored. Three armies will attack—the Sixth Panzer, the Fifth Panzer, and the Seventh, plus our Volksgrenadier and infantry divisions."

The Führer trains his dark eyes on Manteuffel. "General, you and the Fifth Panzer Army will attack the center of the American forces, capturing Saint Vith and Brussels."

"My Führer," Manteuffel says, "if this is the case, you will, of course, supply us with additional equipment?"

"No!" Hitler snaps. "I will not! I have given you everything I have from the production lines! And we have set aside five million gallons of fuel for this attack."[1]

Field Marshal Model knits his brow and slightly shakes his head from side to side, attracting Hitler's eye.

"Field Marshal," Hitler says, "do you have an opinion about this offensive? If so, please allow us to hear it."

"I . . . I believe it will be successful, my Führer," Model says.

Hitler smiles and addresses Brandenberger. "Your Seventh Army will attack in the southern flank, creating a buffer zone to prevent American reinforcements from attacking the Fifth Panzer Army."

He stops speaking and notices the puzzled looks on the men's faces. *My plan is brilliant! Yet I see no excitement in their eyes. They look as if they doubt my plan, my good judgment.*

He continues. "The Fifteenth Army will be held in reserve to counter any Allied attacks. Our forces will surround and cut off Canada's First Army, America's First and Ninth armies, and Britain's Second Army."

General Dietrich dares to pose a practical question.

"My Führer," he says, "I do not question your plan, but the enemy has extensive air power, enough to slow us, if not stop our attack."[2]

"Ah, Dietrich," Hitler says, "weather is our weapon. This is why we will attack in the dead of winter. The Allies won't expect it. They require much time to mount a response. The dense fog will thwart aerial observation. With visibility so poor, their spotters and fighters will be grounded."

"*This* winter?" someone asks abruptly, not thinking of the consequences his spontaneous interruption might bring.

"Yes!" Hitler shouts. "*This* winter! The attack will take place on Saturday, December 16, *five days from today.*"

The men's eyes widen, and more than a few mouths drop open. The room falls deadly silent.

"But . . . but my Führer," General Dietrich says after a full moment passes, "can we prepare for such an attack in such a short time?"

"Yes! I have already begun the process," Hitler says. "I have studied our successes of Fall Gelb [Case Yellow] in 1940, when we invaded France. We are much better equipped now. Then we had the core of small panzers. Now we have the impenetrable and larger Tiger II tanks and the heavier Panthers! I have full confidence in this offensive."

"But, my Führer, will not the winter snow, mud, and thick forests of the Ardennes make it difficult, if not impossible, to maneuver our tanks, especially our Tigers? And will we have enough supplies to—"

"Yes! Yes! Yes!" Hitler shouts, cursing and glaring at the highly decorated SS-Oberstgruppenführer. *How dare Sepp question me like this!*

"Yes, we can do this! The ground will be frozen, Dietrich—the trees, mud, and snow will not slow our tanks!" Hitler shouts.

No one else dares to speak.

"It is settled," the Führer states, bringing the meeting to a close. "A two-hour bombardment of the enemy will begin the attack, followed by an armored attack at the Schnee Eifel. No changes will be made to my plans. This discussion is over."

They stand at attention and salute as Hitler turns and leaves the room.[3]

As the commanders begin to leave, Model touches Dietrich's arm and also motions to the general of infantry, Hans Krebs.

"Could we talk for a moment?" he whispers. They linger in the back of the meeting room, out of the hearing range of others.

"I believe the odds of succeeding in this offensive are small," Model whispers. "No more than a ten percent chance of success at best. And if it succeeds," he adds, looking at Krebs, "it will be a miracle."

"The Tigers and Panthers will make pushing through the Ardennes and villages more difficult," Krebs says. "They are much bigger and heavier, and most roads and bridges will not support their weight. They are constantly breaking down, and they consume far too much fuel."

"I do not think Hitler has considered the new Panthers' and Tigers' handicaps in an operation like this one," Model says. "And, Sepp, you've received the toughest, if not most impossible, assignment of all."

General Dietrich's face reddens. "All Hitler wants me to do is to cross a river, capture Brussels, and then go on and take Antwerp!"

He looks up at the ceiling and shakes his head. "And all this in the worst time of the year in the Ardennes. The snow is waist-deep and there isn't room to deploy two tanks abreast, let alone entire panzer divisions! It isn't daylight until 0800, and it's dark again at 1600. We're getting kids and old, sick men as soldiers! And he expects us to prepare such an operation in *five days*—and at Christmastime!"

Model judges by the look on Krebs's face that he's thinking the same thing.

"What can we do about this?" Krebs asks.

"Nothing!" Dietrich says, swearing under his breath. "Nothing at all!"[4]

CHAPTER 67

A SLEEPLESS NIGHT

— SCHÖNBERG, BELGIUM —
DECEMBER 12, 1944

Firing is light for the 333rd during the cold, dark days of December. They fire only 150 rounds per day per battalion, mostly during the hours of darkness. The ground has frozen, but the mud still poses problems. They sleep in newly winterized huts and cabins, sheltering them from hard-blowing blizzards. Snow piles deeper on the ground with each passing hour. With the exception of wool caps to wear under their helmets, the men have received no winter gear.

"Glad the foxholes are already dug," Green says as the men sit around a portable stove warming their hands.

"Ground's too hard to dig now," Moten says.

"Maybe we won't be needing them," Adams says.

"Hope not," Hudson says.

"You taking part in the Christmas play they're planning?" Shomo asks Adams.

"Nope! Don't feel much like celebrating."

"Still goin' home for Christmas, boys?" Forte asks, standing up and turning away.

"Aw, shove it!" Leatherwood says. "Let's make more coffee. Mine's gone cold."

Each day of freezing temperatures makes the GIs' toes and feet swell, hurt, and sometimes turn a strange shade of steel blue. Some must be taken to clinics and hospitals. After four or five days, depending on the condition of their feet, they are sent home, they undergo amputation, or they get well enough to return to combat.

Sergeant Stewart can't sleep this evening. He stands, grabs the blanket, and wraps it around his shoulders. Leaving the hut, he walks slowly in the snow, his eyes scanning the skies. When he inhales, the freezing air stings his lungs. When he exhales, a puff of white escapes from his nose and mouth.

No stars tonight. Fog's too thick.

He shivers, wrapping the wool closer around his neck.

When he tries to drive out memories of the past few months, he cannot. His mind has stored the details—dead men and animals littering battlefields, devastated towns, foul smells, buzzing flies, men's bodies blown apart, cries of the wounded and dying.

Will I ever be able to forget?

He thinks about his family back in West Virginia, recalling each loved one's face. He recalls his fellow players on Piedmont's baseball team, wondering if they, too, are fighting the war somewhere in the world.

He hears a crunch of snow behind him and turns around.

"Sergeant Forte," he says, smiling, "trouble sleeping?"

"I haven't slept through a whole night since I got to Camp Gruber," he responds. "Sure not gonna get any sleep here with Germans on the other side of those woods."

"Think they might attack us?"

"Wouldn't surprise me none. They are sure quiet over there. Don't know what they're plannin'."

"They've been quiet ever since we got here," Stewart says. "Except for playing phonographs of tank sounds over loudspeakers to scare us."

"What's keepin' them from comin' through those woods and attackin' us while we're sleepin'?"

Stewart focuses his eyes on the fog-hazy woods spreading out before them. Thousands of pine trees are bent, straining under the weight of wet snow. Evergreens stand so close together they seem to hug each other, blocking from view everything behind them. Mountains rise up and down through the trees like the old Coney Island roller coaster, creating deep valleys and ice-filled gorges between them. "No idea. Better hope they don't. We're completely on our own in this godforsaken place."

Sergeant Stewart pauses. "But Krauts would have some more trouble getting through those thick woods with tanks and equipment, 'specially in all that snow."

"What about all those tank noises we've been hearin' all fall?" Forte asks. "Sounds to me like they're gettin' ready for something over there. The word is they came through those same woods four years ago. What's to keep 'em from doin' it again?"

"You've got a point, Forte. You know, smarts jus' seem to come natural to you, but I think you're wrong about the Krauts. Our planes are already bombing Berlin. They can't last much longer."

The two stand silent for a few minutes, breathing in the cold air of the Ardennes, watching snowflakes fall around them. Forte breaks the silence.

"I really hate Krauts," he says. "And I really hate white people. They're both treatin' us like dogs."

"I know you hate 'em, son. It comes out in every word you say."

"Don't wanna hate 'em," Forte says softly. "Just the way it is. They're the enemy—both of 'em."

"Gotta forgive, son. All whites aren't bad. It's jus' a few that causes all the problems between the races."

"Don't think I can ever forgive 'em," Forte says. "Not now. Not ever. I've seen too much of the sufferin' they cause."

"I know, Sergeant. I've seen it, too. But when you don't forgive, it doesn't hurt them. It jus' hurts you."

That evening, Hitler settles into a chair and ponders the upcoming Ardennes attack. *Brilliant!*

His plans are set. No one, not even his most senior generals, can change them. *I am the leader of Germany! I make the decisions!*

His assault divisions are already assembled just a dozen miles behind the West Wall.

Twelve miles behind the West Wall tonight. Six miles closer tomorrow. By December 14 or 15, all will be in position and ready to attack.

He smiles, envisioning the Americans' shock when his powerful panzers smash into Belgium on December 16, surprising their unsuspecting troops. He's amassed 250,000 men, more than 2,600 pieces of artillery, 382 tanks, and 335 assault and self-propelled guns.

I will show the world I am still very much in charge.[1]

Before the attack, Hitler speaks to his generals.

"This battle will determine whether we live or die," he tells them. "I want all my soldiers to fight hard and without pity."

Balling his hand into a fist and raising it high for all to see, he continues. "The battle must be fought with brutality and all resistance must be broken by a wave of terror."

He takes a deep breath and shouts, "The enemy *must* be broken! Now or never! Thus lives our Germany!"[2]

CHAPTER 68

"JUST A PHONOGRAPH"

"The troops east of the river continue to report hearing vehicles, tanks, and horses," Captain McLeod tells his commander. "They say the sounds are getting louder each day. They're not buying the bit about phonographs and loudspeakers anymore."

"The men are still reporting hearing phantom noises?"

"Yes, sir. They believe it's German activity."

"Not much we can do about it, Captain, even if it's true. Our spotter planes are grounded. Aerial observation is impossible in this weather."

"I think we should check it out, Colonel, just to see what's going on."

"The war's over, Captain," Kelsey snaps. "Like I've said before, the Krauts are playing tank sounds on phonograph records and loudspeakers, trying to scare our people. They no longer have the men or equipment to fight."

"But what if—"

"Don't worry about it, McLeod. Nothing is going on. Anyway, the Germans aren't stupid enough to attack in the dead of winter through those woods. Just do your job. Those coloreds are afraid of every little noise they hear. They're making a big deal over nothing!"

As quietly as possible, Hitler's generals continue to move their troops nearer to the Allies' front lines. Under strict radio silence, they give hand motions or whisper when they need to talk, trying to keep the operation ultrasecret. Like a quiet snake, the panzer divisions slowly, carefully, make their way down narrow roads through the trees, across frozen streams, and through deep valleys, coming together, assembling a large number of men, equipment, vehicles, and weapons, preparing for the surprise attack at the edge of Belgium's Ardennes Forest. The German columns stretch for miles back into their homeland. The coniferous trees, which keep their cover in winter, hide their invasion apparatus. They are thankful that few, if any, Allied aerial reconnaissance planes are able to fly in such fog.[1]

Even though Hitler has prohibited patrol or preoffensive reconnaissance, General Hasso von Manteuffel disobeys orders, secretly slipping beyond the West Wall to spy on Allied troops. He finds the area thinly guarded by men who seem to suspect nothing. He plans his attack in predawn darkness, hoping to surprise the sleeping enemy with a bombardment of mortars, rockets, and heavy artillery shells. He then plans to crush them with his tanks.[2, 3]

Some of the 333rd hear that movie star Marlene Dietrich[4] and her USO troupe will be touring the Ardennes to entertain the troops.

"Cert'ly would like to get a pass and go hear her sing," Moten tells Turner and Green.

"Maybe she's coming to Schönberg," Green says. "She was born here, you know. She'll be performing in Bastogne tomorrow."[5]

"You just wanna gaze at her million-dollar legs," Turner says, grinning. "I'd much rather go see Glenn Miller. Hear he is performing in Paris soon."

Green starts to hum Miller's "Pennsylvania 6-5000," closing his eyes and moving his body to the rhythm. At just the right time, Turner makes the sound of a bell ringing, and the others shout, laughing, "Pennysylvania 6-5000!"

Sergeant Pritchett hears the singing and joins in. "We Alabama boys like this one," he says, humming the notes of Miller's "Tuxedo Junction" and pretending to play a trombone. The men jump to their feet, humming along, dancing to the jazz.

"Chattanooga Choo Choo" completes the performance.

"Pardon me, boys, is that the *Chattanooga Choo Choo* . . . Track 29 . . . dinner in the diner . . . nothin' could be finer . . ."

"Sure would like to hear Glenn Miller play that trombone in person," Green says.

"Nothing happening here," Turner says. "Maybe Captain McLeod'll give us passes and we can go to both."[6, 7]

O n Friday, December 15, big band superstar Major Glenn Miller and his band catch a single-engine military plane outside London and head to Paris to give a special Christmas show in honor of the American troops who helped liberate Paris. In a storm somewhere over the English Channel, Glenn Miller's plane disappears.

CHAPTER 69

"TOO QUIET!"

On the evening of December 15, at the Bleialf, Germany, observation post near the Siegfried Line, Second Lieutenant Reginald Gibson keeps watch, his binoculars slowly scanning the quiet Ardennes, a darkened landscape of snow-covered forests and gently rolling hills.

"These mountains are awfully quiet tonight," Gibson tells his men. "Too quiet."

"Yes, sir. It's spooky. If the Krauts ever decide to attack, we'll be the first to feel it," Sergeant Coleman says.

"You're right about that, Sergeant," Gibson says. "We're sitting at their front door, the Golden Lions right beside us."

"It's not gonna happen," Private Williams says, rolling his eyes. "HQ wouldn't put the 106th at the front if they expected an attack. Those boys are still trying to figure out how to fire an M1. Anyway, the brass says Jerry's finished."

"You're right. You guys get some sleep," Gibson says. "I'll keep watch tonight."[1]

That evening, the 106th Golden Lions—the 422nd, 423rd, and 424th regiments—listen to Christmas carols, put up a few hand-made decorations, and throw a party. They are protected from the weather, having moved into some of the Germans' West Wall pill-boxes and bunkers. Earlier, the Second Infantry Division had converted the abandoned fortifications into company and platoon command posts.

Major General Alan W. Jones feels uneasy about his few men stationed so close to the front lines. For months, the CO has battled Headquarters about his troops.

"My division has been robbed of men all summer," he complains to HQ. "Every time you need replacement troops, you take mine. Our numbers are seriously down, and my men haven't had the training needed to be on the front lines. They're still rookies."

Time and again, his protests have been disregarded. The 106th has never been under fire. Their training was jammed into their few weeks in England before coming to France on December 6. They have been at the German border for only four days, and the three regiments are stretched over a sector three times longer than normal.

"Only seven weeks to learn how to fire an M1, throw a grenade, fire a bazooka, and strip a .30-caliber machine gun," Gibson grumbles to HQ. "Then you make them wait for days in the pouring rain, load them into open trucks, drive them for three days nonstop in freezing weather to the Siegfried Line, and spread them across twenty-two miles. They haven't had time to dry off, much less settle in."

"It's a stagnant front, General," Headquarters tells Jones. "Your men will see no action. This will give them time to cut their teeth on combat patrolling before we go into Germany."

"At least send us more mines, ammunition, and barbed wire," Jones says. "We need to strengthen our defenses."

"We see no urgency to send you more supplies," HQ tells him. "Anyway, ammunition won't be available until December 16 or later."[2]

Late that quiet Friday night in the rugged Ardennes Forest, only a few miles away from the point where Belgium, Luxembourg, and Germany meet, the GIs bed down in their bunkers, dreading the morning and another boring day on the "Ghost Front."[3, 4]

———

Just a few miles away, Waffen-SS soldiers, in their camouflage blouses and helmets, stand at attention, listening to Field Marshal Gerd von Rundstedt's final exhortation before they attack.

"Soldiers of the West Front," Rundstedt tells them, "your great hour has arrived. Large attacking armies have started against the Anglo-Americans. I do not have to tell you anything more than that. You feel it yourself. We gamble everything."

He pauses, looking into the faces of the men, some old, others sick, and some with peach fuzz still on their chins. They tremble in the cold, their eyes wide with fear. The officer continues. "You carry with you the holy obligation to give everything to achieve things beyond human possibilities for our Vaterland and for our Führer!"

He raises his arm stiffly in the freezing air, shouting, "Heil, Hitler!"[5]

CHAPTER 70

DARKNESS IN THE SCHNEE EIFEL

Snow swirls through the valley below the West Wall of the Schnee Eifel. Save for the occasional call of an owl, it is as quiet as it is dark. At 0100, in his snug observation post, Second Lieutenant Reginald Gibson listens for some hints of activity coming from the east—a panzer's growl, a restless horse, a truck engine. The town of Bleialf, just inside the German border, is blacked out. Nothing is stirring. The below-zero weather makes it difficult for Gibson's shivering hands to steady his binoculors as he scans the blackness to his front.

Can't see anything in this mess. Daylight before long. If only this fog would lift!

While he waits for dawn, he thinks about Coleman, Williams, and Harris, black GIs who have become his good buddies since they met at Utah Beach. Together, they melded into a team, fighting their way across France.

Good men in the 333rd. They have certainly impressed the brass with their skill and courage. Pleasure serving with them.

He feels terribly alone, even though his comrades rest nearby.

Great they can doze awhile. Hard to relax when you realize you're the closest Americans to the Kraut front lines.

He reassures himself by remembering that the 424th is a few miles south of him, the 423rd and 422nd a few miles north, the Fourteenth Cavalry just south of the Losheim Gap, and the 333rd in nearby Schönberg.

Why can't I shake this sense of extreme isolation I feel? Wish the Second Division was still here. Can't expect much protection from the "Golden Lions" if the fat hits the fire.

Time drags as the night reluctantly yields its dark hold on the thick forests rising to the east.

As silent as ghosts, white-clad German patrols slip behind American lines, severing Allied communication lines. They move swiftly, knowing that within hours, like lightning, they will strike the thinly manned front.

At 0300, Gibson sees unusual flashes of bright light pierce the distant black skies above him. Suddenly the forests light up like daytime.

"On your feet, men!" he shouts. "We're under attack!"

The men wake up and struggle to their feet, rubbing the sleep from their eyes. Gibson hears the banshee screams of Nebelwerfers soaring in their direction.

"Incoming!" Gibson shouts. "Take cover!"

He scrambles to the radio.

"This is King Charlie Three!" he yells. "We've got heavy artillery across our front! Repeat. Heavy coordinated artillery—"

The loud booms of 88s shake the ground. The chatter of machine guns and the din of heavy artillery echo through the snow-laden forests. For the next two and a half hours, thousands of shells pummel the crossroads of Bleialf.

"I don't know how many Krauts are out there," Gibson tells his men. "But we will hold this post with everything we've got!"

"Yes, sir!" the men respond, scurrying to their places of cover. "Hopefully we'll get some air support."

"Not likely," Gibson says. "Planes'll be grounded until this blasted fog clears. Lord only knows when that'll be."[1]

From the Schnee Eifel, Sepp Dietrich peers through his binoculars, announcing to the white-clad Grenadiers and Volksgrenadiers, "We will strike with armor, mortars, and machine guns, encircling the enemy. It should not be difficult to overcome regiments spread so thinly along the West Wall. Then we will move west and seize Schönberg."

He pauses before he addresses the Volksgrenadiers. The eyes of frightened old men and young boys make him wince, his steel heart unexpectedly and strangely touched. *Retirees and children! Have we come to this?*

"Volksgrenadiers!" he calls. "At my command, you will move out in front of the tanks."

Again he pauses, knowing the Volksgrenadiers will take the enemy's bullets before his Panthers, Tigers, and Grenadiers follow behind them.

But he has no time to fret about such things. He has a job to do, and little time to do it. *We must hurry if we are to catch the Amis slumbering under their blankets.* His heart hardens, and he orders the Volksgrenadiers forward.

On December 16, at SHAEF headquarters just outside Paris, General Eisenhower dresses and eats breakfast. The night before, he learned that President Roosevelt had nominated him to become General of the Army, one of only four five-star generals, the highest rank in the U.S. Army. This morning he hears the Senate has approved the nomination, confirming his promotion.

Eisenhower is delighted with the news. He smiles. *In under three years and four months, I have gone from a lieutenant colonel to a five-star general. Not bad for a Kansas farmhand!*[2]

Major Gustav Knittel's fists tap nervously on his knees as he awaits the order to advance his First SS Panzer Reconnaissance Battalion west. He gazes at the dark sky. *It will be daylight soon. We must get under way while it is still dark.*

He smiles. *It is no surprise the Führer chose me to lead my "fast group" battalion to capture a Meuse River bridge. I have certainly proven myself under fire on more than a few occasions.*

He removes his glove and touches the coveted Ritterkreuz des Eisernen Kreuzes (Knight's Cross) at his throat, the highest award Nazi Germany gives for extreme battlefield bravery and outstanding military leadership. Pinned to the pocket on the right side of his blouse is the German Cross in Gold, a prestigious award for bravery in the face of the enemy.

As he waits, stinging crystals of sleet pelt his smooth-shaven face. He reflects on an outstanding career with the SS—leading his troops in seizing the Ukrainian town of Divin, securing defensive positions that allowed the German Army to escape the Russian trap, cross the Zbruck River, and retreat to Lemberg.

He smiles, recalling his successful campaigns in France, Yugoslavia, Greece, and Russia. *We were the "fire brigade," always rescuing some outfit in trouble. Wounded four times. A cat who has used up his nine lives, yet seems to make it through to see another day.*

Knittel ponders his orders. He will lead his reinforced Schnellegruppe behind Joachim Peiper's First SS Panzer Division and Max Hansen's battle groups in their dash for the Meuse.

Time is short.

He takes deep breaths, exhaling them slowly, trying to harness his mounting impatience. *Surely the Führer's timetable is impossible.*

CHAPTER 71

THE ATTACK

Lieutenant Colonel Kelsey is still asleep in Schönberg on the west side of Our River when Captain McLeod knocks on his bedroom door, abruptly awakening him.

"Sir, I've received an urgent report from our observation post in Bleialf. Gibson reports heavy coordinated artillery fire coming from the east. They think they are under attack."

"An attack?" Kelsey responds. "It's probably just to keep us on edge. But I'll ring up General Middleton."

Kelsey telephones General Middleton at VIII Corps HQ in Bastogne.

"You are probably right, Colonel," Middleton says after hearing the report. "No doubt it's just a spoiling attack. Probably won't last long. Let's wait to see what happens."[1]

The next report Kelsey receives comes at 0530.

"German artillery fire has ceased, sir," Gibson tells Kelsey.

"Then I see no reason to withdraw from your posts, Lieutenant," Kelsey says. "Keep me informed."

In the Schnee Eifel, the signal is given and German forces begin moving west. They quickly surround the Bleialf observation post but are unable to seize it. Germans storm the 422nd and 423rd regiments north of Bleialf with a direct and heavy artillery assault.

When Major General Alan W. Jones, asleep in his bedroom in Saint Vith, hears that his two Golden Lions regiments are being bombarded with artillery, he calls General Middleton.

"Sir?" he says. But he is unable to hear, heavy static interfering with the reception. "Sir, the 422nd and 423rd are under artillery fire," he shouts into the mouthpiece.

The telephone line crackles, preventing him from hearing clearly the general's words. He presses the receiver hard to his ear. He tries again.

"Sir? Can I move my regiments farther west? They are too close to the Schnee Eifel. They are receiving heavy fire."

Please, please tell me to withdraw my regiments immediately—all of them.

Jones hears only a few words of the general's response, but he cannot understand the instructions. The phone goes dead. General Jones keeps his troops in position, believing that's what Middleton has requested.[2]

Early that morning, General Eisenhower receives a regular report from Field Marshal Bernard Montgomery, Twenty-first Army Group. Unaware of the sudden German attack at the Siegfried Line, Montgomery states that the "general situation" at the front lines is uneventful.

"The enemy is at present fighting a defensive campaign on all fronts," Montgomery tells him. "He has not the transport or the petrol necessary for mobile operations, nor could his tanks compete with ours in a mobile battle."

Eisenhower sends Montgomery a brief reply: "That's good. The enemy is in a bad way. He has had a tremendous battering and has lost heavily in both men and equipment. We must continue to fight the enemy hard during the winter months."[3]

At 0530, after the heavy bombardment, the Germans push through the American front lines with their three main armies: the Sixth Panzer Army, led by Dietrich; the Fifth Panzer Army, led by Manteuffel; and the Seventh Army, led by Brandenberger. Field Marshal Gerd von Rundstedt's three panzer armies storm through Allied lines. German tanks surround the two Bleialf observation posts, as well as most of the Fourteenth Cavalry and the 106th's most exposed regiments, the 422nd and 423rd.

At the same time, the enemy begins bombarding the Schönberg area with heavy artillery, firing first on the east side of Our River, where Able, Baker, Charley, and part of Service Battery are stationed. Then they bombard the area of Schönberg located west of Our River, where Kelsey, McLeod, and most of Service Battery camps. The Germans are unhindered by USAAF Mustang fighters and RAF tank-busting Typhoons, the planes grounded by low clouds and thick fog.

The well-equipped, winter-clad Wehrmacht troops outnumber the Allied defenders ten to one. The lumbering, heavily armored German Tigers, and the slightly more maneuverable Panthers, armed with 88mm, 7.92 MG34, and 75mm guns, prove far superior to the American lighter and lesser-armored Shermans, armed with the short 75mm guns. Unless fired at point-blank range, the 75mm shells simply bounce off the Tiger and Panther tanks' thick armor.[4, 5]

Gustav Knittel looks at his watch and grits his teeth.

"We are already behind schedule!" he curses. "Idiots!"

Knittel is no longer the brash SS officer of 1940 who believed his Führer's words of final victory. He will obey Hitler's orders, but his memories of the catastrophes of Mortain and Falaise have convinced him Germany cannot win the war.

CHAPTER 72

"SCREAMING MEEMIES!"

— SCHÖNBERG, BELGIUM —
DECEMBER 16, 1944

At 0500, Stewart, Adams, Forte, Davis, and Shomo, stationed near Schönberg east of the Our River, sit outside in the dark around the portable gas stove, sipping coffee, eating their K ration breakfast, and trying to stay warm as they wait for the new day.[1]

Stewart glances at Davis's face, noticing his three-day beard.

"Private," he says softly, "you need a shave. Your skin's gonna freeze under that beard."

"It's too cold to shave and the water's frozen," Davis says.[2]

"Forget the shave," Forte says, wiggling his nose. "I need a bath!"

"Best thing is a quick dry rub—just get your feet, crotch, and underarms," Stewart says. "We don't mind how bad you smell. We don't smell so good ourselves."

Sergeant Shomo refills his coffee cup. "Did I ever tell you guys the story of my great-great-granddaddy fighting in the Civil War?"

"No," Stewart says. "Don't believe so."

Shomo chews on a rock-hard Hershey's bar, offering some silence before he speaks.

"His name was Henry N. Adkins. He was a sergeant major with the Thirty-sixth U.S. Colored Troops. He once asked his commanding officer if he could be promoted to a second lieutenant. His commander said no, that President Lincoln hadn't approved promoting coloreds to officers."

"Whatever happened to him?" Davis asks.

"Well, he survived the war, changed his name to Henry Nepean, and became principal at the Fair Haven Colored School. Settled in Monmouth County, New Jersey, where I was born on February 27, 1921."

"Did you ever meet him?" Stewart asks.

"Nope. He died in his fifties, back in 1899."

"He'd be proud of you," Stewart says. "I wish he could've seen you back in Brittany."

"Me, too," Shomo says. "Been thinking a lot about ol' Henry. Also been wondering about my friend from Jersey, Wesley Forehand. We got drafted at the same time. Wonder if he's still alive." Shomo smiles. "He was sweet on my sister."

S tewart lifts his head. "I'm hearing artillery fire coming from the east," he says.

"Probably just a phonograph record playin' over loudspeakers," Forte snorts. "That's the word from the brass."

"It's more than that, Sergeant," Stewart responds, standing.

Suddenly, at 0535, powerful Nebelwerfer rockets scream overhead, their high-pitched cries sending the GIs diving into snow-filled foxholes.

"Screaming Meemies!" Stewart shouts. "Somebody call McLeod!"

A rocket explodes in the trees above them, smashing branches and raining sharp limbs down on the GIs. The men of Able, Baker, Charley, and Service Batteries jump from their cots, leaving the huts and rushing outside. More rockets hit the treetops, explode with fury, and send sharp spears of branches onto unsuspecting troops. Heavy shrapnel finds several victims, knocking them down, ripping their flesh.

Adams grabs a first-aid kit and races from one wounded GI to another, trying to tie off blood-spurting arteries and splint broken bones.

"Medics!" he shouts. "I need help!"

In the chaos, noise, screams, and smoke, Able, Baker, and Charley Batteries scurry to the 155s. Not yet receiving firing coordinates, they direct their guns to possible enemy positions and start firing.

Stewart's mind spins, his stomach churns, and his ears ache from the violence and sounds of battle coming closer toward them—piercing screams from Nebelwerfer rockets, deafening blasts from exploding mortar rounds, cries from the wounded.

He looks around him. The snow is black from explosions and red from blood. GIs lie facedown in foxholes and on the frozen ground, their bodies twisted into unnatural shapes. Those still alive scream for help, agonizing cries, some with arms and legs torn away and scattered in the snow.

> *"Shell HE, charge five."*
> *"Fuse quick."*
> *"Base deflection."*
> *"Right two-niner-five."*
> *"SI three-zero-two."*
> *"Number two, one round."*
> *"Elevation three-seven-one."*

When the firing coordinates finally start coming in, the GIs pinpoint the enemies' positions. With precision and skill, the guns erupt. "Ready! Stand back! Fire!" They work at record-breaking speeds, launching one heavy shell after another, providing support fire for the infantry regiments several miles to the east.

"Sure hope the Golden Lions can hold!" Stewart shouts.

CHAPTER 73

THE DEATH SENTENCE

On receiving word of the German assault, Captain McLeod jumps into a jeep, ordering his driver to head east, cross the Our River, and try to reach his men stationed on the other side. They race along icy roads, skidding, sliding, the driver gripping the wheel and struggling to keep the jeep on the road. In the noise and confusion, crowds of terrified civilians pack the snow-covered streets, scrambling in all directions, blocking traffic. McLeod and his driver become entangled in a bottleneck of trucks, jeeps, half-tracks, and tanks choking the roadways, some moving, some wrecked, some stranded. McLeod's driver darts around the vehicles, careful not to run over frantic women with crying children pulling their few earthly belongings in wooden carts.

Finally they come to the ancient stone bridge.

"Hurry!" McLeod tells the driver. "We've got to make it across before—"

But it's too late. "Halt!" The enemy surrounds them, pointing rifles at their heads. The driver and McLeod raise their arms above their heads and surrender.

I've got to reach my men!

A German soldier demands the jeep and driver. In the mayhem, McLeod escapes. He dashes through the people, dodging a shower of bullets and scrambling into the trees.[1]

L ater that morning, General Eisenhower receives reports of the German attack. *Brad feels it's only a spoiling attack.*

He pauses, rubbing his chin. *If this is a real offensive, the attack might be a good thing. By rushing out from their fixed defenses, the Germans may give us the chance to turn their great gamble into his worst defeat.*[2]

That afternoon near Paris, counting on General Bradley's lack of alarm about the German spoiling attack, General Eisenhower attends the wedding of two SHAEF staff members: Corporal Pearlie Hargrove and Sergeant Michael McKeogh. Hargrove has been given special permission to be out of her uniform for the occasion. She wears a wedding gown and veil designed by a leading Paris fashion house. After the ceremony, Eisenhower plants a kiss on the bride's cheek and gives the couple a hundred-dollar war bond.[3]

A t his camp in Schönberg, west of the Our River, Colonel Kelsey receives an urgent report from one of the two observation posts in Bleialf. Lieutenant Reginald Gibson tries to explain the emergency situation—the gruesome scene—to Kelsey, but the telephone lines, heavy with static, continue to drop calls.

"We've got to pull out!" Gibson tells Kelsey. "We'll be surrounded if we don't. The 106th can't hold."

"Have you heard from Able, Baker, and Charley?"

"Yes, sir. They've been supporting us with heavy reinforcing fire all morning. They're the reason we're still holding on."

I n the midst of crowds and chaos, Captain McLeod sees a chance to emerge from the trees where he's been hiding. He runs as fast as he can and crosses the bridge. Cold, wet, and exhausted, he races toward his men.

When he steps onto the campgrounds, horror meets his eyes. Dead GIs are scattered everywhere, victims of shell attacks and tree bursts. Others lie in the snow, crying and screaming with pain, their open wounds trickling blood. Shells sail overhead, hitting the ground, exploding, and piercing the living with deadly shrapnel.

McLeod telephones Kelsey, shouting into the mouthpiece, "We've got to get our men out of here! We're taking heavy fire, sustaining heavy casualties. Sir, we're losing them fast!"

"Run!" he hears someone outside scream. Still holding the phone, McLeod ducks under a table. From the window, through the smoke and haze, he sees a large shell land dead center on top of the ammunition dump a few feet away. Men run in all directions, trying to get as far away as possible from the dump. McLeod braces himself for the explosion. He knows that when the shell explodes, it will detonate all the ammunition in the dump, destroying the entire camp and everyone in it. Arms covering his head, he holds his breath and waits for Armageddon.

One, two, three seconds pass, but nothing happens. He raises his head, peeks out the window, and discovers the shell has failed to go off. It lies dead on top of the ammunition dump. He takes a deep breath of relief. "It's a dud, thank God!"

He hears Kelsey's voice shouting from the phone's receiver.

"What's going on!"

"Colonel, we need to pull out all our troops and regiments east of the river: the 106th, the Fourteenth Cavalry, Able, Baker, Charley, and Service Batteries—all of them. We can't hold up under this heavy shelling. I fear the Germans will break through our front lines at any moment."

"I'll contact Middleton!" Kelsey shouts. "I'll call you right back."

Several minutes later, McLeod answers Kelsey's return call.

"Okay, Captain, I've got orders from Middleton to pull them out," Kelsey says. "All of them except Charley and part of Service Battery. General McMahon, the 106th Division artillery officer, has requested they stay in position. The 106th needs the fire support."

"But, sir, that's a death sentence!"

"I'm sorry, Captain, but it's an order."

"In that case, I request permission to stay here with my men, Colonel."

"Permission granted."

CHAPTER 74

A LONG AND DEADLY DAY

— SCHÖNBERG, BELGIUM —
DECEMBER 16, 1944

By afternoon, General Sepp Dietrich's Sixth Panzer Army advances to the edge of Schönberg, east of the Our River. He hopes to overtake the American troops there quickly, cross the bridge and head to Saint Vith, and then continue to the Meuse River.

Dietrich feels great frustration. He hasn't counted on such fierce resistance from the 333rd's howitzers. He knows he is moving far too slowly to satisfy the impatient Hitler.

"Our orders are to fight, kill, and take no prisoners," he tells his troops through clenched teeth.

Following the Sixth Panzer Army is the fearsome First SS Division, which includes Max Hansen's Panzergrenadier Regiment and Gustav Knittel's Reconnaissance Battalion. On Dietrich's command, they move forward in droves, sweeping into Schönberg and crushing everything in their path.

That afternoon, Able and Baker Batteries quickly load the wounded into ambulances and depart in the few trucks available. Behind them, they leave switchboards, telephones, generators, and one-ton trailers, as well as individual equipment and clothes. They race across the old stone bridge, heading southwest to Bastogne.

The men ordered to stay behind continue firing the 155s, holding back the enemy while the rest of the GIs displace.

Left behind are Stewart, Forte, Davis, Adams, Leatherwood, Bradley, Moten, Turner, Green, Moss, Pritchett, Shomo, Hudson, McLeod, and other members of Charley and Service Batteries still alive and standing.

Receiving coordinates, the GIs load, position, and fire the 155s without stopping to rest, eat, drink, or visit the latrines. Late that night, they are still launching shells, supporting the troops in front of them, who struggle to hold their positions.

Long after darkness descends on the campgrounds, and before the new morning dawns, Stewart turns to McLeod, a worried look on his tired face.

"Ammo's almost gone, Captain," he says.

"Just keep firing until we run out, Sergeant."

Standing nearby, Sergeant Forte overhears the conversation.

"We're done for," he says aloud. "We're all dead."

At first light on Sunday morning, December 17, Colonel Kelsey receives word that the two observation posts near Bleialf have been overrun by the enemy, the status of the men there unknown, but presumed to be captured or killed. He also learns that General Jones, the commander of the Golden Lions, is completely surrounded by the enemy and the death rate is very high. He is still in position, having received no orders from HQ to displace.[1, 2]

Colonel Kelsey receives instructions from HQ ordering the displacement of Service Battery, located west of the Our River. He telephones their commander, Captain James Edmundson, ordering him to destroy all the equipment with thermite grenades, leaving nothing behind for the Germans to take and use against them.

When Kelsey finally receives word from HQ ordering the displacement of Charley and the remainder of Service Battery, located east of the Our River, he telephones McLeod.

"I'm bringing trucks," he says. "We will evacuate as many men as we can."

Kelsey, with operations officer Captain Kline L. Roberts, commands three deuce-and-a-half trucks and drivers and leaves Schönberg, speeding along icy roads leading to the Our River Bridge. With Captain Edmundson's Service Battery departing, scores of Service troops, as well as other soldiers heading to Bastogne, clog the route. Women with crying children and frightened farm animals add to the crushing crowds and confusion. Snarled in traffic jams, Kelsey struggles to make his way east. He wonders what he will find when he reaches Charley Battery, and tries hard to prepare his heart and mind for the worst.

Is anyone still alive? Have the Krauts penetrated the grounds, breaking through, killing, maiming, and capturing the men of Charley and Service Batteries?

"What are we driving into?" he asks aloud.

W hen Captain McLeod receives Kelsey's orders to displace, he shouts to his men, "We're leaving! Destroy the equipment! The colonel's bringing trucks to evacuate us!"

The men of Charley and Service Batteries grab thermite grenades and scramble to incinerate the equipment. Filthy, hungry, thirsty, and out of ammunition, they obey orders, praying Kelsey will arrive in time. When Kelsey and his drivers rush into camp, the men run to gather the wounded lying on the bloodied battlefield, picking them up in their arms and racing to evacuate them first.

But Kelsey's trucks are too late.

CHAPTER 75

THE BREAKTHROUGH

— SCHÖNBERG, EAST OF THE OUR RIVER —
DECEMBER 17, 1944

Running toward the waiting trucks, Sergeant Stewart carries an injured man on his back. Before he reaches Kelsey, however, he sees movement in the thick snow-laden trees of the Ardenne Forest behind him. He stops, turns around, and strains to focus his eyes through the heavy fog.

Suddenly he sees thousands of German soldiers burst through the fog and forest. They are well armed, running, yelling, and heading right for him.

"They've broken through!" he screams to the other men. "Run!"

He races toward the trucks, the wounded GI hanging on to his back. Streams of Germans pour from the forest, screaming and blazing away with automatic weapons. Setting up MG42 machine guns, they attack Charley Battery, mowing down artillerymen trying to carry the wounded.[1]

Stewart reaches the trucks, placing the man on the ground beside them. But the soldier is dead, his eyes open and fixed.

The next scene unfolds as if in slow motion as Stewart watches from the trucks. Robert Hudson's childhood friend is struck by an MG42, ripping his body in two, sending his torso and legs flying in different directions. Mortar fragments hit Hudson in the ear and leg. Hudson sprawls out on the ground, moaning in pain, bleeding profusely. Adams runs to help him, quickly pulling him across the ground toward Stewart and the trucks. GIs grab the few rifles and carbines available to them, and with the last of their loaded ammo they fire until it runs out.

Somehow, in the noisy chaos, some of the remaining GIs help Stewart load the injured and dying into the trucks and jump in behind them.

"Go! Go! Go!" they shout.

German soldiers follow them, shooting, grabbing, and pulling them from the trucks. Kelsey and his drivers, their three trucks full, race their engines and floor the accelerators. With tires spinning, they escape the enemy and head west to the bridge.

With no weapons but their hands, Captain McLeod and the rest of the Charley and Service Batteries continue the violent fight that leaves both Germans and GIs wounded or dead. George Shomo finds a trench knife, then stabs and kills two Germans. Robert Hudson, even though seriously wounded, crawls to help injured comrades. As McLeod fights, he sees his men around him shot, stabbed, and butchered without mercy, one after another falling to his death.

No choice now. If I'm to save the rest of my guys, we must call it quits. No other way.

He removes a white wound dressing from its pouch on his belt, tearing off its wrapper. Lifting it high, he waves the symbolic white flag until the enemy stops its frenzied massacre. The downhearted GIs clasp their hands behind their heads, their eyes showing fear and dread. The Germans shove the prisoners into a column.

A grizzled *Landser* grins as he approaches McLeod. "For you, Captain," he says in passable English, "the war is over!"

McLeod watches German photographers snap propaganda pictures and film, as if wishing to further humiliate the captured troops. One lensman points his camera into Shomo's face, pressing the shutter, capturing for posterity his doleful downcast gaze.

CHAPTER 76

CAPTURED!

Jammed in the back of the lead truck, Adams doctors a GI's injured leg as Colonel Kelsey's convoy speeds along the icy and congested Schönberg–Andler road, the main thoroughfare to Saint Vith.

"Compound fracture," he tells Stewart, Fort, and Davis, who sit around him. They help him splint the bloody femur, sickened upon seeing the sharp broken bone jutting through the skin.

"You'll feel lots better in about twenty minutes," Adams tells the soldier, jabbing a dose of morphine into his arm. They remove their jackets, placing the filthy but warm rags on top of the groaning man.

"McLeod's gonna have to surrender the rest of Charley," Stewart tells them. "They won't like it, but there's no way they can hold out for long."

M oten, Leatherwood, Turner, Bradley, and a crowd of other GIs sit in the back of the second truck. They hold on tightly as the truck slips and slides over the snow-covered road. They are quiet, most of them hurt, their eyes closed and heads bobbing. Some are unconscious. Two have already died.

Leatherwood pulls the metal sealing tape from his first-aid packet, unwrapping the sterile dressings and pressing them against stab wounds in a GI's chest. He feels relieved when the pressure stops the bleeding. Moten, Turner, and Bradley follow suit, applying dressings to those with slashed backs, arms, and hands.

In the back of the third truck, Pritchett, Green, and Moss bind a soldier's bleeding stump just below the shoulder of his missing arm. Another victim has a thin ribbon of skin keeping his severed leg attached. Just below the GI's crotch, Moss ties off the thigh with a makeshift tourniquet, pulling it tight and stopping the flow of blood.

At the campgrounds after the surrender, Captain McLeod shouts to his men, "We are now the Germans' prisoners. They will take us to a POW camp. To save your lives, do as they tell you."

McLeod sees a young GI crying and clutching his chest, trying to stop the bleeding. He walks toward him, his hands still clasped behind his head. But before he can help him, a teenage German private steps forward, aiming his rifle at the GI's head. He pulls the trigger at close range. *Crack!* The young GI's body jerks as the bullet smashes his skull, sending a small river of blood seeping onto the snow-crusted ground.

"No!" McLeod screams, turning his body sharply toward the private holding the rifle. "We're prisoners! Under the rules of the Geneva Convention, you—"

The private points his rifle at McLeod, daring him to move closer.

Trying to protect McLeod, Sergeant Shomo lunges at the German. A rifle-butt blow to his shoulder stops him and sends him crumpling to the ground. Grabbing his shoulder, Shomo rises slowly to his feet. Narrowing his eyes, he glares unblinking into the face of the murderous teenager.

McLeod can do nothing as German soldiers walk from one wounded GI to the next, aiming pistols at their heads, pulling triggers— *Crack! Crack! Crack!* With single shots, they shatter skulls. McLeod sees Hudson pull himself to his feet, hiding his wounds and saving his life. Squeezing his eyes shut, McLeod can no longer look at his men's mutilated bodies.

CHAPTER 77

THE P-47 THUNDERBOLT

Colonel Kelsey and his trucks speed down the Schönberg–Andler road at 0900, hoping to reach the safety of Saint Vith. Rounding a curve, Kelsey's driver suddenly swerves and slams his brakes. Coming toward him a short distance away is a line of enemy half-tracks loaded with infantry, most carrying automatic weapons. Tanks follow behind.

"No!" he shouts. "Jump! Run!" he yells to the GIs in the trucks.

Kelsey, the drivers, and the passenger GIs grab the wounded and leap from the backs of the trucks.

"Every man for himself!" Kelsey yells.

They hit the ground, scores of Germans surrounding them, pointing their weapons at their heads, and laughing. One of the Panthers refuses to stop. Without slowing down, it runs over Kelsey's truck, smashing it flat into the road.

Kelsey surrenders his men. They clasp their hands behind their heads.

Suddenly an American P-47 Thunderbolt appears overhead. A GI cheers, "Jabos!"

The Germans point their carbines to the sky, firing at the plane. Kelsey knows how Germans fear the rugged Thunderbolt, the P-47 capable of carrying thousand-pound bombs or eight rockets, and each armed with eight .50-caliber machine guns. The Thunderbolt escapes the carbine fire unscathed. A few minutes later, it returns, circling above them and firing the .50-caliber machine guns, strafing both Germans and POWs on the ground below.

Ack! Ack! Ack! Ack! Ack! Ack! Ack!

Circling again and again, it repeats the firing, causing panic and confusion.

Ack! Ack! Ack! Ack! Ack! Ack! Ack![1]

As the Germans hit the ground on their bellies, firing weapons at the deadly P-47, Kelsey shouts to his troops, *"Run!"*

As he stays behind with the wounded, Kelsey watches the able-bodied GIs jump to their feet, scatter in all directions, running into the forest and out of sight as fast as they can move. When the Thunderbolt leaves, scores of dead and wounded Germans and POWs line the roadway, filling the fields and ditches. Kelsey and his remaining men are rounded up and forced to march.

Some men escape, heading southwest on foot, hoping to reach Bastogne. Others run straight west, deeper into Belgium, not caring where they end up. Adams, Davis, Forte, and Stewart flee north. Along the way, they meet up with Leatherwood, Pritchett, Bradley, and Moss. Soon they encounter Moten, Turner, and Green, who gratefully join the growing group. The eleven black men of the 333rd Field Artillery Battalion race through the dark, dense forest, struggling to stay on their feet as they plow through snow. Sleet rains down upon them, stinging their faces and drenching their clothes.

"Where we goin'?" Forte shouts as he runs.

"Don't know, don't care!" Davis shouts back. "Just away from Germans!"

"Anybody hurt?" Adams yells.

"We're all okay," Stewart responds.

Without stopping, the eleven GIs run for three hours. When they reach the outskirts of the small village of Herresbach—wet, freezing, exhausted, and gasping for breath—they stop among the thick trees, hiding, resting, and keeping watch for German patrols.[2]

CHAPTER 78

MASSACRE AT
THE BAUGNEZ CROSSROADS

Sunday, sometime before dawn, Colonel Joachim Peiper's men reach Lanzerath. Hours later, the most powerful German unit, Kampfgrüppe Peiper, finally arrives in Honsfeld. Traveling proves a slow and tedious process for Peiper, with his forty-eight hundred men, eight hundred vehicles, and a heavy supply of 105mm, 150mm, and antiaircraft weapons. The Tigers and Panthers break down often, requiring long repair hours. Often he must abandon them, leaving tank carcasses lining the narrow roadsides. Running twelve hours behind schedule, and low on fuel, Peiper is furious that early afternoon when his progress is so slow, hampered by trees, snow, hidden mines, and scattered groups of determined American snipers.[1]

In Honsfeld, Kampfgrüppe Peiper is unexpectedly detained by American troops. Outnumbering them, he kills the GIs and heads to steal petrol at the American fuel dump in Büllingen. After refueling, he leads his massive group forward, cursing every mile of the way. He soon reaches the Malmédy–Vielsalm road at the Baugnez crossroads.

Again Peiper runs into American troops, this time at the Baugnez crossroads, two miles southeast of the town of Malmédy. Kampfgrüppe Peiper's panzer tanks open fire on the battalion. The GIs, clearly outnumbered, quickly abandon their vehicles, toss their weapons, and peaceably surrender to Peiper's First AA Panzer Division.

The one hundred or more American soldiers from Battery B of the 285th Field Artillery Observation Battalion are on their way to Saint Vith. After surrendering, they gather in the roadside field, unarmed, helmets removed, and their hands raised. They wait for an hour, believing they will be taken to German POW camps.

Suddenly, at 1600, they see a Waffen-SS soldier stand up in the back of his half-track. He aims a pistol at their group and fires twice. Two soldiers are hit and crumple to the ground. Shocked and horrified, the GIs scatter in all directions, running for their lives. But they cannot bolt fast enough. Waffen-SS soldiers in nearby half-tracks fire machine guns at the American troops, instantly killing many of them, ripping their bodies to shreds. Some of the men, however, are wounded but still alive. They lie still on the ground, pretending to be dead.

Lying facedown in the bloody snow and struggling not to move, they hear SS men laugh and joke as the enemy walks among them, kicking bodies and making sure each is dead.

"Are you okay?" an English-speaking German soldier asks. "Do you need help?"

When a wounded American responds, Peiper's men shoot him in the head or club him to death. More than eighty U.S. soldiers are murdered that afternoon at the Baugnez crossroads. Only a few GIs live. Faking death, they somehow escape the bullet and club. They wait to hear Kampfgrüppe Peiper move on, and see a chance to run. Standing to their feet, they check for survivors and make their way to Malmédy. There they find a U.S. Army colonel and report the massacre.

Like wildfire, news of the unprovoked killings spreads: "The Germans are shooting American POWs!" Numerous war correspondents and American journalists working in the area write news reports. Soon newspaper headlines across the world shout the appalling story of the tragic and unprovoked Malmédy Massacre.[2]

CHAPTER 79

THE FARMHOUSE

The eleven men from the 333rd rest a few minutes in the little village of Herresbach.

"Okay, we've rested long enough. It's 1200 hours, and we've got to keep moving," Stewart tells the men.

"Sergeant, my feet are froze," Davis says. "Need to change my wet socks before my toes drop off."

"Go ahead, Davis, just hurry," Stewart says.

"Anybody have an extra dry sock or two?" Davis asks.

"I've got two pair," Pritchett responds, pulling the socks from his blouse and tossing one pair to Davis.

"Anybody else got dry socks?" Stewart asks.

Leatherwood, Moss, and Bradley have extras. The men take off their boots and wet socks, rub their feet to get the blood flowing, and pull on dry ones. Wringing out the water, they place the wet socks inside their blouses against their chests, hoping their body heat will dry them.

"I'm starving," Davis says. "Anybody have food?"

The men shake their heads. "Sorry, no food, not even a ration chocolate bar."

"I've got some chewing gum," Stewart says.

"No, thanks, Sergeant," Davis says. "I need something more filling."

Corporal Bradley slips the wedding ring off his frozen finger, stuffing it in his pocket. "Too cold to wear metal," he says.

Above them a tree branch, laden with snow, breaks, falling to the ground with a loud thud and startling them.

"At ease, men," Stewart says. "Just a branch. Not a German. Let's get going."

Frozen and hurting and far from Allied lines, the eleven continue their journey northwest, avoiding the roadways, clawing and climbing through trees and thick forests, stopping and dropping into the deep snow whenever they hear a suspicious noise. With each turn and around every hill, they expect to run into Germans.

After several hours of hiking in the battering sleet, they come to a small hamlet surrounded by woods and snow-covered fields. The small white sign posted at the entrance reads WERETH. Nine modest houses form a line. At the end of the street, they see a large cow pasture.

"Do we dare ask somebody for help?" Stewart asks.

"Can't just go up and knock on the front door," Forte says. "House might be filled with Kraut soldiers."

They hide in the woods while they decide whether to take the risk.

"If we don't get help," Adams says, "we're gonna freeze out here. All of us are soaking wet."

"Adams is right," Pritchett says. "It'll be getting dark in a few hours, and the temps will drop even lower."

Stewart looks through the trees. A stark white house stands on the corner of the narrow road, a small red-roofed shed behind it. He sees two small eyes peeking from a window in the house.

"Looks like a boy inside. Don't want to frighten him or his family."

Stewart pauses, rubbing his face and blowing on his hands. "Anybody have a white flag?"

Private Adams pulls a wound dressing from his web pouch. "Here," he says, handing it to Stewart.

Raising the white bandage above his head, Stewart steps out of the trees. *This could be a huge mistake.*

The other men join him, moving forward slowly. Taking several steps toward the house, they stop often, scanning the neighborhood.

"Papa," Hermann Langer calls to his father as he peers out the window of his family's home. "There are some soldiers outside—Americans, I think—with black skin. One has a white flag. They look very cold. May I invite them inside?"

Mathias steps to the window and calls Maria. Her friend Maria Mertes and daughter Anna are visiting.

"Maria, take the children into the bedroom and wait there," he tells her. "Hermann, you come with me."

Mathias opens the door. "Come in quickly," he tells the men, closing and locking the door behind them. They step inside. Water drips off their clothes and boots onto the wooden floor. A tall, thin man with a kind face speaks first.

"Sir, my name's Sergeant Aubrey Stewart with the U.S. 333rd Field Artillery Battalion. We jus' escaped from Germans who ambushed us. We're on our way to American lines to meet our troops. We're cold, hungry, and exhausted. Would you please help us? We won't cause any trouble."

Mathias and Hermann stare at the shivering men standing pitifully at their front door, dressed in wet, filthy uniforms, layers of mud and snow caking their boots.

"Yes, of course, we will help you!" Mathias says. "Hermann, call your mother and tell her to bring blankets."

CHAPTER 80

UNEXPECTED HOSPITALITY

"Come into the dining room," Mathias says, leading them to the large family table. "Hermann, bring more chairs.

"Take off your boots and socks," he tells the shivering soldiers. Collecting them, he lays them on and around a large wood-burning stove.

The women and children bring blankets from the bedroom. Maria, a plain middle-aged woman with a smooth gray bun gathered at the nape of her neck, walks around the table, placing a coverlet over each man's shoulders, tucking the wool close around his ears.

"Tina," she says, "close the curtains. The neighbors must not see our guests."

"I'm sorry," Mathias says to the men. "Some of the neighbors are still loyal to Germany and do not tolerate Americans or Jews. If they see you, they will report you to the SS."

At Mathias's invitation, the men sit down at the long, cloth-covered table. A wooden and glass buffet, filled with dishes, is built into one wall. On the other side of the room, a mountain stone wall opens to a large window, surrounded by white curtains. Dark decorative wooden panels, matching the floor, line the lower walls. The wood-burning stove breathes warm air into the room. Its metal front is covered with inlaid designs—trees, a log cabin, and several antelopes with large antlers. Extra logs are piled neatly in a black iron holder near the stove. A crucifix hangs prominently above the door.

Mathias notices one of the men has an injured hand. "Maria, fetch the medicine and bandages." He glances at his children—Hans, Gertrud, Leo, and Resi—standing in the back of the room, silently staring at the strange, dark men.

"It is okay, my *Kinder.* These men are Americans. They are our friends."

"Are they our friends like the ones hiding in the cellar?" one of the children asks, referring to the two Belgians, deserters from the German Army, whom Mathias has been protecting for months.

Mathias nods and smiles. "Yes, little one," he says. "But we must keep their staying with us a secret."

When Maria returns with a first-aid kit, she takes Sergeant Forte's hand gently in hers, dabbing it with ointment and wrapping it with fresh gauze.

"Keep your hand warm inside the blanket," Maria tells him, and pats his back.

Forte looks up into Maria's compassionate face.

"Thankin' you, ma'am," he says. "That's very kind of you." For the first time in a long while, Forte smiles.

"We don't want to cause you any trouble," Adams says. "If the Krauts find us here, they'll—"

"Do not worry," Mathias interrupts. "We understand the risks. After you are warm and fed, you will want to take the path at the back of the house to Meyerode. It will be safer there for you."

Maria places a large platter of homemade bread and butter on the table. "Please eat," she says. "I wish we could offer you more, but this is all we have." She reaches into the buffet, brings out a small jar of homemade preserves, and sets it in front of the men. "We have been saving this sweetened fruit for a special occasion," she says. She motions for the children to come to the table. They stand beside the GIs, passing the plate around, offering each man bread, butter, and jam.

Maria pours steaming coffee into cups, adding a tad of cream. "This will warm you inside," she says, patting her heart.

"Thank you, ma'am," Stewart says. He wraps his hands around the cup of hot liquid. "This is a feast. We haven't eaten in two days."

"How did you escape from the Germans?" Hermann asks, his eyes wide.

"Jus' got lucky, son," Stewart tells him, purposely leaving out the gruesome details.

"Do you have families back home?" Maria asks. "Any children?"

Private Adams reaches into his pocket and shows Maria the photograph of Catherine and Jesse. "Only saw my son one time," he says. "I hope God'll keep him safe till I can get home." He glances at the crucifix above the door. "I pray for my boy every day, I do."

"I, too, pray for my *Kinder*," Maria says, "especially for my three older sons hiding in Belgium." She touches the silver crucifix on the end of her necklace. "I pray they will survive the war and avoid German conscription."

"That's a beautiful crucifix," Adams says, noticing Maria's necklace.

Maria pauses and smiles. She slips the crucifix from its delicate chain, holds it in her hand, and looks at it for a long time. Then she places it in Adams's hand. "This will help you pray for your son," she says. "God will protect him."

Adams stares at the crucifix and then raises his eyes to Maria's face. "Thank you. I'll pray for your children, too." He puts the crucifix in the pocket that holds Catherine's dog-eared little Bible.

"I wish we had something to give you—a gift to thank you for your hospitality," Stewart tells Mathias. "But we've jus' got the uniforms on our backs."

Forte, Davis, and Adams dig into their pockets and, with open palms, each offers Mathias coins—several French francs and German Reichsmarks.

Mathias thanks them but shakes his head. "We will not take your money. You will need it for your journey."

Stewart pulls a box of Chiclets chewing gum out of his pocket. "Here, kids—hold out your hands." He empties the sugar-covered chewing gum into the children's cupped hands.

"How many children do you have?" Stewart asks.

Maria blinks her eyes, her expression serious.

"We have ten children," she says. "Two little ones died at birth." She hugs her *Kinder* close to her, smiling and patting her eyes with a lace handkerchief.

"You've got a beautiful family," Stewart says.

Corporal Bradley searches his pockets. He finds the new bar of Woodbury soap and hands it to Maria.

"My woman gave it to me," he says. "It's special soap. Real special."

Maria puts the bar to her nose, sniffing it, smiling, and passing it to her children to smell its fragance.

While the men eat warm bread and butter, Maria walks to the window and peeks through the curtains. Suddenly her mouth drops open and her hand flies up to cover it. "Mathias! There are four SS soldiers in a Schwimmwagen outside our door."[1]

CHAPTER 81

THE ARREST

A hard pounding on the front door vibrates throughout the house. Maria, her seventeen-year-old daughter, Tina, and their visiting friend and child grab the younger children, run into the bedroom, and shut the door. Hermann, Mathias, and the eleven men jump from their chairs.

"I know you are in there, Herr Langer!" a husky voice calls from outside. "Open the door and let us inside."

"Hermann," Mathias says, "quickly! Take the men to the cellar to hide. The SS must not find them."

"No," Stewart says abruptly. "We're not gonna hide and put the lives of your family in danger." He glances back to the men. "We've gotta give ourselves up."

The GIs nod in agreement.

Sergeant Forte turns to Mathias. "Thankin' you again, sir. Not many people would've done this for us. We'll always be grateful to you," he says, and smiles.

"Our prayers go with you all," Mathias says, placing his hand tenderly on Forte's back.

Opening the front door, Mathias acknowledges the SS troops. An officer wearing a black-billed cap emblazoned with a death's-head, and a scar on his cheek as big as a silver dollar, points his pistol at the Americans and motions them outside.

"Papa!" Hermann shouts, visibly upset, tears dropping off his chin. "Where are they taking our new friends?"

"Friends!" the scar-faced officer blurts out. "You call these Negro American soldiers your 'friends'? Mathias, you would be wise to teach your son who the enemy is and who their *real* friends are!"

Mathias puts his arm around Hermann's shoulders. "He is just a boy," he tells the officer. "He means no harm."

The soldiers shove the Americans into the yard. "Sit down against the house," they demand. "Wait here until we return."

The men walk to the side of the house, sit down in deep snow, and lean against the wall of the house, icy sleet beating down hard on them.

"Wait!" Mathias calls to the officer. "Won't you please allow the men to take shelter in our shed while they wait? It is warm there."

"No!" the officer says. "They will wait here. You will remain inside. We will come get them soon. They will warm up when they run in front of the cars."

He posts a patrol inside the Schimmwagen to guard the men and steps inside the warm house. "I am hungry," he tells Mathias. For the next hour, he sits at the table, chatting with Mathias and eating bread and butter.

Mathias locks the door when the scar-faced officer leaves. Maria rushes out from the bedroom.

"When the Germans come back for the men, Mathias, they will arrest us and our *Kinder*. We will all be punished. What if . . . what if we are deported or hurt . . . or maybe even killed?"

"We will wait here, Maria, and pray."

"I am sure it was Greta who betrayed us," Maria says. "She always watches the house."

"Papa," Hermann asks. "What will happen to the men?"

Mathias bends down, hugging the boy. "They are prisoners now, son. The SS will take them to a camp where they will be warm and have food to eat. When the war is over, they will go home to the United States."

Hermann cries, opening his fist and staring at the handful of Chiclets. "Papa, they are such nice men. It is so cold outside. Won't the Americans freeze sitting in the snow?"

"They will be okay, Hermann."

Mathias walks to the window and looks outside. *I wish I could help them.*

CHAPTER 82

THE LONG WAIT

—WERETH, BELGIUM—
DECEMBER 17, 1944

Private Davis takes his granddaddy's old watch from his pocket, checking the time. "We've been sitting here half an hour," he says. "We're gonna freeze before they come get us."

"They'll be coming soon," Stewart says. "We can't do nothing but wait."

"We can make a run for it," Forte says.

"Do you see that guard in the Schwimmwagen pointing his rifle at us, Sergeant?" Stewart says. "He'll shoot us the minute we stand up. And if some of us did escape, he might get mad enough to shoot the Langer family. Can't take that chance."

Georgie Davis holds his granddaddy's watch, sitting quietly in deep reflection. He is no longer the immature kid he was back in Bessemer, Alabama. He closes his eyes, recalling the previous summer and fall—the months of war that grew him up, made him a man. He wonders if he'll ever forget the images and smells of combat in France and Belgium—bloated, rotting bodies covered with flies and rats. He puts his hand to his nose as if to block out the mental stench of dead men and animals lying on battlefields and roads. Never before has he been so cold, so hungry, and so tired. War has tested the limits of his human endurance, and somehow he has served his country well and survived.

He opens his eyes and stares at the pocket watch in his hand, thinking about his parents. He can hardly wait to go home. Smiling, he remembers sitting with his parents in the warm, cozy front room, his belly filled with his mama's home cooking, familiar family photographs watching him from the wall. He returns the watch to his pocket.

Daylight begins to fade in the tiny village of Wereth as the eleven men sit helpless and freezing in the snow.

"Your bandage's coming off," Adams tells Forte. He reaches over to the sergeant, takes his hand, and rewraps the gauze. Forte slides his injured hand inside his jacket.

"My feet's frozen," Pritchett says. "My toes ain't never gonna thaw out."

"Don't wanna get frostbite," Adams says. "Take off your shoes and socks. Let's get the blood flowing to your toes."

Adams cups Pritchett's feet between his cold hands, massaging them forcefully.

"Won't be long till the Krauts come back and take us to a POW camp," Stewart says. "We can tend to our feet there."

"We'll be war heroes when we get home," Davis says. "My parents'll be so proud of me."

"They sure will be, Private First Class George Davis," Stewart says. "They sure will be, son."

"Bet we get some medals for this," Davis says. "Maybe even a promotion. Can you hardly believe we got written up in *Yank*?"

"Don't care much about medals or promotions or magazines," Adams says. "More concerned about staying alive, getting back to my family." He pulls from his pocket the photograph made at Camp Gruber and for a long time stares at the smiling faces of Jesse and Catherine.

"We're all gonna make it," Stewart tells Adams. "Me and Jesse gonna play baseball one day. Want to teach that boy how to pitch for the major league."

Sergeant Forte frowns at Stewart, who is opening his mouth to speak.

"No, Sergeant Forte," Stewart interrupts, his voice raised. "Don't you say that coloreds won't ever be major leaguers. You jus' keep quiet. I've got a feeling our children and grandchildren'll be pitching with the whites before long. Jus' be a crying shame if they don't."

"I wasn't gonna say that, Sergeant," Forte says, his face sullen. "I'm just hopin' the Langers don't get hurt for takin' us in. They're the nicest white folks I ever met."

"There's lots of good whites like the Langers," Stewart says. "Captain McLeod's another one who's been real kind and encouraging to us. People are people, Sergeant. There are good ones, and there are bad ones. Don't much matter what color skin's on the outside. More important what kinda heart's on the inside."

"I'm beginnin' to see that," Forte whispers. "I'm *really* beginnin' to see that."

"Captain McLeod's a straight-up guy," Green says. "Hope he and the other boys are safe."

"Probably eating hot kraut and sausage in a warm German POW camp," Stewart says.

The men huddle closer together, their bodies shivering uncontrollably.

Adams changes the subject. "You ever find Angelina that diamond wedding ring in Paris, Forte?" he asks.

"Sure did." He takes a thin gold ring from his pocket. "Real diamond, too." The men strain their eyes, trying to find the chip of diamond in the center of the ring.

"Real nice, Forte," Adams says.

"Wish we were still sitting inside by that warm stove with the antelopes on it," Forte says. "Never saw one like that before."

Long minutes tick away in silence. Davis closes his eyes, and with a soft voice and a steady rhythm, he begins to sing the old spiritual he had heard all the mothers before him sing. "Roll, Jordan, roll. Roll, Jordan, roll. . . . I wanter go to heav'n when I die, to hear ol' Jordan roll. . . ." Some of the other men join in. After the first verse ends, they again sit quietly.

"Remember when George taught us that song at Camp Gruber?" Stewart says, breaking the silence.

Some of the men smile, remembering the days when they struggled to learn how to operate the 155.

Forte gazes deep into Stewart's eyes, tightly wrinkling his brow. "They're gonna kill us, aren't they, Sergeant?" Forte asks. "Why would they keep us alive? We'd just be extra mouths for 'em to feed."

Stewart takes a deep breath, looking into the face of each frightened man. "Whatever happens, men, we did our jobs the best we could. We served our country. That's what's most important right now."

Adams reaches into his pocket, wrapping his hand around Catherine's childhood Bible. He begins to say softly from memory, "The Lord's my shepherd; I'll not want. He lays me down in green grassy pastures, and leads me to still waters—"

Davis joins him, whispering the words of the psalm he learned as a child: "He restores my soul. Leads me along paths of righteousness for His name's sake."

The other men, searching old memories, blend in with low voices: "Yes, even when I walk through the valleys, and the death shadows hang long and heavy over me, I won't fear no evil and no Krauts; for God is right here with me. . . ." Their voices fade with each word, finally growing quiet, the shadows of death too real, and hanging too heavy over them.

Private Adams continues. "God sets a table before me with my enemies all around. . . ."

He pauses for several seconds. "We certainly got enemies all around us now," he says, and continues. "Surely goodness and mercy'll follow me—and follow *all of us*—all the days of—" His voice choking, Adams stops.

"All the days of *our* lives," Stewart says. "And *we* will go home and live in the house with our dear loving Lord—where's it's warm and we're at peace—forever and ever and ever."[1]

Tears fall from the men's eyes, freezing to ice on their cheeks as they wait, as each deeply contemplates the psalm's timeless message.

CHAPTER 83

"THOUGH I WALK
THROUGH THE VALLEY"

— WERETH, BELGIUM —
DECEMBER 17, 1944

Hermann stands at the window, crying, watching, and worrying about the men.

"Please, Papa," he whines. "Can I take them some hot coffee?"

"No, son. It's too dangerous. We must stay inside as we've been told."

Suddenly the boy sees headlights shining from several cars coming down the road toward the house. With his hand, he shields his eyes from the bright beams of light.

"Papa!" he shouts. "The SS has returned."

Mathias, Maria, and Hermann stare out the window. They watch the SS officers approach the eleven men, poking them with rifle butts and demanding they stand up.

"We need not worry about the Americans now, Hermann," Mathias says. "The Germans will take care of them."

"But, Papa—"

Mathias puts his arms around his wife and son, gently moving them away from the window, not wanting them to witness what he hopes and prays won't happen.

He closes the curtain, lowers his head, and makes the sign of the cross over his heart.

The men struggle to their feet. "Can't feel my legs," Pritchett tells Adams. "Don't think I can stand up."

"You've got to," Adams says, reaching around Pritchett's chest and helping him.

When the men are finally on their feet, the scar-faced officer orders them to stand in front of the cars. The men smell petrol and feel the faint warmth of headlights against their skin. The cars' engines race, loud roars filling the sky.

"March!" the officer orders.

The men try to straighten their backs, hobbling forward slowly.

"Run!" the officer shouts. "Run fast, or else the vehicles will crush you!"

The Americans jog slowly in front of the cars, the headlights reflecting their agony in each labored step. They come to the end of the neighborhood street, a few yards from the cow pasture.

But Pritchett moves too slowly, his toes and feet like blocks of ice. The driver again races the engine, threatening to mow him down. Stewart and Adams rush to help him, but before they can reach Pritchett, the driver lurches the car forward, plowing over Pritchett, buckling his legs beneath him and knocking him hard to the ground. Stewart and Adams jump out of the way, both landing facedown in the snow. The driver laughs as he shifts the car into reverse, backs up, guns the motor, lunges forward, and runs over Pritchett's legs again and again. Paralyzed, moaning, and bleeding, Pritchett lies on the ground, the ends of both leg bones piercing through his skin.

A soldier jumps from the car, shoots a bullet into Pritchett's shoulder, and with his rifle butt rams him in the face, shattering his jaw.

"No!" Forte screams, and rushes to help Pritchett. The driver then turns his car in Forte's direction, gunning his engine and charging forward. The front of the car hits Forte, pushing him down into the snow. The driver slowly runs his tires again and again over Forte's back. When he screams out in pain, another German attacks him with a knife, laughing as he severs four of Forte's fingers.

The sport continues as soldiers plow into Adams and Green, breaking their necks and crushing their skulls. A German stoops in the snow, slices off Adams's ring finger, and steals his wedding band, Catherine's gift to him forever gone.

Stewart tries to stop the slaughter. A German attacks him, shooting him in his left arm and then hitting him hard in the stomach with his boot. From the ground, Stewart looks up into the soldier's face and asks softly, "Why?" The German stabs a bayonet into his eyes. When the dying baseball pitcher moans, the soldier strikes the back of his head with a rifle butt, bashing in his skull.

Like wild animals excited by a bloody kill, the soldiers grab Moten and Davis, using them for target practice, bayoneting their chests, backs, eyes, and groins until the two GIs lie silent and unmoving in the snow.

Leatherwood and Bradley dart toward the woods, but they are caught, stabbed again and again, and left in the pasture. The soldiers then aim their rifles at Moss and Turner, firing multiple times, peppering their faces, necks, and shoulders with bullets. They shoot each man again and again, just in case one is still alive.

The Germans then speed away, their taste for blood and brutality seemingly satisfied. Brains, guts, and severed fingers lie strewn in a bloody corner of the cow pasture.

Throughout the silent night, a heavy shroud of snow falls, blanketing the eleven mangled black bodies now resting in peace . . . forever and ever and ever. . . .

THE REST OF THE STORY

The Discovery

The violent world war continues, resulting in more killing and dying. On the day after Christmas 1944, an airplane drops a bomb in front of the Langers' home, exploding and injuring Hermann, Leo, Tina, and the baby, Anneliese. They are transported to a hospital in Halenfeld by an army truck filled with wounded German POWs. Later, the Langer children are moved to Mirfeld to receive more treatment. They heal, recovering and returning home to their family in Wereth.[1]

The Langers' German-loyal neighbors turn against them, shunning them and accusing Mathias of sheltering American soldiers, Jews, and others. Heavy fighting between Allies and Axis comes into Wereth, continuing for many weeks. Mathias and Maria keep their children safely locked inside their home until the fighting in Wereth ends.

They venture out of their home for the first time in February 1945, dressed warmly and heading to Sunday morning Mass at a nearby church.

Hermann runs ahead of his family, happy to be outside, thankful the fighting in Wereth has stopped. He looks forward to the coming of spring, noticing that some of winter's snow has already begun to melt. Skipping through the cow pasture on his way to Mass, he spots something on the ground. He walks closer, leaning down and straining his eyes to see. A hand sticks out of the snow. The twelve-year-old boy screams, running back to his parents, crying inconsolably as he describes what he saw.

Maria takes the children back to the house as Mathias examines the bodies, solidly frozen in the cow pasture. He contacts the U.S. Ninety-ninth Division unit in the area. Sending out authorities, they examine, snap photographs of, and remove the eleven mutilated bodies. The Langers hear no more about their American friends, and the residents of Wereth dare not discuss it.

What Happened to the Eleven Men

On February 15, 1945, Army captain William Everett examines the frozen bodies, their deaths unacknowledged, and their bodies buried in snow for almost two months. He reports that the men are believed to have been massacred by the Waffen-SS, part of Major Gustav Knittel's First SS Panzer Reconnaissance Battalion. But Captain Everett isn't certain, and he cannot prove it.

In his official medical report, he writes that the eleven GIs have been systematically and severely tortured, suffering multiple wounds all over their bodies. He notes some of the injuries:

Sergeant William Pritchett's legs have been broken, and his jaw has been fractured in two places.

Sergeant Aubrey Stewart and Privates Curtis Adams and Robert Green have had their skulls bashed in, hit with a hard object from behind.

Sergeant Forte's four fingers have been removed, along with the fingers of some of the other men, their wedding rings gone.

Many of the men's eyes have been bayoneted out, and their heads and bodies stabbed multiple times. Most have suffered fractures to

their skulls, believed to have been made by rifle butt blows to the head.
Tire marks on their bodies indicate some of the men have been run
over by vehicles before dying. All the men have been shot, the bul-
let wounds designed to inflict pain and anguish, rather than cause
immediate death.

When Captain Everett empties the men's pockets, he finds some
interesting objects. Besides a few coins and pictures, he discovers a
Bible, a fountain pen, letters from Catherine, and a crucifix in Private
Curtis Adams's pocket; a woman's broken diamond wedding ring in
Sergeant Thomas Forte's pocket; a man's wedding ring in Corporal
Bradley's pocket; and, in Private First Class George Davis's pocket, a
Bible, an old pocket watch, and a faded newspaper photograph of Olym-
pic star Jesse Owens.

The men's families receive the dreaded "killed in action" telegrams,
but for the next half century or so, they have no idea what happened,
or how their loved ones died.[2]

The Investigation

Colonel Burton Ellis, the lead war crimes investigator, officially inves-
tigates the massacre at Wereth. He interrogates more than one thousand members of the First SS Panzer Division. But afterward, he claims
the evidence proves inconclusive, and that he can turn up no positive
identification of those who committed the brutal murders. He makes
a note on his pad: "The perpetrators were undoubtedly SS enlisted
men, but available testimony is insufficient to establish definite unit
identification." Most place the blame on Gustav Knittel's First SS
Reconnaissance Battalion. In the end, however, no one is held responsible or punished for the murders at Wereth.[3, 4] No newspapers carry
headlines of the massacre.

In 1947, exactly two years to the day after the bodies are discovered, the government investigation is officially closed. It is given a "secret" classification, sealed and locked in a government file drawer, and completely forgotten. A 1949 Senate Armed Services Committee carefully documents, in official records, twelve specific incidents of American troop and Belgian civilian massacres by Nazi troops, publishing them in the final 1949 Congressional Report on War Crimes. They list, in detail, all the names of the massacred victims—both civilian and military—and where each crime took place. The eleven black American GIs, massacred on December 17, 1944, in Wereth, Belgium, are omitted from the report.[5]

The bodies of the eleven forgotten men were buried in temporary graves in Europe. In 1947, their families were contacted about permanent burial options. Seven of the men now rest in Belgium's Henri-Chapelle American Cemetery: Tech Sergeant Thomas J. Forte, Tech Sergeant James Aubrey Stewart, Private First Class George Davis, Private First Class George W. Moten, Private First Class Due W. Turner, Private Curtis Adams, and Private Nathanial Moss. The remains of the other four soldiers were requested by their families and buried in the United States: Corporal Mager Bradley, Staff Sergeant William Edward Pritchett, Private First Class James Leatherwood, and Private Robert Green.[6]

For the next fifty years or more, the tragedy at Wereth was forgotten by everyone, except one person, Hermann Langer, the twelve-year-old Belgian boy with a bar of soap and a fistful of Chiclets in his hands at the time of the killings. He never forgot the kind American GIs he and his family welcomed into their home one cold December afternoon. He also never forgot the nightmare of finding their mutilated bodies months later, scattered in the cow pasture behind his family's home.

The War Ends

Months before the war ended, the surviving men of the all-African-American 333rd Field Artillery Battalion were absorbed into their sister unit, the 969th Field Artillery Battalion. They provided support fire for the 101st Airborne Division in the Seige of Bastogne (December 19–23, 1944), suffering many casualties.[7]

For their extraordinary courage and undaunted determination in the defense of Bastogne, the 969th (including the 333rd) was awarded the Presidential Distinguished Unit Citation, the highest honor bestowed by the president of the United States upon an army unit. They were the first African-American combat unit to receive this award during World War II. The battalion also received the Belgian Croix de Guerre (War Cross) with Palm for their heroic actions defending Bastogne.

During the Battle of the Bulge, the 333rd Field Artillery Battalion sustained more casualties than any other VIII Corps field artillery battalion. Of the 500 officers and men serving in the battalion, at least 220 or more were killed, wounded, or captured. The 333rd Field Artillery Battalion was officially dissolved in late December 1944. During their courageous advance from Utah Beach, throughout France, and to the Belgian Siegfried Line, the 333rd Field Artillery Battalion's extraordinary performance earned it the reputation of one of the best field artillery units in the European theater of operations (ETO).[8]

After the Battle of the Bulge

By the time the bodies of the eleven men of the 333rd Field Artillery Battalion were discovered in February 1945, the Battle of the Bulge had ended. The rapid gains made by the Germans in mid-December were slowed by various isolated units, including the 333rd, giving the U.S. First and Ninth Armies time to shift against the German northern flank. The British sent reserves to secure the Meuse River. General Patton's Third Army shut down the enemy attack in the south. The cost of victory in the Bulge proved heavy, with high American casualties.

World War II, in the European theater of operations, ended on

May 8, 1945. German troops throughout Europe laid down their weapons and surrendered.[9]

After the December 17, 1944, surrender of Charley Battery near Schönberg, Sergeant George Shomo, Corporal Robert Hudson, Captain William Gene McLeod, and many others were loaded on trains, transported to German POW camps, and imprisoned for months. Held behind barbed wire and monitored by guards in tall towers, they settled into wooden barracks heated with charcoal-burning stoves. They lived on two meager meals a day, usually black bread and thin soup, and were always cold and hungry. They endured hard work and beatings, and wondered if their comrades were alive or dead. They struggled to survive throughout the long winter and spring, threatened with execution if they tried to escape, and waited for the war to end. They were all released in the summer of 1945.

More than one million African-Americans served in World War II, fighting with every branch of the military and in every theater of operation. Their service helped to win the fight for freedom. As Tech Sergeant James Aubrey Stewart said shortly before he was murdered, the men served America the best they could, and that's what's important.

Army chief of staff General Omar N. Bradley had earlier stated that desegregation would come to the army only when it became a fact in the rest of American society.[10]

On July 26, 1948, President Harry Truman signed Executive Order 9981, abolishing racial discrimination in the United States Armed Forces. The order eventually led to the end of segregation in the military.[11, 12]

In 1954, the United States Board of Education outlawed segregated public education facilities for blacks and whites at the state level. The Civil Rights Act of 1964 ended all U.S. state and local laws requiring segregation.[13]

The Eleven Men Honored

Hermann Langer moved away from Wereth in 1961. But on September 11, 1994, on the fiftieth anniversary of the massacre, Hermann revisited his old homeplace, reflecting deeply as he walked through the pasture where the murders had taken place when he was a boy. Using pieces of his own family's gravestones, he made a cross, erecting it on the exact spot where the eleven men had been murdered on December 17, 1944.

The story, however, does not end there. Several years later, others began to hear about the killing of the eleven men. Year after year, on the anniversary, people began to gather at the site where they were killed. In 1998, the group of people held the first official memorial at the cow pasture in Wereth, Belgium, coming together to "celebrate, honor, and recognize eleven African-American soldiers who fought and were massacred during World War II."[14]

On that occasion, Major General James W. Monroe, commander of the U.S. Army Industrial Operations Command, presented posthumous awards to Sergeant Forte's relatives, saying, "Staff Sergeant Forte and his fellow soldiers risked their lives and epitomized the army core values with their exemplary behavior, efficiency, and fidelity during their military service. . . . He and the other ten courageous soldiers shared the common bonds of the Armed Forces, which is duty and sacrifice."[15]

Since then, growing crowds from all over the world have gathered annually at the memorial site to honor the eleven lost men, members of the 333rd Field Artillery Battalion.

In 2001, three Belgians, including Adda Rikken, president of the U.S. Wereth Memorial Committee, began to raise funds to create a more fitting and permanent memorial to the Americans. The committee raised enough money to purchase much of the pastureland that surrounded the original monument. They created and erected a permanent memorial, monument, and plaque, dedicating it at the site in a ceremony on May 23, 2004. They also erected a beautifully designed monument at the wall of the house, marking the place where the eleven men were ordered to wait.

"What began with hate, we now end with honor," Adda Rikken said at the 2004 dedication.[16]

The memorial honors the memory of the eleven African-American soldiers, as well as all black GIs and segregated units who fought in Europe during World War II. It is believed to be the only memorial of its type in Europe.[17]

Should Never Be Forgotten

On May 1, 2007, at the annual remembrance ceremony in Wereth, Belgium, Brigader General Dennis L. Via, commander of the Fifth Signal Command in Mannheim, Germany, told the crowd:

"What happened on December 17, 1944, should never be forgotten. However, we are not here today to focus on the crime and the pain; we are here today to focus on the heroic lives of these eleven Americans."[18]

At the annual remembrance ceremony on May 17, 2014, Colonel L. Mitchell Kilgo, commandant, Fifth Signal Command, U.S. Army, stated, "We know [about these eleven GIs] largely because a young twelve-year-old boy could not forget what he had witnessed on a cold winter [afternoon] in 1944. Throughout his lifetime, Hermann Langer could not forget the desperation he saw in the eyes of the soldiers that appeared at his home—nor could he forget the dignity in their eyes when they faced their captors. He could not forget the compassionate example of his father. And he could not forget the liberty that their sacrifice purchased."[19]

Through the efforts of Hermann Langer and other private citizens in Belgium, as well as members of the U.S. armed forces and compassionate individuals like Norman Lichtenfeld, a physician in Mobile,

Alabama, the Wereth Memorial site survives as a lasting remembrance to the final acts of courage of the eleven men of the 333rd Field Artillery Battalion. Road signs now direct visitors to the memorial site in Wereth, and the Belgian Tourist Bureau lists it in their brochures.[20]

The Lost Eleven Officially Recognized

In 2013, a resolution, House of Representatives Concurrent Resolution 68, called on the U.S. Senate's Armed Services Committe to "correct the omission" of the 1949 subcommittee report to include appropriate recognition of the massacre of the eleven black soldiers of the 333rd Field Artillery Battalion of the U.S. Army who were murdered by Nazi captors almost seven decades before. The original subcommittee report had documented a dozen similar massacres during the Battle of the Bulge but did not include any reference to the killings in Wereth, Belgium.

The new Statement on the Resolution read: "Our country shall be forever grateful to every member of the 'Greatest Generation' who contributed to the defeat of fascism in Europe and laid down their lives so that future generations could enjoy the blessing of freedom. Every now and then, it takes history a while to accurately reflect the monumental moments that have helped chart its course. That's certainly the case with these eleven black soldiers who courageously fought on the front line in the Ardennes against a relentless enemy and eventually made the ultimate sacrifice for their fellow soldiers and our nation. This resolution is a tribute nearly seven decades overdue. And it is indeed a privilege to . . . ensure that the story of the exemplary service and incredible sacrifice of these eleven black soldiers is always remembered."[21]

Representative Chaka Fattah (D-PA) stated, "The valiant efforts and unequal sacrifice of the Wereth 11 soldiers deserves to be commemorated in our country's history. These are men whose heroic story has been lost to time, but whose names must be honored, and whose accounts we must share today and into the future. I am proud to join with my colleague Representative Gerlach in paying reverence to their courage and bravery, recalling their lives of service, and ensuring their story of fighting for freedom over tyranny is told for decades to come."[22]

The eleven massacred men of the 333rd Field Artillery Battalion were posthumously awarded five combat decorations, including the Bronze Star, Purple Heart, and World War II Victory Medal.[23]

WHAT HAPPENED
TO THE OTHERS?

The 333rd POWs

Battalion Commander Lieutenant Colonel Harmon S. Kelsey: Colonel Kelsey, born on December 28, 1895, in San Bruno, California, was captured with most of his men on December 17, 1944, as he tried to rescue the troops stationed at Schönberg during the German attack. Released after the war, Kelsey died on March 10, 1965, at sixty-nine. He is buried in Golden Gate National Cemetery in San Bruno, California.[1]

Captain William Gene McLeod: Captain McLeod, born April 25, 1921, at Granite, Oklahoma, rose to the rank of major general and corps commander of artillery, retiring from the army in 1979 and settling in Lawton, Oklahoma. Captured on December 17, 1944, in Belgium, he spent time in a German POW camp until the war's end. On his final tour of duty, he was assigned to Commander in Chief Pacific (CINCPAC) with headquarters in Hawaii. During his long career, he received the army's highest noncombat award, the Distinguished Service Medal, was awarded three times the Legion of Merit, received the Bronze Star with "V," the Purple Heart, the Joint Services Commendation Medal, two Army Commendation Medals, the Republic of

Korea Cheon-Su Medal, and numerous other service medals and badges. After retiring from the army, he was appointed by Governor George High as a member of the Oklahoma Board of Corrections, where he held the positions of vice president and president. He died in August 2005, at age eighty-four. He was buried with full military honors at Fort Sill National Cemetery, Elgin, Oklahoma.

Captain McLeod was greatly loved by his men, especially by Sergeant George Shomo. Shomo lost touch with McLeod after the war, assuming he was dead. Two weeks before McLeod died, Shomo and McLeod were reunited by phone. At the end of the conversation, Shomo expressed his admiration for and gratitude to Captain McLeod, telling him he would have followed him anywhere.[2]

Sergeant George E. Shomo: George Shomo, born in Red Bank, New Jersey, on February 27, 1921, was captured during World War II on December 17, 1944, and spent time in a German POW camp. George Shomo's childhood friend Wesley Forehand entered the army with Shomo and they trained together, went overseas together, and were captured, both spending time in a German POW camp. After the war, Shomo and Forehand were released. Shomo settled in northern New Jersey, where he and his wife raised seven children. Forehand married George Shomo's sister, Helen, together raising three children and eight grandchildren. Forehand died in September 1978 at age fifty-six.

After the war, George Shomo worked for thirty-nine years at the former Bendix Corporation before retiring. His wife, Inice Rock Shomo, died in 1995. George Shomo died on December 22, 2014, and was buried in Red Bank, New Jersey. He was survived by six children, eleven grandchildren, and fifteen great-grandchildren.

George's son, **Rob Shomo**, visited France, traveling the same path to Belgium that his father took back in 1944. Rob is now doing family research at an old African-American cemetery in Red Bank. He has discovered many family members there, tracing them back to slavery in New Jersey. Rob Shomo lives in Asheville, North Carolina.

On his father's birthday in 2013, Rob presented him with a family tree, having spent several years digging into the Shomo family history. His father was recently honored with a paver in the new Veterans Park in Neptune, New Jersey, the guest of honor in the Memorial Day parade there. George Shomo's uncle, Private First Class Randolph V. Shomo, who was twelve years older than George, also served in Europe during World War II (April 1944–October 1945), enlisting as a Duty Soldier III 590 and assigned to the 682 U.S. General Hospital Unit.

Corporal Robert Rolland Hudson Sr.: Corporal Robert R. Hudson, twenty-four (333rd FAB, Battalion C), was wounded (shell fragments, left leg) and captured in the Ardennes during the German attack on December 17, 1944. He received medical treatment aboard a German Red Cross hospital train on Christmas Day, 1944. He spent four months in a German prison camp (Stalag 6c Lingen, Germany—December 24, 1944, to February 20, 1945; Stalag 11b Fallenbostel, Germany—February 24, 1945, to April 16, 1945) and was liberated by the British Eighth Army in June 1945. In the POW camps, he was given only grass soup, four small potatoes, and three slices of black bread a day.

Robert Hudson's mother received a Western Union telegram regarding her son sometime after December 17, 1944 (no date listed on telegram):

MRS. FLORENCE HUDSON: THE SECRETARY OF WAR DESIRES
ME TO EXPRESS HIS DEEP REGRET THAT YOUR SON
CORPORAL ROBERT R HUDSON HAS BEEN REPORTED MISSING
IN ACTION SINCE SEVENTEEN DECEMBER IN BELGIUM. IF
FURTHER DETAILS OR OTHER INFORMATION ARE RECEIVED
YOU WILL BE PROMPTLY NOTIFIED. DUNLOP ACTING THE
ADJUTANT GENERAL.

Robert Hudson's mother received a second Western Union telegram regarding her son on April 16, 1945:

MRS. FLORENCE HUDSON: THE SECRETARY OF WAR DESIRES
ME TO INFORM YOU THAT YOUR SON CPL ROBERT R HUDSON
IS A PRISONER OF WAR OF GERMAN GOVERNMENT BASED ON
INFORMATION RECEIVED THROUGH PROVOST MARSHAL
GENERAL. FURTHER INFORMATION RECEIVED WILL BE
FURNISHED BY PROVOST MARSHAL GENERAL. J A UL10 THE
ADJUTANT GENERAL.

While in the POW camp in Germany, Robert wrote several post-cards and letters to his mother.

December 28, 1944 (from Stalag VI-C, L.L.):

Dear Mother. I am a prisoner; slightly wounded. For information contact the Red Cross. The treatment is good here. I pray often and thank God. Say hello to all and keep faith. Love-Son-Bob.

January 3, 1945:

Dear Mother: By the time this letter reaches you, I hope you will have received my first one. Thank God I have improved. My health is good, am treated fine as a prisoner of war. I miss you all very much. Try not to worry too much. I received Red Cross boxes here. They are very good containing food. See the Red Cross and try sending me a box with can goods and candy. They say it takes 2–3 months for the package to arrive here. Send a dollar-watch, one that can be seen at night with radium hands and numbers. I will close now. Love, Son-Bob.

February 20, 1945:

Dearest Mother: This letter leaves me well and the weather improving here. While in the hospital here I read books to past [sic] away the time.

As you can see there is not much to write about, as being a prisoner I am confined. Nevertheless I am treated well. I thank God that I have improved. Love to all, Son-Bob.[2]

When Corporal Hudson returned to the United States, he married (1946), settled in Chicago, and worked for the post office for forty years as a postal clerk. He died on May 6, 1995.

Corporal Hudson's son, **Robert Hudson Jr.**, made a recent trip to Belgium to retrace the ten-mile journey the eleven men took in their flight to freedom. He also delivered the memorial speech in Belgium on September 26, 2009. (Please see Appendix 1 to read the Wereth 11 Memorial Speech written and delivered by Robert Hudson Jr.)

Tech Sergeant William Pritchett never married but had one daughter, born in 1943, a schoolteacher, who recently retired. She lives in New Jersey. Pritchett is buried in the McCastar Cemetery in Wilcox, Alabama.

Tech Sergeant James Aubrey Stewart's parents, in West Virginia, died never knowing how their son, Aubrey, was killed. In the mid-1990s, fifty years later, his nephew heard about his uncle's murder, traveled to Wereth, and visited with Hermann and Tina Langer. They told him the whole story. In 2012, the West Virginia House of Delegates honored Stewart by passing a resolution officially naming state Route 46 (between Keyser and Piedmont) "The James Aubrey Stewart Memorial Highway."[4]

Corporal Mager Bradley: Owing to the wishes of his wife, Eva Mae, Bradley's body was buried in the Fort Gibson National Cemetery in Oklahoma. A U.S. flag at half-staff flies over his tombstone. Tina Langer, the daughter of Mathias and Maria, remembers Corporal Bradley giving her family a bar of soap, a treasure they hadn't seen after the war started.[5]

Private George Moten was single when he was murdered, and had no children.

Sergeant Thomas Forte's wife, Angelina, died on May 12, 1973, at the age of sixty-six. The Fortes had no children.

Private First Class Due W. Turner for many years was the "unknown soldier of Columbia County, Arkansas." In October 2014 his name was added to the monument dedicated to the country's veterans on the courthouse square in Magnolia, Arkansas. His body is buried at Henri-Chapelle Cemetery.[6]

Private First Class Jimmie Lee Leatherwood's body was returned to Pontotoc, Mississippi, in 1947, and he was buried in College Hill Cemetery between two cedar trees. He lay in an unmarked grave for many years. Recently Leatherwood's family, friends, and community came together and bought him an engraved headstone. The back of the headstone tells the story of the Wereth massacre and quotes the Scripture verse from John 15:13: "Greater love hath no man than this, that a man lay down his life for his friends."

His daughter, **Jimmie Mae Leatherwood** of Tupelo, Mississippi, was a baby when her father was murdered. She doesn't remember ever seeing him. Neither Jimmie Mae nor her son, Steve, has ever seen a picture of him. They attended a ceremony to honor her father and his grandfather in May 2012 and were thrilled to receive a presidential memorial certificate signed by President Barack Obama.[7]

The Langer Family: Mathias Langer was the mayor of the small farming hamlet of Wereth, Belgium. He and his wife, Maria, had thirteen children, two of whom died during difficult births. Of the surviving eleven living children, the last one was born in 1946.

Hermann Langer, who placed a memorial cross on the massacre spot on the fiftieth anniversary of the murder, told his brother-in-law,

"I will be very surprised if, one day, an American came here to see this cross. Who knows, maybe, if one comes, he would give us a Chiclet like the GIs did in 1944."

When Hermann died on June 21, 2013, the village planted a beech tree in Wereth beside the memorial, dedicating it to Hermann Langer in celebration of his life. At the time of his death, a newspaper reporter wrote:

"Hermann, you don't receive a Chiclet today, but much more: you receive the recognition from the 11 families [whose] children finally emerge from obscurity. Now, more and more people, Americans and from other nations, are coming to your monument to pay tribute to all African-American soldiers who gave their youth and their life for our liberty, and they say: Thank you so much, Hermann. Rest in peace."

Mathias Langer died on May 14, 1974, at age eighty-five. His wife, Maria, seventy-two, died on July 15, 1974, three months later. Walter Langer lived until June 14, 1995. Paul died on March 3, 2013. His brother, Hermann, died three months later, on June 21, 2013. Johann (Hans) died on March 30, 2004. Leo lived until November 8, 2011. Therese (Resi) died on October 21, 2014. At this writing, Katharine (Tina), Heinrich (Heinz), Gertrud (Traudchen), Anneliese, and Joseph Langer are still alive.[8]

The Americans

President Franklin Delano Roosevelt: President Roosevelt died on April 12, 1945, after more than three momentous terms in office, leaving Vice President Harry S. Truman as commander in chief of the United States as the war still raged on. After Roosevelt's death, President Truman asked Roosevelt's wife, Eleanor, if there was anything he could do for her. She replied, "Is there anything we can do for *you*? For you are the one in trouble now."[9]

Franklin D. Roosevelt's body was carried from Warm Springs,

Georgia, to Washington, D.C., and he was buried at his family's home in Hyde Park, New York.

Mrs. Franklin D. (Ann Eleanor) Roosevelt: Mrs. Roosevelt, born on October 11, 1884, in New York, was often called the world's most admired woman, although she was not without critics and controversy. She served for twelve years as America's First Lady and was involved in civil rights activism. After her husband's death, President Harry Truman appointed Mrs. Roosevelt (1945) as a delegate to the UN General Assembly. She died on November 7, 1962, at age seventy-eight. At her funeral services, Adlai Stevenson said, "What other single human being has touched and transformed the existence of so many? She would rather light a candle than curse the darkness, and her glow has warmed the world." She is buried next to her husband at Springwood, the Roosevelt family home.[10]

General Dwight David Eisenhower: A popular leader, Eisenhower (Ike) is associated with "victory in war and a tireless crusade for peace." Born in Kansas in 1891, he became the Supreme Allied Commander, conquering the Axis powers during World War II. He retired from the army in 1948, becoming president of Columbia University and then, in 1950, head of NATO. He was elected the thirty-fourth president of the United States in 1952 (sworn into the office in 1953) and served two terms. He died on March 28, 1969, at age seventy-eight, after a long battle against coronary heart disease. Eisenhower, and his wife, Mamie, are buried on the grounds of the Eisenhower Library in Abilene, Kansas.[11]

General Troy Houston Middleton: General Middleton, born near Georgetown, Mississippi, on October 12, 1889, was dove hunting with his son when he heard about the December 7, 1941, Japanese attack on Pearl Harbor. The next day, he sent a telegram to the War Department and reported for active duty as a lieutenant colonel on January 20, 1942.

Middleton was a distinguished soldier-educator, serving as VIII Corps commander in Europe during World War II. The U.S. VIII Corps was activated on June 15, 1944, their divisions assuming responsibility for defensive positions west of the town of Carentan on the Cotentin Peninsula as part of the U.S. First Army. They secured Coutances and Avranches at the end of July. In the summer and fall of 1944, divisions of the VIII were: Second Infantry Division, Fourth Infantry Division, Eighth Infantry Division, Eighty-second Airborne Division, and 101st Airborne Division. After the war, in 1951, Middleton served as the president of Louisiana State University, retiring in 1973 at eighty-three. He died in Baton Rouge on October 9, 1976.[12]

General George Smith Patton: Often called "Old Blood and Guts," General Patton was born on the family ranch at San Gabriel, California, on November 11, 1885. He has been regarded as one of the most brilliant soldiers in American history, serving in World War I and leading his troops in World War II to victories in North Africa and Sicily and as leader of the Third Army on the Western Front. Patton died on December 21, 1945, two weeks after he suffered a broken neck in a car crash.[13]

General Omar Nelson Bradley: Called the "GI General," Bradley was born to an impoverished family on February 12, 1893, in Clark, Missouri. He graduated from West Point in 1915. As one of the towering American military leaders of the twentieth century, Bradley commanded more troops during World War II than any general in American history, including four armies, twelve corps, and forty-eight divisions—over 1.3 million troops. After the war, Bradley headed the Veterans Administration, later becoming a five-star general and first chairman of the Joint Chiefs of Staff, where he served two terms. Retiring in 1953 after thirty-eight years of distinguished military service, he died in 1981, at the age of eighty-eight, in New York City.[14]

Field Marshal Bernard Law Montgomery: Nicknamed "Monty," Montgomery was a senior officer in the British Army, serving in both World War I and World War II. Born on November 17, 1887, in Kensington, United Kingdom, he became known as a "meticulous planner who worked tirelessly to integrate the operations of the infantry, engineers, and artillery." He served in France, North Africa, Sicily, and Italy, and as commander of the Twenty-first Army Group, he participated in the Normandy Invasion on June 6, 1944, and the Battle of the Bulge. After World War II, Montgomery became commander of the British occupation forces, Allied Control Council. He became Viscount Montgomery of Alamein in 1946, served as chief of the Imperial General Staff, duty commander of NATO's European forces, retiring in 1958. He died on March 24, 1976, and was buried at Binsted.[15]

Major Glenn Miller: Miller, a successful trombonist and bandleader superstar, entered the army in 1942, forming a new fifty-piece USAAF dance band and giving performances for Allied troops in the ETO. General James Doolittle, USAAF, praised Miller: "Next to a letter from home, Captain Miller, your organization is the greatest morale builder in the European Theater of Operations." As he was flying to France on December 15, 1944, to entertain troops who had helped liberate Paris, Miller's single-engine military aircraft disappeared. It was never found. His official military status remains to this day: Missing in Action.[16]

Mess Attendant Third Class Doris Miller: "Dorie" Miller, from Waco, Texas, was aboard the USS *West Viginia* at Pearl Harbor when it was attacked by the Japanese on December 7, 1941. He became a naval hero after his efforts to save the injured captain of the ship and shoot down enemy planes. The Navy Cross citation read: ". . . distinguished devotion to duty, extraordinary courage and disregard of his personal safety during the attack on the Fleet in Pearl Harbor on 7 December

1941. While at the side of his Captain on the bridge, Miller, despite enemy strafing and bombing, and in the face of serious fire, assisted in moving his Captain, who had been mortally wounded, to a place of greater safety, and later manned and operated a machine gun . . . until ordered to leave the bridge."

He was awarded the Navy Cross by Admiral Chester W. Nimitz from Fredericksburg, Texas. The navy also promoted him to mess attendant first class. Unfortunately Doris Miller was killed in action when the USS *Liscome Bay* was sunk in November 1943 during operations in the Gilbert Islands.[17]

Jesse Owens: African-American athlete Jesse Owens won four gold medals at the 1936 Olympic Games in Berlin, Germany, upsetting and embarrassing Adolf Hitler and disproving the Führer's myth of Aryan superiority. Owens's achievement stood unequaled until the 1984 Olympic Games in Los Angeles, when American Carl Lewis matched Jesse's record. Owens spent the rest of his life working with underprivileged youth and helping others. President Gerald Ford presented him with the Medal of Freedom, the highest civilian honor in the United States. In February 1979, President Jimmy Carter presented him with the Living Legend Award. He was posthumously awarded the Congressional Gold Medal in 1990 by President George H. W. Bush. Owens died from complications owing to lung cancer on March 31, 1980, in Tucson, Arizona.

"Perhaps no athlete better symbolized the human struggle against tyranny, poverty, and racial bigotry," President Carter told the world. "His personal triumphs as a world-class athlete and record holder were the prelude to a career devoted to helping others. His work with young athletes, as an unofficial ambassador overseas and a spokesman for freedom, are a rich legacy to his fellow Americans."

Jesse's three daughters, Gloria, Marlene, and Beverly, are continuing with his work through the Jesse Owens Foundation.[18]

The Germans

Adolf Hitler: Hitler was born in Braunau am Inn, Austria, in 1889 and became the leader of the Nazi Party (1933–1945) and chancellor of Germany (1934–1945). After serving in World War I, he rose to power in the National Socialist German Workers Party, becoming one of the most powerful dictators of the twentieth century. Responsible for the deaths of more than six million Jews, and millions of non-Jews, he started World War II in 1939 when he attacked Poland. Germany occupied much of Europe and North Africa by 1941, but following his Russian invasion and the United States entering the war, his dictatorship began to decline. He married his mistress, Eva Braun, on April 29, 1945, dictated his final political testament, and shot and killed himself. Eva Braun also committed suicide. Their bodies were reported to be burned on the day of their mutual deaths. The Germanic Reich collapsed after Hitler's death, Nazi Germany surrendering on May 7, 1945.[19]

Propaganda Minister Joseph Goebbels: Born in the Rhineland on October 29, 1897, Goebbels was the master propagandist of the Nazi regime for twelve years. A foot deformity kept him out of the military during World War I. In the fall of 1924, Goebbels became district administrator of the Nationalsozialistische Deutsche Arbeiterpartei (NSDAP: the National Socialist German Workers' Party, or the Nazi Party). Impressed by his intellect and powerful organizational and verbal skills, Hitler appointed him in 1929 as Reich propaganda leader of the NSDAP. Goebbels became the creator of the Führer myth, painting Hitler in the image of a messiah-redeemer. Known for his hatred of Jews, he became one of the chief secret abettors of the Final Solution program. After Hitler's suicide on April 29, 1945, he poisoned his six children, and he and his wife took their own lives.[20]

Hermann Göring: Born in Rosenheim, Bavaria, on January 12, 1893, Göring was a decorated fighter pilot during World War I, joining the

Nazi Party in 1923 after hearing a speech by Adolf Hitler, and becoming part of Hitler's inner circle. He served as commander in chief of the Luftwaffe and director of the Four Year Plan in the German economy. He also took part in organizing the Final Solution program, setting up concentration camps and striving to eliminate Germany's and Europe's Jewish population. After the war, the International Military Tribunal, during the trials in Nuremberg, charged Göring with crimes against peace, war crimes, crimes against humanity, and conspiracy to commit crimes. Convicted and sentenced to death by hanging, on the eve of his execution in 1946 he killed himself in his prison cell.[21]

General der Fallschirmtruppe Hermann-Bernhard Ramcke: General Ramcke, born on January 24, 1889, in Schleswig-Friedrichsberg/Schleswig-Holstein, and married with seven children, entered the Imperial German Navy at age sixteen. Serving with distinction in World War I and World War II with the German Navy, Army, and Luftwaffe, Ramcke served as commandant of Fortress Brest, France, in August and September 1944, telling his men to defend the city to the "last grenade." After holding out against General Middleton's VIII Corps for over a month, the general surrendered on September 19, 1944. He was a prisoner of war from September 20, 1944, to June 23, 1951. He died at Kappelin/Schlei/Schleswig-Holstein on July 5, 1968, at age seventy-nine.[22]

Heinrich Luitpold Himmler, Reichsführer-SS and head of the Gestapo and Waffen-SS, was the Nazi organizer of the mass murder of Jews. He served as Nazi minister of the interior from 1943 to 1945. Born on October 7, 1900, in Munich, Germany, he set up the first concentration camp in Dachau in 1933. Hoping to create a race of German "supermen," he founded the breeding program Lebensborn ("wellspring of life") on December 12, 1935, selecting young German girls with Nordic traits to procreate with SS men. (Himmler's "Procreation Order" of October 28, 1939, directs: "SS-Men and you mothers of these children which Germany has hoped for, show that you are ready, through your faith in the Führer and for the sake of the life of our blood and people, to regenerate life for Germany just as bravely as you know how to fight and die for Germany.")[23]

On May 23, 1945, Himmler killed himself in Lunberg, Germany, to escape capture.[24, 25]

Field Marshal Gerd von Rundstedt: A member of an aristocratic Prussian family, born December 12, 1875, in Aschersleben, Germany, Rundstedt entered the Germany Army at age sixteen, serving as a captain in World War I. Throughout his life, he suffered with heart problems, leading to several heart attacks. Promoted to field marshal during World War II, he took part in the Battle of Britain, Operation Sea Lion, and Operation Barbarossa. Disobeying one of Hitler's commands regarding Rostov, Rundstedt was replaced by Field Marshal Walther von Reichenau. Advocating for peace after the German defeat near Caen on July 1, 1944, Rundstedt was removed from command and replaced with Field Marshal Gunther von Kluge. After the plot to kill Hitler on July 20, 1944, Rundstedt served on a court of honor to examine the Wehrmacht's loyalty to Hitler. He was opposed to Hitler's counterattack (resulting in the Battle of the Bulge). Captured by American troops in Bavaria on May 1, 1945, he was turned over to the British for trial, but, because of his poor health, his trial never took place, and he was released from a British military hospital four years later. He died on February 24, 1953, at age seventy-eight in Hanover, Germany.[26]

Field Marshal Walter Model: Born on January 24, 1891, Model joined the German Army in 1909, serving on the Western Front as part of the Fifth Division in World War I. In World War II, he fought in the attack on Poland, Western Europe, and the Soviet Union, commanding the Third Panzer Division. In 1942, Model was given the command of the Ninth Army, the Army Group North the next year, and promoted to field marshal on March 1, 1944. Model helped plan the Ardennes Offensive. He disbanded his army command on April 15, 1945, and rather than surrender to the Allies, he killed himself on April 21.[27]

Major Gustav Knittel: Born to a baker on November 27, 1914, in Neu-Ulm, Bavaria, Knittel joined the Nazi Party in 1934. Honored and decorated with numerous awards, Knittel also received the following promotions and commands:

- Adjutant, SS-Kradschützen-Reserve Battalion "Ellwangen," August 26, 1939–May 1940. He took part in the Battle for France, where he was wounded on June 19, 1940.
- Platoon Commander, 15 Company/LSSAH, May–August 1940.
- Commander, Fourth Company, First Reconnaissance Battalion LSSAH, August 19, 1940–March 1942. He took part in the attack on Yugoslavia, the Battle for Greece, and Operation Barbarossa in the Soviet Union. He was wounded on July 11, 1941.
- Commander, Third Company, First Reconnaissance Battalion LSSAH, March 1942–April 1943.
- Commander, First SS Panzer Reconnaissance Battalion LSSAH, April 1943–August 1944.
- Commander, SS Field Reserve Battalion LSSAH, September 1944–December 12, 1944.
- Commander, First SS Panzer Reconnaissance Battalion, First SS Panzer Division LSSAH, December 14, 1944–December 31, 1944. He was briefed on December 14, 1944, about his part in Operation Wacht am Rhein and ordered to capture a bridge across the Meuse River.

On December 16, the day of the offensive, Knittel marched over Holzheim, Hosingen, Honsfeld, and Born. On December 17, Knittel's men were believed to have murdered the eleven African-American soldiers at Wereth. After the war, he was sentenced to life imprisonment

(July 16, 1946), a sentence that was reduced to fifteen years, and again to twelve years. He was released from Landsberg Prison on December 7, 1953, working as a car salesman until retiring in 1970 with heart problems. He died on June 30, 1976, in Ulm Hospital.[28]

Colonel Joachim Peiper: Born on January 30, 1915, in Berlin, Peiper was a senior Waffen-SS officer and commander in the panzer campaigns of 1939–1945. He was the youngest regimental colonel in the Waffen-SS, serving as an adjutant on Heinrich Himmler's staff, and then commanding various panzer units within First SS Leibstandarte Adolf Hitler. Peiper was responsible for the massacres at Malmédy (December 17, 1944), where more than eighty American soldiers were shot and killed after they surrendered, and Stavelot, Belgium (December 18, 1944), where a hundred and thirty Belgian civilians were executed after being charged with sheltering American soldiers. At the end of the war, Peiper was found guilty of the massacres and, along with many of his men, sentenced to death by hanging. His sentence was later commuted to life imprisonment. He spent only eleven and a half years in prison and was released on parole in December 1956. After his release, he worked with Porsche in Stuttgart, later settling in Traves, Haute-Saône, France. On the night of July 13, 1976, his house was firebombed, burning him to death. His murderers, believed to be former French Resistance members, were never caught.[29, 30, 31]

General Hasso Eccard von Manteuffel: Born in Potsdam, Germany, in 1897, into a Prussian aristocractic family, Manteuffel joined the army as a cadet in 1915. During World War II, he took part in Operation Barbarossa (June 1941). In 1942, he was sent to Tunisia. In August 1943, he was given command of the Seventh Panzer Division. Serving in the Soviet Union, he captured Zhitomyr and was promoted to lieutenant general. In 1944, Manteuffel took command of the Fifth Panzer Army during the Battle of the Bulge. Manteuffel was forced to surrender to the U.S. Army on May 8, 1945. Held as a prisoner until

September 1947, he began a political career when released, serving as a member of the Bundestag for the Free Democratic Party from 1953 to 1957. Hasso Manteuffel died in Austria on September 28, 1978.[32]

General Josef Dietrich: Born on May 28, 1892, in a small village in Swabia, "Sepp" was a butcher's apprentice as a boy, joining the German Army in 1911 and rising to the rank of sergeant during World War I. A longtime friend of Adolf Hitler, and once serving as Hitler's bodyguard, Dietrich participated in France (1940), Yugoslavia, Greece, Russia, the German recapture of Kharkov, and the Battle of Normandy. A member of the Leibstandarte-SS Adolf Hitler, General Josef Sepp Dietrich commanded the Sixth Panzer Army during the Ardennes Offensive. His assignment was to move his divisions across the Schnee Eifel region and then capture the Belgian towns of Schönberg and Saint Vith. Although he was known for his bravery, his officers despised him, describing him as a man of "no great intelligence." He surrendered to General George C. Patton on May 8, 1945. For war crimes, he was sentenced to twenty-five years in prison. He was released, however, after serving only ten years of his sentence. In 1957, he was convicted of another war crime, serving another twenty months in prison. He died after a heart attack on April 21, 1966, in Ludwigsburg, West Germany. More than seven thousand comrades attended his funeral.[33]

Colonel Max Hansen: Born on July 31, 1908, in Niebüll, Germany, Hansen became one of the most highly decorated officers in the Waffen-SS. By 1939, he commanded the Twelfth Company in the Leibstandarte-SS Adolf Hitler, receiving a promotion to Sturmbannführer (major), and given command of the II/1st Panzergrenadier Regiment LSSAH. He was awarded the Knight's Cross after the Third Battle of Kharkov in March 1943, his battalion breaking through to Red Square in Kharkov. Later he commanded the First SS Panzergrenadier Regiment LSSAH, taking part in the Ardennes Offensive in 1944 and the offensive in Hungary, Operation Spring Awakening, in 1945. After the war, he settled in his hometown, Niebüll, and eventually ran a laundry. Alzheimer's overtook him later in life, and he died on March 7, 1990, at age eighty-one.[34]

Field Marshal Friedrich Wilhelm Ernst Paulus: Born in Breitenau, Germany, on September 23, 1890, Paulus joined the German Army in 1910 after the German Navy rejected him. During World War I, he served on the Eastern and Western Fronts. During World War II, he took part in the invasions of Poland, Belgium, France, and the Soviet Union. He was promoted to general in January 1942 and began an advance toward Stalingrad. Hitler had ordered Paulus to take Stalingrad, but bad weather, lack of food and supplies, and a counterattack by the Red Army prevented it. On January 30, 1943, Hitler promoted Paulus to field marshal. Paulus surrendered to the Red Army the next day. He turned against Hitler, becoming the spokesman of the Committee for a Free Germany, calling for the overthrow of Hitler and peace with the Allies. In the winter of 1953, Marshal Paulus was released from Soviet Union captivity, having been held prisoner in Moscow for a decade. He arrived in the city of Dresden in Soviet-occupied East Germany. Two years later, on February 1, 1957, at age sixty-seven, he died of amyelstrophic lateral sclerosis (motor neuron disease) in a Dresden clinic.[35]

General Friedrich Fromm: Born in Berlin on October 8, 1888, Fromm served in both World War I (as a lieutenant) and World War II. The commander of the German Home Army, General Fromm was a quiet conspirator in the assassination attempt of Adolf Hitler, lying about his involvement with Colonel Claus von Stauffenberg in the Valkyrie Conspiracy of July 20, 1944. General Fromm ordered the murder of four conspirators, including Stauffenberg, the man who planted the briefcase bomb under Hitler's table at the Wolf's Lair.

Adolf Hitler suspected that Fromm had a part in the conspiracy.

He ordered Heinrich Himmler to arrest him on July 21, 1944. Fromm was brought before the People's Court, charged with not reporting the conspiracy plot, found guilty, and executed (shot) on March 19, 1945.[36]

Major General Siegfried von Waldenburg: Born on December 30, 1898, Waldenburg entered World War I at age seventeen, becoming a soldier in the Emperor Alexander Grenadier Guards regiment on the Western Front. Wounded three times, he was awarded the Iron Cross First Class. The highly decorated commander of the 116th Panzer Division in World War II, honored by Hitler on December 11–12, 1944, at the Adlerhorst, died on March 27, 1973.[37]

Major General Baron Harald Gustav von Elverfeldt: Born in 1900 in Hildesheim and serving in both World War I and World War II, the German commander of the Ninth Panzer was honored by Hitler at the December 11–12, 1944, meeting at the Adlerhorst. Elverfeldt participated in the invasion of Poland, the Battle of France, Operation Barbarossa, the battles of Moscow, Rzhev, and Kursk, the Siegfried Line Campaign, the Battle of the Bulge, and the Western Allied invasion of Germany. Killed in action by Allied forces in March 1945, he was posthumously promoted to Generalleutnant.[38]

SS-Obersturmbannführer Otto Skorzeny: Skorzeny was considered the most dangerous man in Europe. Born on June 12, 1908, in Vienna, Austria, Skorzeny worked at the request of Adolf Hitler in Operation Greif, gathering a team of German imposters (English-speaking spies), dressing them in stolen American uniforms, infiltrating France before Hitler's Ardennes counterattack, and wreaking havoc on the Allies stationed there.[39]

Skorzeny's spies, when caught, were shot after a court-martial. Skorzeny always regarded the mission as a failure. Forty-four of the German imposters survived, returning to Germany. Eight were killed, and eighteen were captured and executed. The Dachau Military

Tribunal acquitted Skorzeny after the war. He escaped from his holding prison in 1948, fleeing to France and then to Spain. He died on
July 5, 1975.[40]

Others

Sir Winston Leonard Spencer Churchill: Churchill was a British
statesman and prime minister of the United Kingdom from 1940 to
1945, and again from 1951 to 1955. He was born to an aristocractic
family on November 30, 1874, in Blenheim Palace, U.K., served in the
British military, and worked as a journalist before beginning his political career. As prime minister during World War II, Winston Churchill worked with the U.S. and Russia, planning a successful Allied
strategy to defeat Germany, and led the British people to victory. He
died in London on January 24, 1965, at age ninety.[41]

Joseph Stalin (real name: Iosif Vissarionovich Dzhugashvili): Born
an only child to a poor alcoholic father in Gori, Georgia, on December 18, 1878, Joseph Stalin became the general secretary of the Central
Committee of the Communist Party of the Soviet Union from 1929
to 1953, coming to power after the death of Bolshevik leader Vladimir
Lenin. Stalin (who named himself the "Man of Steel") transformed
the Soviet Union from a peasant society into an industrial and military
superpower. Stalin had signed a nonaggression pact with Hitler in
1939, before World War II began. Germany broke the Nazi-Soviet
pact in June 1941 and invaded the USSR. The Red Army defeated the
Germans at the Battle of Stalingrad (August 1942 to February 1943).
An ally of Britain and the U.S. in World War II, Stalin developed a
strained, hostile relationship with the West (the Cold War) that lasted
from 1946 to 1991.

Stalin and his first wife, Ekaterina ("Kato"), had one son, Yakov,
born in 1907. Ekaterina died from typhus when Yakov was an infant.
Yakov died as a prisoner in Germany during World War II. Stalin's

second wife, Nadezhda, gave him two children, a boy and a girl. Nadezhda committed suicide in her early thirties.

Stalin ruled the USSR with terror. Millions of Soviet citizens died during his cruel regime. (Some estimate he is responsible for the deaths of twenty million people.) He suffered a stroke and died on March 5, 1953, at age seventy-four.[42]

Nina Stauffenberg and her children: Nina was the wife of Claus von Stauffenberg, who tried to assassinate Hitler on July 20, 1944. After the failed assassination attempt, Hitler rounded up almost five thousand Germans believed to be participants in the scheme. Wanting them to suffer a slow, agonizing death, Hitler ordered them hanged by the neck with piano wire from meat hooks. He also ordered that the Stauffenberg children, renamed "Meister," be put on a train and taken to the concentration camp at Buchenwald.

While waiting to be taken to Buchenwald, the children were cared for (until the spring of 1945) at Bad Sachsa, near Nordhausen, in a children's home run by a Nazi Party member. On Easter 1945, Berthold and his siblings, as well as the children of other conspirators, were loaded into an army truck headed toward Nordhausen Station and then on to Buchenwald.

But when they reached the town's suburbs, they encountered an Allied air raid that bombed and destroyed the station, as well as much of the town. Berthold saw the ensuing chaos and later heard about a Nazi official who tried to restore some order. The townspeople, having already lost much of their loyalty for Hitler's regime, captured and lynched the Nazi official.

Fortunately the children were driven back to Bad Sachsa after the raid interrupted their route to Buchenwald. On April 12, 1945, they watched the violent battles from their window as the American army fought and liberated the city.[43]

The Stauffenberg children survived. As an adult, Berthold followed in his father's footsteps, joining the German Army, always aware he lived under the shadow of his father's crime. He commanded a panzer brigade, rising to the head of the army and retiring in 1994.

Pregnant with her husband's child, Nina Stauffenberg was harshly interrogated by the Gestapo and sent to Ravensbrück, the concentration camp for women. She was released and in January 1945 gave birth to her fifth child at a maternity home in Frankfurt-on-the-Oder. She lived until her ninety-second year, dying in 2006.[44]

Dr. Theodor Morell: Dr. Morell was one of Hitler's personal physicians. Half Jewish and born in Munzenberg on July 22, 1890, he earned a medical degree and worked on a ship. Establishing a medical practice in Beth, he specialized in skin and venereal disease. Morell's treatments were unconventional, testing numerous unknown drugs on Hitler. He endured much criticism from others for the ways in which he treated Hitler's illnesses. Hitler, however, was devoted to him, completely trusting his treatments. Dr. Morell profited greatly from the promotion he received while treating Hitler, patenting new remedies, building factories, and amassing a fortune.

In May 1945, after Hitler's suicide, Dr. Morell told a newspaper reporter from the U.K. that he didn't believe Hitler killed himself because "Hitler is not that type." He had examined Hitler daily for nine years, admitting that Hitler "flew into rages . . . would go as white as a sheet and tightly clench his jaws, while his eyes would dilate. Everyone . . . would get panicky because these fits were always followed by an order to dismiss or to execute somebody."

Dr. Morell examined Hitler after the July 20, 1944, attempt on his life. He found Hitler sitting with singed hair, torn uniform, and blood on his face, banging his knees with both hands, saying, "Nothing can happen to me." He described Hitler as having a split personality, one half iron will, determination, forcefulness, and cruelty, the other uncertainty, fits of depression, and shyness, particularly with women.

Captured by the U.S. Army at the end of World War II, Morell was interrogated by British intelligence, charged with no crimes, and released. Dr. Morell died on May 26, 1948, at Tegernsee.[45]

Hitler's Alsatian, Blondi: The dog Hitler loved so much had been a gift to him. Blondi slept in his bedroom in the bunker during Hitler's final days in April 1945. Eva Braun did not share his devotion to Blondi, and would often kick the dog under the table. She preferred her two Scottish terriers, Negus and Stasi.

Before Hitler and Eva's suicide, a glass cyanide tablet was placed in Blondi's mouth, her jaw pushed down to break the glass. Hitler watched without emotion. Blondi had just delivered a litter of Alsatian puppies. Hitler's dog handler, Feldwebel Fritz Tornow, took Blondi's puppies outside the bunker and shot them.[46]

Additional Information

Executive Order 9066: The Detainment of Japanese-Americans in the United States: "President Franklin D. Roosevelt signed Executive Order 9066 on February 19, 1942, authorizing military leaders to detain Japanese-Americans in camps, en masse, without due process. Although the Department of Justice and the Federal Bureau of Investigation insisted that people of Japanese descent did not pose a security threat, the internment process began soon after President Roosevelt signed the order. In March 1942, the United States military ordered all individuals of Japanese ancestry residing on the West Coast to report to internment centers within seven days. This applied to more than 120,000 people, 70,000 of whom were American citizens."[47]

When the Japanese internment order was officially rescinded in January 1945, individuals were released from internment but received no compensation after the end of the war for lost property and mistreatment. Forty years later, in 1988, President Ronald Reagan signed an act apologizing for the internment, authorizing a twenty-thousand-dollar redress payment be made to each living internment survivor.[48]

The Role of Black Americans in World War II: African-Americans have volunteered to serve their country in times of war dating back to the American Revolution. More than 185,000 African-Americans served in the United States Colored Troops (USCT) during the Civil War. During World War I, after America's entry into the war, one million black Americans responded to their draft calls, with some 370,000 inducted into the army. For black Americans, fighting in the Great War offered them a chance to show their patriotism and improve their situations at home.

Black Americans in World War II fought battles on two fronts: the enemy overseas and racism at home. More than 2.5 million African-American men registered for the draft. Large numbers of black women also volunteered. They also served at home in many vital services. In the military, however, they faced continuing discrimination and segregation, many comparing the way Jews were treated in Germany to the way they were treated in America. The majority of black soldiers worked in service jobs, transporting supplies, burying the dead, digging ditches, cleaning latrines, working on docks, performing maintenance jobs, etc. However, by 1944, black soldiers, like the 333rd and 969th Field Artillery Battalions and others, were involved in combat. By 1945, the military placed more African-American troops in positions as infantrymen, tankers, medics, pilots, and officers.

World War II helped lay the foundation for postwar integration in the military.[49]

The Problems of Frostbite and Trench Foot: Frostbite happens when the skin and underlying tissues freeze, occurring most frequently to the fingers, toes, nose, ears, cheeks, and chin. It was especially common during the winter months of World War I and World War II when GIs spent time outside at the mercy of dropping temperatures, snow, and sleet. Frostbite can cause infection, nerve damage, various degrees of pain, and numbness, and in severe cases can result in amputation.

Trench foot caused the soldiers many problems during World War II, developing when their feet were exposed to damp, cold, and unsanitary conditions as well as ill-fitting footwear. Trench foot caused the soldiers' feet to swell, go numb, and be painful. Untreated, it often led to gangrene and amputation.[50]

APPENDIX 1

THE WERETH 11 MEMORIAL SPEECH: "THE BOYS OF SAINT VITH" BY ROBERT R. HUDSON JR., SEPTEMBER 26, 2009, BELGIUM

"Good day, ladies and gentlemen, citizens of Belgium and Europe, veterans, survivors, patriots, relatives, and distinguished U.S. military personnel. It is a tremendous honor for me to speak to you today, for I am the son of Robert R. Hudson Sr., corporal, U.S. Army, 333rd Field Artillery Battalion C, and I am here to tell my father's story of captivity by Axis forces and to honor all Black GIs of World War II whose experiences are symbolized by the tragedy of the Wereth 11 massacre.

"We're also here to remember that year in history when the Allied armies joined in battle to reclaim this continent to liberty. For four long years, much of Europe had been under a terrible shadow. Free nations had fallen, Jews suffered and died in camps, and millions cried out for liberation. Europe was enslaved, and the world prayed for its rescue. It was here in Belgium that the final rescue began. Here the Allies stood and fought against tyranny in an epic battle. Here the fate of the Second World War hung in the balance. Here the Battle of the Bulge was both decisive and consequential.

"We stand today in the beautiful Liège province of Belgium where the air is soft. Sixty-five years ago in December 1944, the air was dense with smoke, the ground was soaked with blood and guts, and the only sounds were the screams of men, the crack of rifle fire, and the roar of tanks and artillery.

"In late 1944, Hitler hatched a desperate plot, one last giant offensive to turn the tide of the war—an all-out counteroffensive to split the Allied armies in half by capturing the strategic port of Antwerp. This effort was led by General Walther Model, known as 'Hitler's Father' because of his ruthless prosecution of prior military campaigns.

"Let's go back in time as these events happened through my father's recollection. On December fifteenth, the 333rd Field Artillery had been relaxing in the vicinity of Saint Vith. They watched a Marlene Dietrich movie that evening and were in good spirits. They were looking forward to Christmas Day and anticipating large turkey dinners being delivered to them. Their commanders were comfortable with the knowledge that no army had ever mounted an armored attack at night through a forest—in particular, a forest as dense and as steep as the Ardennes.

"Little did my dad's small battalion of approximately a hundred and fifteen men realize as they slept the night of December 15, 1944, that fate had dealt them a bad hand. They had no forewarning that a mere stone's throw away from them stood a quarter million elite German troops—specifically three German armies, including two armor divisions. Little did they know that by morning they would be in the meat grinder of the Wehrmacht war machines with no armor cover of their own.

"On December 16, 1944, just before dawn, German Field Artillery laid down on my dad's unit a forty-eight-hour-long raging storm of fire. After the second day of shelling, out of the morning mist, my dad's unit heard an awful roar—falling trees, the shaking earth, the sound of armor approaching, tracks rumbling, an incessant squeaking noise of gears and the clash of tanks' guns. In moments they were face-to-face with massive German Tiger tanks annihilating them with turret blasts followed by ruthless Panzergrenadiers on half-tracks, wiping out everything in sight. My dad heard the horrific screams of his best friend, Lester, as he was eviscerated by machine-gun fire. Dad was seriously wounded by mortar fragments and was bleeding profusely from ear and leg wounds. Dazed and confused, he was captured by the Germans. They pointed to the medic cot, and he crawled to it with his limited strength. He later recalled to me that all men who were not able to crawl to a cot were shot.

"Dad was treated aboard a German Red Cross hospital train. He was taken to Stalag VI C near Bremen, Germany. At the German prison camp he was fed only grass soup, four small potatoes, and three slices of black bread daily, and was cuffed about by guards. He bartered his Red Cross cigarettes with the German guards for additional food. My dad was liberated by the British in April 1945, ultimately returning to the U.S., where he married my mother, his high school sweetheart, in 1946. Dad passed away in 1995. My mother is now eighty-seven years old and lives close to me in Chicago. I am their only son.

"Sixty-five summers have passed since the battle was fought here. Most of my dad's GI friends have faded away. . . . When I think about Dad's GI buddies, I realize that they were hardly more than boys with the deepest joys of life before them. Yet they risked everything here. Why did they do it? What compelled them to put aside the instinct for self-preservation and risk their lives? What inspired all of the men that fought here?

"I have thought about those questions all my life, and only now do I know the answers. It was faith and belief. It was loyalty, love, and optimism. The Black GIs and specifically the Wereth 11 of the segregated 333rd Field Artillery should not be enlarged more in death than they were in life. They were simple men with a simple faith that what they were doing was right, faith in their fight for all humanity. Faith that a just God would grant them mercy on this battlefield or on the next. To them, uncommon valor was a common virtue.

"In addition, it was their deep knowledge that there is a difference between the use of force for liberation and the use of force for conquest. I worry sometimes today that nations forget this lesson.

"They all knew some things were worth dying for. One's country is worth dying for and democracy is worth dying for, because, despite its imperfections, it is the most deeply honorable form of government ever devised by man.

"It is ironic that these Black GIs fought for freedom on foreign soil despite the fact that they faced racial segregation at home and on the battlefield. They did not share first-class citizenship with their white comrades, yet they bled and died for the same flag. They knew from their personal experiences that, as long as one person is enslaved, none of mankind is free. They remained optimistic about the future and the ultimate triumph of the human spirit.

"It must be said that in all the annals of human conflict, Black GIs have always been patriotic. They have always been willing to make the ultimate sacrifice on foreign soil. The only thing they have ever asked our nation is that no man be left behind. The only soil they have ever desired in battle was enough to bury those who could not return home.

". . . As we think about this place where the Allied forces held together, let us make a vow to our dead. Let us show them by our actions that we understand what they died for. These soldiers fought for universal values which transcend place and time. When the eyes of the world were upon them, when the hopes and prayers of liberty-loving people marched with them: They accepted nothing less than full victory; they refused to shrink beneath the level of events; and they nudged history in the right direction. Let us continue to stand for the ideals for which they lived and died.

"Thank you very much, and God bless you."

(Robert Hudson Jr. delivered this address at the 2009 Wereth 11 Memorial in Wereth, Belgium. Hudson is a senior business executive, with extensive work history in manufacturing, distribution, logistics, and nonprofit consults, working with Inland Steel, A.M. Castle, U.S. Foodservice, and ADS Logistics, where he served as vice president, division vice president, president, and board member, respectively. Bob is a past president of the Delta Institute, a nonprofit organization focused on the creation of green jobs. Bob is currently a board member of the Chicago Social Enterprise Alliance and a senior adviser for G2 Capital Advisors, a corporate restructuring firm based in Boston, Massachusetts. Bob has a BS in economics from Fisk University and an MBA in finance from Atlanta University.

Bob Hudson's father, Corporal Robert Rolland Hudson Sr., served in Battalion C, 333rd Field Artillery Battalion.)[1]

APPENDIX 2

U.S. MEMORIAL WERETH
INFO ABOUT MEMORIAL AND
ANNUAL SERVICES, ETC.

U.S. Memorial Wereth Staff Members (June 25, 2015)

HONORARY MEMBERS
Hermann Langer (deceased 6/21/2013)
Katharina Langer
Mathilde Langer

ADMINISTRATOR DELEGATES
Beatrix Langer (Treasurer)
Silvia Langer
Patrick Langer (Vice President)

ADMINISTRATORS
Solange Dekeyser (President/Secretary)
Marion Freyaldenhoven
Thierry Mercier

MEMBERS
Alois Hennes
Willy Rikken
Heinz Lentz

ACKNOWLEDGMENTS

A huge heartfelt thank-you to Harlan Hobart Grooms Jr., colonel, U.S. Marine Corps Reserve (Ret.), former president of the Birmingham Bar Association, Birmingham, Alabama, for bringing the men of the 333rd Field Artillery Battalion to my attention, suggesting we write the book, finding the right books to study, and offering his expertise of all things military as well as editoral. I am deeply indebted to Colonel Grooms for his help with this project.

Thank you to Rebecca Pounds George, my daughter-in-law, who helped me with research at the Eisenhower Library in Abilene, Kansas.

My gratitude to my book agent, Greg Johnson, president of WordServe Literary and FaithHappenings, for all the wonderful work he does on my behalf; to the fabulous people at Penguin Random House, especially my editor, Allison Janice, and all those who worked on this book.

A special note of gratitude to Dr. Fred Moss, who lent me valuable books from his personal library; to friends who encouraged me throughout the writing, including my mother, Willene Williams Wyse; to my son, Dr. Christian George; to my daughter, Alyce Elizabeth George; to Carolyn Tomlin; to Pat Batson; to Doris Hughston; to Dr. Lucien Coleman; and to many others.

I can't begin to thank my husband, Dr. Timothy F. George, founding dean of Beeson Divinity School, Samford University, Birmingham, Alabama, and the author of more than thirty books. He gave me much help, and showed great understanding, throughout the process of putting together a book of this magnitude.

I also want to say a word of gratitude to my dad, Robert C. Wyse (1927–1999), for his six years of service during World War II, in both the Pacific and Europe.

And thank you to Robert Child, my coauthor, who was a joy to work with.

Denise George

At this writing I have been involved with the "Wereth Story" for more than seven years. And I owe a debt of gratitude to a number of people, beginning with Norman Lichtenfeld. Norman was the man who contacted me originally about the Wereth 11 back in 2009, urging me to write and direct a film on the story. Norman also introduced me to Joseph Small, the visionary producer of the film *Wereth Eleven*.

I owe a sincere debt of gratitude to Joe for his tireless pursuit of the truth in the story. He and Joe Springer were responsible for securing many of the government records and much of the backstory on who these men were.

On that note I want to acknowledge my London-based crew, Jamie Hobbis, Robert Linnell, Tim Deacon, and Sam Howson, who helped bring the documentary version of this story to life. In addition, I must mention Jonathan Gibson and Frederic Lumiere, who were integral to the effort.

Heartfelt thanks go out to George Shomo of the 333rd FAB. It was a distinct honor and pleasure to know him. He epitomized the no-nonsense courageous soldier of World War II.

I would also like to thank my wonderful friends in Belgium who maintain the memorial and who have made certain this story is not forgotten. It was an honor to get to know Herman and Tina Langer and the entire Langer family, who still own the home in Wereth that sheltered the eleven soldiers. Other folks in Belgium whom I must acknowledge include Solange Dekeyser, president of U.S. Memorial Wereth, who helped so much with organizing the information, and Patrick Langer for securing the photos of the home as well as his family.

I would also like to make special mention of Erwin Peters, who was my military guide in Belgium, and who led us on the trail retracing the steps of the eleven men. His contributions were invaluable.

A special note of gratitude goes out to Robert Hudson Jr., Robert DeShay, and Robert Shomo, who shared the stories of their fathers' harrowing experiences in the 333rd.

I also have to mention T. J. Colemen, a veteran who has worked tirelessly in West Virginia to make sure James Aubury Stewart's life and service are not forgotten.

And last, but certainly not least, I would like to sincerely thank my coauthor, Denise George, for her talent and efforts in raising the bar on the telling of this story. I know it will touch many people for generations to come.

Robert Child

"These brave soldiers . . . did not have an opportunity to see the world that they aimed to create. Yet, because of their actions, we enjoy the world they envisioned, the world they fought for. These men were brothers, sons, and fathers. They served because, like us, they believed in the values we hold dear—freedom, justice, liberty. They believed in the greater good. For this, we are thankful for their service."

General Dennis Via, speaking about the lost eleven men at a memorial ceremony in Wereth[1]

ENDNOTES

PART 1

1 Quoted from: http://www.nationalww2museum.org/assets/pdfs/african-americans-in-world .pdf. Accessed: October 3, 2015.

CHAPTER 2

1 Some information found at: http://timesmachine.nytimes.com/timesmachine/1936/07 /13/93523339.html?pageNumber=10. Accessed: November 30, 2015.

2 Quoted from: http://timesmachine.nytimes.com/timesmachine/1936/07/13/93523339 .html?pageNumber=10. Accessed: November 30, 2015.

3 Quote found at: https://www.jewishvirtuallibrary.org/jsource/Holocaust/olympics.html. Accessed: October 17, 2015.

CHAPTER 3

1 *New York Times*, Monday, August 3, 1936. Found at: http://timesmachine.nytimes.com /timesmachine/1936/08/03/93526149.html?pageNumber=19. Accessed: November 30, 2015.

2 Quoted from: https://www.jewishvirtuallibrary.org/jsource/Holocaust/olympics.html. Accessed: October 17, 2015.

3 Ten African-American athletes were 1936 Olympic medalists: David Albritton (high jump, silver), Cornelius Johnson (high jump, gold), James LuValle (400-meter run, bronze), Ralph Metcalfe (4 x 100-meter relay, gold; 100-meter dash, silver), Jesse Owens (100-meter dash, gold; 200-meter dash, gold; broad long jump, gold; 4 x 100-meter relay, gold), Frederick Pollard Jr. (100-meter hurdles, bronze), Matthew Robinson (200-meter dash, silver), Archie Williams (400-meter run, gold), Jack Wilson (bantam-weight boxing, silver), and John Woodruff (800-meter run, gold). Found at: https:// www.jewishvirtuallibrary.org/jsource/Holocaust/olympics.html; http://www .jesseowens.com/about/; https://www.jewishvirtuallibrary.org/jsource/Holocaust /olympics.html; http://www.historyplace.com/worldwar2/triumph/tr-olympics.htm. Accessed: October 17, 2015.

CHAPTER 4

1 Some information found at: https://en.wikipedia.org/wiki/Bessemer,_Alabama; http:// blog.al.com/spotnews/2013/04/bessemer_historical_society_to.html; https://www.flickr

.com/photos/cdjunkie/12806286625/; and http://www.encyclopediaofalabama.org
/article/h-2328. Accessed: October 4, 2015.

2 Found at: http://www.searsarchives.com/people/juliusrosenwald.htm. Accessed: October 2, 2015.

CHAPTER 5

1 Adolf Hitler, *New York Times*, Sunday, September 3, 1933. Found at: http://timesmachine
.nytimes.com/timesmachine/1933/09/03/issue.html. Accessed: November 30, 2015.

2 Attending the meeting are: Colonel Count Friedrich Hossbach (Hitler's military adjutant); Baron Konstantin von Neurath (Reich foreign minister); Field Marshal Werner von Blomberg (Reich war minister); General Werner Freiherr von Fritsch (commander in chief of the armed forces); Admiral Erich Raeder (commander in chief of the navy [Kriegsmarine]); and Hitler's close confidant, Hermann Göring (commander in chief of the Luftwaffe).

3 Scholars have argued and disagreed for decades about the primary purpose of this meeting, as well as the discussions that took place. The Hossbach Memorandum was written five days after the conference, on November 10, 1937, and was used as evidence on November 24, 1945, during the Nuremberg Trials.

4 Some information found at: r.org/jhr/v04/v04p372_Weber.html; http://avalon.law.yale.edu
/imt/hossbach.asp; and http://www.historylearningsite.co.uk/world-war-two/causes
-of-ww2/the-hossbach-conference-of-1937/. All accessed: November 26, 2015.

CHAPTER 6

1 Some information found at: http://www.historynet.com/negro-league; and http://www
.wvculture.org/history/wvmemory/vets/Sergeant Stewartjames/Sergeant Stewartjames
.html. Accessed: November 26, 2015.

CHAPTER 7

1 Attending the meeting are: Wilhelm Keitel (chief of the High Command), Walter von Reichenau (commander of army troops along the German-Austrian border), Hugo Sperrle (air force general), and Joachim von Ribbentrop (Germany's new foreign minister).

2 *New York Times*, Tuesday, February 6, 1934. Found at: http://timesmachine.nytimes
.com/timesmachine/1934/02/06/94490678.html?pageNumber=20. Accessed: November 30, 2015.

3 Quoted from: *New York Times*, Sunday, February 20, 1938. Found at: http://timesmachine
.nytimes.com/timesmachine/1938/02/20/issue.html. Accessed: November 30, 2015.

CHAPTER 8

1 *New York Times*, Friday, August 5, 1938. Found at: http://timesmachine.nytimes.com
/timesmachine/1938/08/05/98174369.html?pageNumber=9. Accessed: November 30, 2015.

2 Information found at: http://www.ushmm.org/outreach/en/article.php?ModuleId
=10007698. Accessed: November 26, 2015.

3 Some information found at: http://www.history.com/this-day-in-history/germany
-annexes-austria; and http://www.historyplace.com/worldwar2/triumph/tr-austria.htm.
Accessed: November 26, 2015.

CHAPTER 9

1 Prayer found at: http://www.catholic.org/prayers/prayer.php?p=2727. Accessed:
November 28, 2015.

2 Found at: https://www.quora.com/why-did-time-magazine-designate-hitler-1938-and
-stalin-1939-and-1942-time-person-of-the-year; and http://content.time.com/time/mag
azine/article/0,9171,760539,00.html. Accessed: October 17, 2015.

CHAPTER 10

1 *New York Times.* Found at: http://timesmachine.nytimes.com/timesmachine/1940/09
/01/113103600.html?pageNumber=50. Accessed: November 30, 2015.

2 Quoted from: http://www.historyplace.com/worldwar2/holocaust/timeline.html. Accessed: October 17, 2015.

3 Some information found at: http://www.ushmm.org/wlc/en/article.php?ModuleId
=10005070; http://www.history.com/this-day-in-history/germany-invades-poland; http://
www.yadvashem.org/yv/en/holocaust/about/01/crucial_year.asp; http://www.historyplace
.com/worldwar2/holocaust/timeline.html; http://www.ushmm.org/wlc/en/article.php?
moduleid=10007762; http://www.ushmm.org/learn/timeline-of-events/1933-1938; http://
www.ushmm.org/learn/timeline-of-events/1939-1941; and http://www.ushmm.org/wlc
/en/article.php?ModuleId=10007761. Accessed: October 17, 2015. Information also found
at: http://www.history.com/this-day-in-history/germany-invades-poland. Accessed:
November 26, 2015.

4 The Battle of the Atlantic began on September 3, 1939, when Britain and France entered
the war, and the Kriegsmarine began its campaign against Allied supply ships in the
Atlantic. German U-boats ("Wolf Packs") inflicted heavy losses. It ended on May 8,
1945. Found at: http://militaryhistory.about.com/od/worldwari1/p/World
-War-II-Battle-Of-The-Atlantic.htm. Accessed: January 29, 2016.

5 Found at: http://digitalcommons.conncoll.edu/cgi/viewcontent.cgi?article=1005&
context=histhp&sei-redir=1&referer=http%3A%2F%2F; and www.google.com%
2Fsearch%3Fclient%3Dsafari%26rls%3Den%26q%3Dwhat%2Bdid%2Bpoor%2BBel
giums%2Beat%2Bin%2B1940%253F%26ie%3DUTF-8%26oe%3DUTF-8#search=%
22what%20did%20poor%20Belgiums%20eat%201940%3F%22. Accessed: July 22, 2015.

6 Found at: http://ww2db.com/country/Belgium. Accessed: October 8, 2015.

7 The Dunkirk Evacuation took place between May 25, 1940, and June 4, 1940. German
panzers had secretly moved through the dense forests of the Ardennes, surprising the
Allies and driving them to Dunkirk, pushing the Allies out of northern France on June
4, 1940. The Allies successfully evacuated more than 330,000 troops using a fleet of
destroyers, merchant ships, and hundreds of small boats. British losses in men, equipment,
and supplies proved unusually heavy. Found at: http://militaryhistory.about.com/od
/worldwarii/p/dunkirk.htm. Accessed: January 29, 2016.

8 *New York Times*, Saturday, May 11, 1940. Found at: http://timesmachine.nytimes.com/timesmachine/1940/05/11/92973383.html?pageNumber=6. Accessed: November 30, 2015.

CHAPTER 11

1 Found at: https://en.wikipedia.org/wiki/Gustav_Knittel. Accessed: October 15, 2015.

2 Information from: Butler, Rupert. *SS-Liebstandarte: The History of the First SS Division 1933–45*. St. Paul, MN: MBI Publishing Company, 2001, p. 61.

3 Information from Butler, Rupert. *SS-Liebstandarte: The History of the First SS Division 1933–45*. St. Paul, MN: MBI Publishing Company, 2001, p. 63.

4 Found at: https://www.jewishvirtuallibrary.org/jsource/biography/Dietrich.html. Accessed: January 27, 2016.

5 Found at: http://www.historylearningsite.co.uk/world-war-two/famous-battles-of-world-war-two/the-battle-of-the-bulge/sepp-dietrich/. Accessed: October 7, 2015.

6 Found at: http://www.imdb.com/name/nm0226281/bio. Accessed: July 27, 2015; and http://militaryhistory.about.com/od/aerialcampaigns/a/battle-of-britain.htm. Accessed: January 29, 2016.

7 Some information found at: Peter Caddick-Private Adams. *Snow & Steel: The Battle of the Bulge, 1944–45*. Oxford, England: Oxford University Press, 2015, p. 236.

8 Some information found at: https://books.google.com/books?id=NKj0BwAAQBAJ&pg=PA406&lpg=PA406&dq=Jochen+Peiper+bio&source=bl&ots=nC8hTpcs_8&sig=zymbUu8Gr8TNWFA0uPCFF0gHF54&hl=en&sa=X&ved=0ahUKEwiNyKX3x8rKAhUDcD4KHfspD6s4FBDoAQhHMAc#v=onepage&q=Sigurd&f=false. Accessed: January 27, 2016.

9 "Peiper was the most dynamic man I ever met," writes Hans Hennecke. "He just got things done . . . He was mature, spoke languages, was clever." Found at: Peter Caddick-Private Adams. *Snow & Steel: The Battle of the Bulge, 1944–45*. Oxford, England: Oxford University Press, 2015, p. 246.

CHAPTER 12

1 Found at: http://timesmachine.nytimes.com/timesmachine/1941/09/18/issue.html. Accessed: November 30, 2015.

2 Three days after the signing, Hitler destroyed the 1918 Armistice site, taking the famed railway car to Berlin as a trophy of war. It was moved to Crawinkel in Thuringia in 1945; SS troops demolished the car and buried the remains. Found at: https://en.wikipedia.org/wiki/Armistice_of_22_June_1940#Destruction_of_the_armistice_site_in_Compi.C3.A8gne. Accessed: November 27, 2015.

3 Found at: http://learning.blogs.nytimes.com/2011/06/22/june-22-1940-hitler-gains-victory-over-france/?_r=0. Accessed: October 7, 2015.

4 Found at: http://www.eyewitnesstohistory.com/hitlerparis.htm. Accessed: July 27, 2015.

5 Found at: http://www.eyewitnesstohistory.com/hitlerparis.htm. Accessed: July 27, 2015.

6 The German-Soviet nonaggression pact was signed on August 23, 1939. Found at: http://www.ushmm.org/wlc/en/article.php?ModuleId=10005164. Accessed: January 14, 2016.

7 Hitler's siege of Leningrad on the Eastern Front began on September 8, 1941, and ended on January 27, 1944. Found at: http://militaryhistory.about.com/od/worldwarii /a/world-war-2-battles.htm. Accessed: January 29, 2016.

8 Some information found at: http://militaryhistory.about.com/od/WWIIEasternFront /p/World-War-Ii-Battle-Of-Moscow.htm; http://www.ushmm.org/outreach/en/article .php?ModuleId=10007681. Accessed: October 7, 2015.

9 Some information found at: http://www.yivoencyclopedia.org/article.aspx/Zhytomyr. Accessed: October 11, 2015.

10 Found at: http://www.ww1battlefields.co.uk/somme/albert.html. Accessed: October 7, 2015.

11 Note: German soldiers believed that the war wouldn't end until the statue fell. The Golden Virgin held her child above the Basilica until the Germans advanced into Albert during their Spring Offensive in 1918. British artillery destroyed the statue for fear the Germans might use it as an observation point. The Basilica of Notre-Dame de Brebières was rebuilt after the war, and the golden Madonna and child restored. Found at: http:// www.ww1battlefields.co.uk/somme/albert.html; and http://www.1914-1918.net/battle field_somme.html. Accessed: July 31, 2015.

12 Some information found at: https://en.wikipedia.org/wiki/Oberst; and https://en.wiki pedia.org/wiki/Hasso_von_Manteuffel. Accessed: October 12, 2015.

13 To read the entire article, please see: http://research.calvin.edu/german -propaganda-archive/goeb15.htm.

14 Quoted from: http://research.calvin.edu/german-propaganda-archive/goeb15.htm. Accessed: December 5, 2015.

CHAPTER 13

1 Found at: http://timesmachine.nytimes.com/timesmachine/1948/01/25/86014414.html? pageNumber=105. Accessed: November 30, 2015.

2 Found at: http://www.ushmm.org/wlc/en/article.php?ModuleId=10005164; and http:// news.bbc.co.uk/onthisday/hi/dates/stories/june/22/newsid_3526000/3526691.stm. Ac- cessed: October 10, 2015.

3 Quote found at: http://www.secondworldwarhistory.com/soviet-offensive-the-battle -for-russia.asp. Accessed: October 11, 2015.

4 Found at: http://news.bbc.co.uk/onthisday/hi/dates/stories/june/22/newsid_3526000 /3526691.stm. Accessed: October 10, 2015.

5 For more details about the battles, please see the timeline at: http://ww2db.com /battle_spec.php?battle_id=37. Accessed: October 11, 2015.

6 Found at: http://ww2db.com/battle_spec.php?battle_id=37; and http://news.bbc.co.uk/on thisday/hi/dates/stories/june/22/newsid_3526000/3526691.stm. Accessed: October 11, 2015.

7 Found at: http://militaryhistory.about.com/od/WWIIEasternFront/p/World -War-Ii-Battle-Of-Moscow.htm. Accessed: December 1, 2015.

8 The Battle of Moscow began on October 2, 1941 and ended on January 7, 1942.

PART 2

1 Quoted from: http://www.post-gazette.com/news/nation/2011/12/25/Christmas-1941
-With-world-at-war-Churchill-joins-FDR-for-Washington-Yule/stories/201112250236.
Accessed: October 2, 2015.

CHAPTER 14

1 Some information found at: http://www.blackpast.org/aah/miller-doris-dorie-1919–1943.
Accessed: October 3, 2015; and http://www.usswestvirginia.org/veterans/personalpage
.php?id=241. Accessed: October 4, 2015.

2 Found at: http://www.history.com/topics/world-war-ii/pearl-harbor. Accessed: October
3, 2015; and http://www.history.com/this-day-in-history/fdr-reacts-to-news-of-pearl
-harbor-bombing. Accessed: October 3, 2015.

CHAPTER 15

1 Some information found at: http://www.thirdreichruins.com/wolfschanze.htm; http://
wolfschanze.pl/index.php/history. Accessed: December 5, 2015.

2 Quoted from: http://www.history.co.uk/study-topics/history-of-ww2/pearl-harbor.
Accessed: December 5, 2015.

3 The agreement was called the Tripartite Pact. Found at: http://www.historyplace.com
/worldwar2/defeat/america-enters.htm; http://rarehistoricalphotos.com/the-speech-where
-adolf-hitler-declared-war-on-the-usa-1941/; and http://historynewsnetwork.org/article
/32084. Accessed: October 10, 2015.

CHAPTER 16

1 Found at: http://www.let.rug.nl/usa/presidents/franklin-delano-roosevelt/pearl-harbor
-speech-december-8-1941.php. Accessed: July 3, 2015.

2 "Roll, Jordan, Roll" was written by Charles Wesley in the eighteenth century. It became
a well-known song among slaves in the nineteenth century. Found at: https://en.wiki
pedia.org/wiki/Roll,_Jordan,_Roll. Accessed: December 18, 2015.

3 Found at: http://www.encyclopediaofalabama.org/article/h-1460. Accessed: October 2,
2015.

4 Found at: http://www.encyclopediaofalabama.org/article/h-1460. Accessed: October 2,
2015.

5 Found at: http://examples.yourdictionary.com/examples-of-jim-crow-laws.html.
Accessed: October 2, 2015.

CHAPTER 17

1 Found at: http://www.historyplace.com/worldwar2/defeat/america-enters.htm. Accessed:
October 10, 2015.

2 Found at: http://www.historyplace.com/worldwar2/defeat/america-enters.htm. Accessed:
October 10, 2015.

3 From: "Verändertes Weltbild," *Das eherne Herz* (Munich: Zentralverlag der NSDAP, 1943), pp. 124–130. Information found at and quoted from: http://research.calvin.edu /german-propaganda-archive/goeb7.htm. Accessed: December 5, 2015.

4 Quoted from: http://www.winstonchurchill.org/resources/speeches/802-christmas. Accessed: March 10, 2016.

CHAPTER 18

1 Found at: http://research.calvin.edu/german-propaganda-archive/goeb34.htm. Accessed: October 3, 2015.

2 Found at: http://www.eisenhowerinstitute.org/about/living_history/wwii_soviet _experience.dot. Accessed: October 3, 2015.

3 Some information and quotes found at: http://www.history.com/news/history-lists /8-things-you-should-know-about-wwiis-eastern-front. Accessed: October 3, 2015.

4 Found at: http://www.telegraph.co.uk/history/world-war-two/8978732/Images -of-Adolf-Hitler-celebrating-Christmas-emerge.html; and http://io9.com/5970184 /this-nazi-christmas-party-must-have-been-the-worst-ever. Accessed: October 11, 2015.

5 Quoted from: http://www.history.army.mil/books/amh-v2/amh%20v2/chapter3.htm. Accessed: December 6, 2015.

6 Information found at: http://www.history.army.mil/books/amh-v2/amh%20v2/chapter3 .htm. Accessed: December 6, 2015.

7 Found at and quoted from: http://www.post-gazette.com/news/nation/2011/12/25 /Christmas-1941-With-world-at-war-Churchill-joins-FDR-for-Washington-Yule /stories/201112250236. Accessed: October 2, 2015.

8 Found at: http://www.history.army.mil/books/amh-v2/amh%20v2/chapter3.htm. Accessed: December 6, 2015.

9 Some information found at: http://www.nationalww2museum.org/learn/education /for-students/ww2-history/america-goes-to-war.html. Accessed: October 3, 2015.

10 Found at: http://www.nationalww2museum.org/assets/pdfs/african-americans-in-world .pdf. Accessed: October 3, 2015.

11 Quoted from the United States Military. Found at: http://www.nps.gov/malu/forteachers /jim_crow_laws.htm. Accessed: December 22, 2014.

12 Found at: http://www.nationalww2museum.org/assets/pdfs/african-americans-in-world .pdf. Accessed: October 3, 2015.

CHAPTER 19

1 Found at: https://en.wikipedia.org/wiki/Richard_W._Leche. Accessed: July 17, 2015.

2 Information found at: http://www.jstor.org/stable/4233092?seq=1#page_scan_tab _contents; http://library.duke.edu/rubenstein/uarchives/history/articles/rose-bowl; and http://mentalfloss.com/article/29618/after-pearl-harbor-rose-bowl-was-forced -relocate-—-north-carolina. Accessed: October 1, 2015.

3 Found at: https://news.google.com/newspapers?nid=2211&dat=19420124&id
   =9epfAAAAIBAJ&sjid=QgMGAAAAIBAJ&pg=4200,5048139&hl=en. Accessed:
   September 19, 2015.

4 Found at: http://www.blackpast.org/aah/pittsburgh-courier-1907. Accessed: July 15,
   2015.

5 Some information found at: http://www.blackpast.org/aah/pittsburgh-courier-1907.
   Accessed: July 15, 2015.

6 You can read Thompson's original letter, published in the *Pittsburgh Courier* on January
   31, 1942, at this Web site: http://www.learner.org/courses/amerhistory
   /resource_archive/resource.php?unitChoice=19&ThemeNum=3&resourceType=2&
   resourceID=10106.

7 Some information about the Lee Street Riots found at: https://alexcenla.wordpress.com/
   2009/05/25/lee-street-riot-lets-set-the-record-straight-what-really-happened/; and
   https://books.google.com/books?id=_BSfa33RD1UC&pg=PA27&lpg=PA27&dq=the+
   lee+street+riots&source=bl&ots=LLk1yeEnVK&sig=eZ0yzWbZuD6ruG8
   Unsj5W7H54i8&hl=en&sa=X&ei=dXqZVdzvEoTAsAXska-ICw&ved=0CCYQ
   6AEwAw#v=onepage&q=the%20lee%20street%20riots&f=false. Accessed: July 14,
   2015.

CHAPTER 20

1 Found at: http://www.3riversmuseum.com/camp-gruber-the-war-years.html. Accessed:
   July 20, 2015.

CHAPTER 21

1 Some sources estimate between 70,000 and 90,000 Jews lived in Belgium at that time.
   Found at: http://www.ushmm.org/wlc/en/article.php?ModuleId=10005432; https://
   books.google.com/books?id=VOJpAgAAQBAJ&pg=PA22&lpg=PA22&dq=Hitler's+
   abuse+to+Belgium+Jews&source=bl&ots=DFQiAloAGS&sig=Xa10OJMVDzcQu
   -pVZ1YfJCgz5ag&hl=en&sa=X&ved=0CBkQ6AEwAWoVChMI6MjAh_GwyAIVR
   JMNCh27Pwjl#v=onepage&q=Hitler's%20abuse%20to%20Belgium%20Jews&f=false.
   Accessed: October 7, 2015.

2 Found at: http://www.ushmm.org/exhibition/hidden-children/insideX/. Accessed:
   October 7, 2015.

3 Found at: http://www.ushmm.org/exhibition/hidden-children/insideX/. Accessed:
   October 7, 2015.

4 A Schwimmwagen was an amphibious four-wheel drive "floating/swimming" car used
   by German ground forces during World War II, produced by Volkswagen.

5 The Langers had German-loyal neighbors in Wereth, especially one particular neighbor (believed to be the wife of an SS member) who suspected the Langers of hiding
   Jews. Since no records exist giving the neighbor's name, the name "Greta" has been
   created for her. The Langers took a great risk opening their home to Jews and others,
   since three of the nine farmhomes in Wereth were still loyal to Germany.

CHAPTER 23

1 Found at: https://en.wikipedia.org/wiki/Pontotoc,_Mississippi; and http://www.bringing historyhome.org/assets/bringinghistoryhome/3rd-grade/unit-2/activity-5/3_Missis sippi_JimCrow.pdf. Accessed: July 14, 2015.

2 The 333rd and the 969th were sister battalions that served together in the same Field Artillery Group. They were among nine black units serving in Europe during World War II and operating the M1 155mm howitzer.

3 Some information found at: http://cisupa.proquest.com/ksc_assets/catalog/1538 _PapersNAACPPart9SerB.pdf. Accessed: July 20, 2015.

4 Found at: http://www.pacificwarmuseum.org/your-visit/african-americans-in-wwii/. Accessed: October 2, 2015.

5 Found at: http://www.npr.org/sections/pictureshow/2011/03/25/134769323/black _aviators; http://cisupa.proquest.com/ksc_assets/catalog/1538_PapersNAACPPart9SerB .pdf; and http://www.tuskegee.edu/sites/www/Uploads/files/About%20US/Airmen /TUSKEGEE_AIRMEN_CHRONOLOGY12.2011.pdf. Accessed: July 18, 2015.

6 The Tuskegee Airmen flew more than 15,000 sorties from May 1943 to June 1945, 66 airmen dying in combat. http://www.nationalww2museum.org/assets/pdfs/african -americans-in-world.pdf. Accessed: February 16, 2016.

CHAPTER 24

1 Information found at: http://www.nationalww2museum.org/learn/education/for -students/ww2-history/take-a-closer-look/draft-registration-documents.html. Accessed: November 27, 2015.

2 Found at: http://www.nationalww2museum.org/assets/pdfs/african-americans-in-world .pdf. Accessed: October 3, 2015.

3 Found at: http://www.biography.com/people/benjamin-o-Private First Class -jr-37840. Accessed: November 27, 2015.

4 Found at: http://www.nationalww2museum.org/learn/education/for-teachers/lesson -plans/take-a-memo.html. Accessed: October 3, 2015.

5 Found at: http://www.fdrlibrary.marist.edu/education/resources/pdfs/tusk_doc_a.pdf. Accessed: December 6, 2015.

6 The H. E. Fly memorandum and report were written on November 10, 1925, placed in the government's Top Secret file, and released to the public in 1988. To read the entire report, please see: http://www.fdrlibrary.marist.edu/education/resources /pdfs/tusk_doc_a.pdf. FDR Library warning: "Some of the historical documents contained in this curriculum guide reflect deep-seated and disturbing racial prejudices regarding African-Americans that were common among many white Americans in the early and middle years of the twentieth century. While offensive to modern readers, they help us understand the intense opposition the Roosevelts and the Tuskegee Airmen faced over the issue of allowing black men to pilot military aircraft."

7 Information and some quotes found at: https://www.gwu.edu/~erpapers/teachinger /glossary/tuskegee-airmen.cfm; and https://www.gwu.edu/~erpapers/teachinger/lesson -plans/notes-er-and-civil-rights.cfm. Accessed: November 27, 2015.

CHAPTER 25

1 The M1 155mm units, like the 333rd Field Artillery Battalion, had three firing batteries of four guns each (Able, Baker, and Charley), a headquarters battery made up of the CO (Lieutenant Colonel Kelsey) and his staff, as well as the fire direction personnel, communications center, and a service battery that included ammunition, mechanics, supplies, etc. Batteries were headed by a captain (Captain William McLeod). The 155mm battalion had 550 enlisted men and 30 officers; each battery had 120 men. Because of significant losses during World War II, however, a battalion usually had fewer men than needed. Some information found at: http://hubpages.com/education/ArtilleryBattalions. Accessed: March 11, 2016.

2 Some information found at: http://hubpages.com/education/ArtilleryBattalions and http://www.militaryfactory.com/armor/detail.asp?armor_id=439. Accessed: July 31, 2015.

CHAPTER 26

1 Found at: http://www.history.com/this-day-in-history/germans-surrender-at-stalingrad. Accessed: November 27, 2015; and http://ww2today.com/12th-january-1943-living -the-german-nightmare-in-berlin. Accessed: November 27, 2015.

2 Found at: http://www.ushmm.org/wlc/en/article.php?ModuleId=10005069. Accessed: November 27, 2015.

3 Some information found at: http://www.jpost.com/Opinion/Op-Ed-Contributors /The-little-known-uprising-Warsaw-Ghetto-January-1943. Accessed: November 27, 2015.

4 The Warsaw Ghetto Uprising began on April 19, 1943, and ended on May 16, 1943.

5 Information found at: https://history.state.gov/milestones/1937-1945/casablanca. Accessed: November 27, 2015. Some information found at: http://learning.blogs.nytimes .com/2012/05/07/may-7-1945-nazi-germany-surrenders-in-world-war-ii/?_r=0. Accessed: November 27, 2015.

6 Found at: http://www.history.com/this-day-in-history/americans-bomb-germans-for -first-time; and http://ww2today.com/27th-january-1943-u-s-bombs-from-u-s-airplanes -with-u-s-crews-hit-germany. Accessed: November 27, 2015.

CHAPTER 27

1 Information found at: https://www.jewishvirtuallibrary.org/jsource/biography/Paulus .html. Accessed: November 27, 2015.

2 Found at: http://www.historyplace.com/worldwar2/defeat/catastrophe-stalingrad.htm; https://www.jewishvirtuallibrary.org/jsource/biography/Paulus.html. Accessed: November 27, 2015.

3 Information found at: https://www.jewishvirtuallibrary.org/jsource/biography/Paulus .html. Accessed: November 27, 2015.

4 Quoted from: http://www.historylearningsite.co.uk/world-war-two/famous-battles -of-world-war-two/the-battle-of-stalingrad/. Accessed: November 27, 2015.

5 Found at: https://www.jewishvirtuallibrary.org/jsource/biography/Paulus.html. Accessed: November 27, 2015; and http://militaryhistory.about.com/od/worldwarii/p/World-War-Ii-Battle-Of-Stalingrad.htm. Accessed: December 1, 2015.

6 Found at: http://www.history.com/this-day-in-history/germans-surrender-at-stalingrad; https://www.jewishvirtuallibrary.org/jsource/biography/Paulus.html; http://www.history learningsite.co.uk/world-war-two/famous-battles-of-world-war-two/the -battle-of-stalingrad/; and http://www.historyplace.com/worldwar2/defeat/catastrophe -stalingrad.htm. Accessed: November 27, 2015.

7 During this three-day period of national mourning in the German Reich, cinemas and theaters were closed. "We must do everything to help the Volk overcome this dark hour," Joseph Goebbels recorded in his diary. Information found at: Jochen Hellbeck. *Stalingrad: The City That Defeated the Third Reich.* New York: Public Affairs, 2015, p. 431.

8 Some information found at: http://research.calvin.edu/german-propaganda-archive /goeb36.htm. Accessed: December 5, 2015.

9 Information found at: http://ww2today.com/30th-january-1943-hitler-only-survivors -and-annihilated-in-this-war. Accessed: January 16, 2016.

10 Some information found at: https://www.jewishvirtuallibrary.org/jsource/biography /Stauffenberg.html. Accessed: February 5, 2016.

CHAPTER 28

1 Some information found at: War Department: Field Artillery Tactical Employment, U.S. Government Printing Office, Washington: February 5, 1944.

2 Some information and quotes from: *Field Artillery Field Manual: Tactics and Technique.* Washington, D.C.: United States Government Printing Office, 1940; and from: War Department, *Field Artillery Field Manual: Firing.* Washington, D.C.: United States Government Printing Office, 1939.

CHAPTER 29

1 Found at: http://www.worldatlas.com/webimage/countrys/namerica/usstates/oktimeln .htm. Accessed: July 17, 2015.

CHAPTER 30

1 Some information from: War Department, *Basic Field Manual: U.S. Rifle, Caliber .30,* August 3, 1942.

2 Some information from: War Department, *Military Sanitation Field Manual,* July 1945.

CHAPTER 31

1 Some information from: War Department, *Medical Field Manual: Transportation of the Sick and Wounded,* February 21, 1941.

2 Found at: http://www.3riversmuseum.com/camp-gruber-the-war-years.html. Accessed: July 20, 2015.

3 Found at: http://www.cmgww.com/sports/louis/bio.htm. Accessed: July 18, 2015.

4 Some information found at: http://www.militaryfactory.com/armor/detail.asp?armor _id=439. Accessed: August 1, 2015.

5 Info found at: https://en.wikipedia.org/wiki/Hal_Newhouser. Accessed: June 27, 2015.

CHAPTER 32

1 Some information found at: http://www.ok.ngb.army.mil/cgts/pdf/historical_photographs _of_camp_gruber.pdf. Accessed: July 18, 2015.

2 Found at: http://www.history.com/this-day-in-history/germans-invade-poland; and http:// www.ushmm.org/wlc/en/article.php?ModuleId=10005070. Accessed: October 1, 2015.

3 Found at: http://www.okhistory.org/publications/enc/entry.php?entry=KU001. Accessed: October 1, 2015.

4 Found at: https://en.wikipedia.org/wiki/Tulsa_race_riot. Accessed: September 21, 2015.

5 Found at: http://www.ok.ngb.army.mil/cgts/pdf/historical_photographs_of_camp _gruber.pdf. Accessed: September 16, 2015.

CHAPTER 33

1 Found at: http://www.3riversmuseum.com/camp-gruber-the-war-years.html. Accessed: October 1, 2015.

2 Some info about Gruber found at: http://www.ok.ngb.army.mil/2011brief/Camp -Gruber-Self-Guided-Historic-Tour.pdf. Accessed: September 21, 2015.

CHAPTER 34

1 Found at: http://www.militaryfactory.com/armor/detail.asp?armor_id=38; and http:// www.britannica.com/technology/panzer. Accessed: October 12, 2015.

2 Found at: http://www.world-war-2-planes.com/ilyushin-il-2-shturmovik.html; and http://www.2worldwar2.com/stuka.htm. Accessed: October 12, 2015.

3 Found at: http://www.historyplace.com/worldwar2/defeat/kursk-gamble.htm. Accessed: October 12, 2015.

4 Found at: http://www.gutenberg.us/articles/Gustav_Knittel. Accessed: December 1, 2015.

5 Found at: http://www.imdb.com/name/nm0226281/bio. Accessed: July 27, 2015.

CHAPTER 35

1 Some information on Stauffenberg found at: https://www.jewishvirtuallibrary.org /jsource/biography/Stauffenberg.html; http://www.historynet.com/claus-von -stauffenberg.htm; and https://www.jewishvirtuallibrary.org/jsource/Holocaust/julyplot .html. Accessed: October 15, 2015.

2 Found at: http://militaryhistory.about.com/od/1900s/p/World-War-Ii-Colonel -General-Ludwig-Beck.htm. Accessed: October 15, 2015.

3 Some information found at: http://militaryhistory.about.com/od/1900s/p/World -War-Ii-Colonel-General-Ludwig-Beck.htm. Accessed: October 15, 2015.

4 On the night of July 24, 1943, the Royal Air Force bombed targets in Hamburg, Germany. The next day, American B-17s struck Hamburg's U-boat pens and shipyards, then destroyed Hamburg's power plant. On the night of July 27, the RAF attacked the city, causing a raging inferno and demolishing the city's infrastructure. Night raids continued for another week, ending on August 3, 1943, causing Hamburg many deaths (40,000–50,000 civilians) and wide destruction. Operation Gomorrah, a success for the Allies, proved a serious concern for Nazi leadership. Information found at: http://militaryhistory.about.com/od/aerialcampaigns/p/gomorrah.htm. Accessed: January 29, 2016.

CHAPTER 36

1 Canoneers often sang songs while they marched, worked, and launched shells. There were many favorites, from popular tunes to old gospel songs, including "Low-down Babe," Doo-wop's "Blue Moon," "Deep River," and many others. Sometimes the 333rd shouted as they loaded the shell, "How many men you got, Rommel?" After launching the shell, they shouted, "How many men you got now, Rommel?"

Note: To listen to the spiritual "Roll, Jordan, Roll," please see: http://www.google .com/search?client=safari&rls=en&q=roll+jordan+roll+12+years+a+slave&ie=UTF-8& oe=UTF-8. Accessed: December 18, 2015.

CHAPTER 37

1 During the war, Detroit's industrial landscape had rapidly expanded, its many production plants used primarily for the war effort. New African-American laborers arrived en masse from the South, causing violent racial tensions that erupted into bloody riots.

Crowds of local whites in Detroit, Michigan, known as the nation's "arsenal of democracy," marched through the new housing project, built to house the large influx of African-Americans escaping the Southern states and harsh Jim Crow laws. Black families, packed and ready to move into the public housing Sojourner Truth Homes, were pelted with rocks, harassed, intimidated, and humiliated. Police arrested 200 African-Americans during the violent protest and only three whites. Another Detroit riot began at the integrated amusement park Belle Isle, on June 20, 1943, when teenagers of both races, as well as white sailors and thousands of white residents, gathered to attack black vacationers.

Riots and strikes broke out that summer when 25,000 white factory workers in Detroit's aircraft assembly-line production went on strike to protest the promotions of three African-American employees. All production stopped for three days.

The wartime riots in Detroit were severe, resulting in the deaths of 25 black residents and 9 white residents. (Detroit, Michigan, February 28, 1942) Found at: http:// racialinjustice.eji.org/timeline/1940s/; http://www.pbs.org/wgbh/americanexperience /features/general-article/eleanor-riots/; and http://time.com/3880177/detroit-race-riots -1943-photos-from-a-city-in-turmoil-during-wwii/. Accessed: October 5, 2015.

2 The event occurred in Sikeston, Missouri, on January 25, 1942. During the early hours of Sunday, January 25, African-American Cleo Wright was accused of assaulting a white woman. Police officers shot him, arrested him, and drove him to Sikeston's local hospital. The hospital refused to treat him. Suffering from gunshot wounds, Wright ended up in the city jail without receiving medical treatment.

The next morning, a mob of 75 whites stormed the jail, abducting the nearly unconscious Wright, dragging him through the streets of Sikeston's black neighborhood, and then forcing Wright's wife to look at his body. Taking Wright to a black church, they burned him in front of hundreds of Sunday churchgoers.

More than 100 black residents fled Sikeston, terrified for their lives. Although the murder made national news, no perpetrators were ever convicted. Found at: http://racialinjustice.eji.org/timeline/1940s/. Accessed: October 5, 2015.

3 Turner is referring to the Elaine Massacre, the deadliest racial confrontation in Arkansas history, which happened on September 30, 1919, when 100 African-Americans, mostly sharecroppers, attended a meeting of the Progressive Farmers and Household Union of America at a church in Phillips County, near Elaine, Arkansas. Some information found at: http://www.encyclopediaofarkansas.net/encyclopedia/entry-detail .aspx?entryID=1102. Accessed: October 10, 2015.

4 Note: Private Turner is referring to the riots that took place in Detroit, Michigan, between black and white workers on February 28, 1942. Found at: http://racialinjustice .eji.org/timeline/1940s/; http://www.pbs.org/wgbh/americanexperience/features /general-article/eleanor-riots/; and http://time.com/3880177/detroit-race-riots-1943 -photos-from-a-city-in-turmoil-during-wwii/. Accessed: October 5, 2015.

5 Found at: http://racialinjustice.eji.org/timeline/1940s/; http://www.kcet.org/updaily /socal_focus/history/la-as-subject/los-angeles-1943-war-on-the-zoot-suit.html; and http://www.britannica.com/event/Zoot-Suit-Riots. Accessed: October 5, 2015.

6 When so many agricultural and service jobs were vacated by men serving in the military, the United States sought an agreement with Mexico to bring in temporary workers, a large influx not welcomed by white Americans. Mexican youths in Los Angeles often wore colorful outfits that became known as "zoot suits," a style of clothing many people considered an un-American challenge to the war effort. Members of the military stationed in Los Angeles, angry that the youths weren't respecting the rationing rules forbidding such clothing production, attacked them with belt buckles, ropes, baseball bats, and sticks and stripped them of their clothes. Instead of halting the attack on the Latino youths, the police arrested hundreds of young Latinos, charging them with violence and vagrancy. The "Zoot Suit Riots," as they came to be called, spread rapidly into other areas, causing serious injuries to clashing Mexican-American and U.S. servicemen. (Los Angeles, California, May 30, 1943) Found at: http://racialinjustice.eji.org/timeline/1940s/; http://www.kcet.org /updaily/socal_focus/history/la-as-subject/los-angeles-1943-war-on-the-zoot-suit.html; and http://www.britannica.com/event/Zoot-Suit-Riots. Accessed: October 5, 2015.

7 America's anti-Japanese bigotry worsened after the Japanese attack on Pearl Harbor. President Roosevelt signed Executive Order 9066, ordering the United States military to move all Japanese-Americans to internment camps, en masse and without due process.

More than 120,000 Japanese, more than half of them American citizens, were rounded up and imprisoned in overcrowded, filthy, barbed-wire-encircled camps. They were held captive until the end of the war. (United States West Coast, February 19, 1942) Found at: http://racialinjustice.eji.org/timeline/1940s/. Accessed: October 5, 2015.

CHAPTER 38

1 Some information found at and quoted from: http://history.howstuffworks.com/world -war-ii/d-day-invasion3.htm; http://ww2today.com/29-january-1944-hitlers-plans -for-a-post-war-breeding-programme; http://germanhistorydocs.ghi-dc.org/docpage .cfm?docpage_id=2336; and http://germanhistorydocs.ghi-dc.org/docpage.cfm?docpage _id=2337. Accessed: November 29, 2015.

PART 3

1 Found at: https://www.gwu.edu/~erpapers/teachinger/lesson-plans/notes-er-and-civil -rights.cfm. Accessed: November 27, 2015.

CHAPTER 39

1 There were nine black field artillery battalions in VIII Corps employed in Europe. All were heavy-caliber units used as corps artillery to support and reinforce one or more divisions. The black battalions were often attached to another group, white or black, as needed. Found at: http://www.history.army.mil/books/wwii/11-4/chapter21.htm. Accessed: February 16, 2016.

2 Information found at: http://www.armystudyguide.com/content/Prep_For_Basic _Training/Prep_for_basic_land_navigation/determine-the-grid-coordi.shtml. Accessed: December 8, 2015.

3 Information found at: https://en.wikipedia.org/wiki/M2_Browning#Features. Accessed: December 8, 2015. Some information found at: http://ww2blancomuseum.com/german _weapons/german_weapons_-_landmines. Accessed: December 9, 2015.

4 Some information found at: http://ww2blancomuseum.com/german_weapons/german _weapons_-_landmines. Accessed: December 9, 2015.

5 Some information found at: http://io9.com/11-jaw-dropping-weapons-from-world -war-ii-you-probably-511010752; and https://armyhistory.org/the-origins-of-u-s-army -explosive-ordnance-disposal/. Accessed: December 8, 2015.

6 Found at: http://www.skylighters.org/encyclopedia/compound219.html. Accessed: December 8, 2015.

CHAPTER 40

1 Some information and quotes found at: http://www.heretical.com/smith/wwar2.html. Accessed: November 29, 2015.

CHAPTER 41

1 Found at: http://www.nationalww2museum.org/learn/education/for-students/ww2 -history/d-day-june-6-1944.html. Accessed: December 9, 2015.

2 Some information found at: http://www.americainwwii.com/articles/pattons-ghost -army/. Accessed: December 11, 2015.

3 Quoted from: http://www.nationalww2museum.org/learn/education/for-students/ww2 -history/d-day-june-6-1944.html. Accessed: December 9, 2015.

4 Quoted from: http://www.nationalww2museum.org/learn/education/for-students/ww2 -history/d-day-june-6-1944.html. Accessed: December 9, 2015.

5 Some information found at: http://www.americainwwii.com/articles/pattons-ghost -army/. Accessed: December 11, 2015.

6 Some information found at: http://www.army.mil/d-day/; http://www.history.army.mil /html/books/072/72-18/CMH_Pub_72-18.pdf; http://www.nationalarchives.gov.uk /cabinetpapers/themes/d-day-preparation-invasion-of-normandy.htm; and http://www .history.army.mil/brochures/brief/overview.htm; Accessed: November 28, 2015.

7 Quoted from: http://www.history.com/topics/world-war-ii/d-day. Accessed: December 10, 2015.

CHAPTER 42

1 Found at: http://www.history.army.mil/html/books/072/72-18/CMH_Pub_72-18.pdf. Accessed: March 11, 2016.

2 Found at: http://www.dailymail.co.uk/news/article-2650423/A-battle-life-death -progress-Read-breaking-news-report-D-Day-happened-70-years-ago.html. Accessed: December 12, 2015.

3 Some information found at: http://www.theatlantic.com/magazine/archive/1960/11 /first-wave-at-omaha-beach/303365/; http://www.history.com/topics/world-war-ii /d-day; http://www.shsu.edu/~his_ncp/Omaha.html; and http://www.britannica.com /place/Omaha-Beach. Accessed: December 10, 2015.

4 Found at: http://www.britannica.com/place/Omaha-Beach. Accessed: December 11, 2015.

5 Some information found at: https://www.army.mil/d-day/; and http://www.britannica .com/place/Omaha-Beach. Accessed: December 10, 2015.

CHAPTER 43

1 Information/quotes from: http://news.bbc.co.uk/onthisday/hi/dates/stories/june/6 /newsid_3499000/3499352.stm. Accessed: December 12, 2015.

2 Found at: http://www.nytimes.com/2014/06/07/world/europe/how-the-times -covered-d-day-in-the-paper-of-june-6-1944.html?_r=0. Accessed: December 12, 2015.

3 Found at: http://www.nytimes.com/2014/06/07/world/europe/how-the-times -covered-d-day-in-the-paper-of-june-6-1944.html?_r=0. Accessed: December 12, 2015.

4 Some information found at: http://www.shsu.edu/~his_ncp/Omaha.html. Accessed: December 10, 2015.

5 More than 1,700 African-American troops participated on D-day on Omaha and Utah beaches, including the 327th Quartermaster Service Company and the 320th Anti-Aircraft Barrage Balloon Battalion. Found at: http://www.nationalww2museum .org/assets/pdfs/african-americans-in-world.pdf. Accessed: February 16, 2016.

6 Found at: http://www.wvculture.org/history/wvmemory/vets/stewartjames/stewart james.html. Accessed: February 17, 2016.

7 In order to hinder German forces in responding to invasion operations on and after D-day, on June 6, the Allies planned to liberate the city of Caen. It took seven weeks of intense fighting to take the city, destroying much of it by the time it ended on July 20, 1944. Operation Goodwood held German forces in place for the July 25 Operation Cobra: an operation for the Allies to break through German lines and push out of Normandy (July 25 to July 31, 1944). Some information found at: http://militaryhistory. about.com/od/WWIIEurope/p/World-War-Ii-Battle-Of-Caen.htm. Accessed: January 29, 2016. To read an interesting first-person account of the Battle of Caen, please see: http://www.bbc.co.uk/history/ww2peopleswar/stories/55/a3621755.shtml. Accessed: January 29, 2016.

8 These German soldiers were from the Third Company of the First Battalion of the Fourth Regiment (Der Führer) of the Second SS-Panzer Division (Das Reich).

9 Some information found at: http://www.oradour.info/ruined/chapter2.htm; http:// spartacus-educational.com/FRoradour.htm; http://www.dailymail.co.uk/news/article -2535926/Prosecutors-charge-88-year-old-man-1944-Nazi-massacre-Oradour-Sur -Glane-642-villagers-shot-burnt.html; http://www.historyplace.com/worldwar2 /timeline/oradour.htm; and http://members.iinet.net.au/~gduncan/massacres.html. Accessed: December 16, 2015.

10 A 1953 report claims that 648 people perished in the massacre. Found at: http://members. iinet.net.au/~gduncan/massacres.html. Accessed: February 14, 2016. The village of Oradour-sur-Glane was never rebuilt. It stands today an empty ghost town, a memorial to Nazi atrocities. The reason for the massacre has been argued but never confirmed. In November 2014, during a reopened investigation, 88-year-old former Nazi "Werner C, from Cologne," was charged with 25 counts of murder, and aiding and abetting the murder of hundreds of people in connection with the June 10, 1944, massacre. Found at: http://www.dailymail.co.uk/news/article-2535926/Prosecutors-charge-88-year-old-man -1944-Nazi-massacre-Oradour-Sur-Glane-642-villagers-shot-burnt.html. Accessed: December 16, 2015.

11 On June 27, 1944, two days before the 333rd FAB arrived in France, Allied forces captured Cherbourg, placing a major port under their control, and allowing them to ship men, vehicles, and tons of supplies to support the Allied invasion of northern France. Found at: http://www.indiana.edu/~league/1944.htm. Accessed: February 11, 2016.

CHAPTER 44

1 Found at: http://www.theatlantic.com/photo/2011/10/world-war-ii-the-allied -invasion-of-europe/100160/. Accessed: December 12, 2015.

2 The 333rd Field Artillery Battalion, like most black artillery battalions, was a nondivi-sional unit under the command of the VIII Corps. Earlier it had been reorganized as

part of the 333rd Field Artillery Group with both black and white units: the 969th, 578th, 741st, 559th, and 740th Field Artillery Battalions. The 333rd FAB and 969th FAB were 155mm howitzer, truck-drawn sister units. Some information found at: http://www.redlegsofthebulge.com/333rd-field-artillery. Accessed: February 12, 2016.

3 Quoted from: Matthew 6:9–13. The Bible, King James Version.

4 Some information found at: http://www.britannica.com/place/Utah-Beach. Accessed: December 11, 2015.

5 General Eisenhower described the German soldiers as "well-trained, well-equipped, and battle-hardened" men who "fight savagely." Found at: http://www.dailymail.co.uk /news/article-2650423/A-battle-life-death-progress-Read-breaking-news-report-D-day -happened-70-years-ago.html. Accessed: December 12, 2015.

CHAPTER 45

1 Found at: http://www.crwflags.com/fotw/flags/fr-29-pb.html. Accessed: January 21, 2016.

2 The 333rd Field Artillery Group consisted of the 733rd, 202nd, and the 333rd Field Artillery Battalions.

CHAPTER 46

1 Quoted from: 333rd Field Artillery Group, Unit Journal, Eisenhower Library, Abilene, KS.

2 Found at: http://www.sextantproperties.com/normandy/manche/property-la-haye -du-puits. Accessed: January 21, 2015; and https://www.ibiblio.org/hyperwar/USA /USA-A-StLo/USA-A-StLo-1.html; http://www.worldwar2history.info/Normandy /hedgerows.html. Accessed: February 11, 2016.

3 Found at: http://yankstories.blogspot.com/2009/08/taking-la-haye-du-puits-part-2 .html. Accessed: December 14, 2015.

4 Note: La Haye-du-Puits was half-destroyed in World War II but today has been restored to its former beauty, the busy shops painted in pastel colors. Found at: http://www .sextantproperties.com/normandy/manche/property-la-haye-du-puits. Accessed: January 21, 2015.

5 Found at: https://books.google.com/books?id=7ko-AQAAMAAJ&pg=PA179&lpg =PA179&dq=Major+John+G.+Workizer,+WWI&source=bl&ots=jcg0XjNqxc&sig =Cl2Qq82CyAJyWsohp5iA1K_c2IA&hl=en&sa=X&ved=0ahUKEwizh671ibnKAhX KRiYKHXS0BxwQ6AEIHDAA#v=onepage&q=Major%20John%20G.%20Workizer% 2C%20WWI&f=false; and https://news.google.com/newspapers?nid=950&dat =19441003&id=UmlIAAAAIBAJ&sjid=JFUDAAAAIBAJ&pg=2793,5440880&hl=en. Accessed: January 20, 2016.

6 Found at: http://www.300thcombatengineersinwwii.com/towns.html. Accessed: December 14, 2015.

7 Some information in this chapter found at: http://www.worldwar2-photofinder.com/city/ basse-normandy/listing/la-haye-du-puits-rue-du-chateau/. Accessed: December 14, 2015.

CHAPTER 47

1 Some information found at: https://www.jewishvirtuallibrary.org/jsource/biography /Stauffenberg.html; http://www.historynet.com/claus-von-stauffenberg.htm; https:// www.jewishvirtuallibrary.org/jsource/Holocaust/julyplot.html. Accessed: March 5, 2016.

2 Some information found at: https://books.google.com/books?id=qBrjZ8-VtEMC&pg =PA44&lpg=PA44&dq=Colonel+Heinz+Brandt&source=bl&ots=SyG-OSnmqQ&sig =NBLvKfB5CjYXRICCbOYEl4iwRU4&hl=en&sa=X&ved=0CFMQ6AEwDmoVCh MItY3zsZjFyAIVV-FjCh2rEAFn#v=onepage&q=Colonel%20Heinz%20Brandt&f =false. Accessed: October 15, 2015.

3 When, two hours later, Tresckow learned that the bottle bombs had not detonated and that Hitler had arrived safely in Rastenburg, he panicked. Tresckow pondered how he would recover the unexploded bombs before Brandt delivered the package to Stieff and his treasonous act would be exposed. Tresckow telephoned Brandt, telling him he had sent the wrong package to Colonel Stieff, and he would pick it up the next day. His plan worked. He recovered the package and the bombs weren't discovered.

Brandt moved the briefcase about six feet away to the other side of the table leg in order to stand closer beside Hitler to better view the map. Some information found at: https://books.google.com/books?id=qBrjZ8-VtEMC&pg=PA44&lpg=PA44&dq=Colonel+ Heinz+Brandt&source=bl&ots=SyG-OSnmqQ&sig=NBLvKfB5CjYXRICCbOYEl4i wRU4&hl=en&sa=X&ved=0CFMQ6AEwDmoVChMItY3zsZjFyAIVV-FjCh2rEAFn#v =onepage&q=Colonel%20Heinz%20Brandt&f=false. Accessed: October 15, 2015.

4 Quoted from: https://books.google.com/books?id=n4AsZq4e5vwC&pg=PA203&lpg =PA203&dq=Colonel+Heinz+Brandt&source=bl&ots=d9Yl5X9j0d&sig=vca_yKJpk fkeiIUTq3dYoUW2JGY&hl=en&sa=X&ved=0CFYQ6AEwD2oVChMItY3zsZj FyAIVV-FjCh2rEAFn#v=onepage&q=Colonel%20Heinz%20Brandt&f=false. Accessed: October 15, 2015.

CHAPTER 48

1 Found at: http://www.telegraph.co.uk/culture/film/3558716/Claus-von-Stauffenberg -the-true-story-behind-the-film-Valkyrie-starring-Tom-Cruise.html. Accessed: October 13, 2015.

2 Some information found at: https://books.google.com/books?id=n4AsZq4e5vwC&pg =PA203&lpg=PA203&dq=Colonel+Heinz+Brandt&source=bl&ots=d9Yl5X9j0d&sig =vca_yKJpkfkeiIUTq3dYoUW2JGY&hl=en&sa=X&ved=0CFYQ6AEwD2oVChMI tY3zsZjFyAIVV-FjCh2rEAFn#v=onepage&q=Colonel%20Heinz%20Brandt&f=false; http://ww2db.com/person_bio.php?person_id=671; http://ww2db.com/person_bio.php? person_id=671; and https://books.google.com/books?id=qBrjZ8-VtEMC&pg=PA44& lpg=PA44&dq=Colonel+Heinz+Brandt&source=bl&ots=SyG-OSnmqQ&sig=NBLvKfB 5CjYXRICCbOYEl4iwRU4&hl=en&sa=X&ved=0CFMQ6AEwDmoVChMItY3zsZ jFyAIVV-FjCh2rEAFn#v=onepage&q=Colonel%20Heinz%20Brandt&f=false; https:// en.wikipedia.org/wiki/Heinz_Brandt. Accessed: October 15, 2015.

3 Some information found at: https://www.jewishvirtuallibrary.org/jsource/biography /Fromm.html; https://en.wikipedia.org/wiki/Albrecht_Mertz_von_Quirnheim. Accessed: October 13, 2015.

4 Some information found at: http://ww2db.com/person_bio.php?person_id=520; http://www.history.com/this-day-in-history/assassination-plot-against-hitler-fails; http://www.history.com/topics/july-plot; https://www.jewishvirtuallibrary.org/jsource/biography/Fromm.html; http://www.bbc.com/news/magazine-28330605; http://www.dw.com/en/germany-remembers-the-plot-to-kill-hitler/a-17792469; http://www.historytoday.com/roger-moorhouse/good-german-von-stauffenberg-and-july-plot; and http://www.historynet.com/claus-von-stauffenberg.htm. Accessed: July 2, 2015.

5 Some information found at: http://ww2db.com/person_bio.php?person_id=520; http://www.history.com/this-day-in-history/assassination-plot-against-hitler-fails; http://www.history.com/topics/july-plot; https://www.jewishvirtuallibrary.org/jsource/biography/Fromm.html; http://www.bbc.com/news/magazine-28330605; http://www.dw.com/en/germany-remembers-the-plot-to-kill-hitler/a-17792469; http://www.historytoday.com/roger-moorhouse/good-german-von-stauffenberg-and-july-plot; and http://www.historynet.com/claus-von-stauffenberg.htm. Accessed: July 2, 2015.

6 Note: The German policy of Sippenhaft required that family members of arrested and/or executed conspirators against Hitler also be punished. Sippenhaft showed no compassion for infants or the elderly, taking innocent family members, imprisoning them in concentration camps, or killing them. Some information about Sippenhaft found at: https://books.google.com/books?id=mSFeAQAAQBAJ&pg=PA126&lpg=PA126&dq=Lt.+Werner+von+Haeften&source=bl&ots=U10zKGUurh&sig=78974cKQfUDTR-y3ZUhDe-LQ33A&hl=en&sa=X&ved=0CDEQ6AEwBTgKahUKEwif1OyolMXIAhUW52MKHS05A9Y#v=onepage&q=Lt.%20Werner%20von%20Haeften&f=false. Accessed: October 15, 2015.

CHAPTER 49

1 Some information found at: http://www.army.mil/article/42658/_quot_Operation_COBRA_and_the_Breakout_at_Normandy__quot_/. Accessed: January 20, 2016.

2 Some information found at: https://translate.google.com/translate?hl=en&sl=fr&u=http://www.infobretagne.com/saint-aubin-daubigne.htm&prev=search. Accessed: January 21, 2016.

3 Some information found at: http://www.encyclopedia.com/topic/Rennes.aspx. Accessed: January 21, 2016.

4 In late November 2014, 3,000 people evacuated the city of Rennes after metro lines workers discovered a gigantic 550-pound World War II bomb, packed with 155 pounds of high-grade explosives, buried near Rennes's town hall. It took two hours to defuse the bomb, believed to have been dropped by the British Royal Air Force between 1943 and 1944. Found at: http://www.nydailynews.com/news/world/thousands-evacuate-french-city-discovery-wwii-bomb-article-1.2021466. Accessed: December 14, 2015.

5 In early August 1944, the VIII Corps had been transferred to General George Patton's Third Army with the intent of seizing the seaports of Saint Malo, Brest, Lorient, and Saint Nazaire. On August 4, the city of Rennes (the "Gateway to Brittany") fell. Nantes fell two days later. The Germans' access to Brest and the Breton ports had been severed. The trapped German forces withdrew to the Atlantic seaports, turning them into

fortresses, and were ordered by Hitler himself to defend them to the death. Found at: http://www.indiana.edu/~league/1944.htm. Accessed: February 11, 2016.

CHAPTER 50

1 Colonel Andreas von Aulock was a highly decorated Oberst in the Wehrmacht, commanding the Seventy-ninth Infantry Division. Found at: http://www.worldlibrary .org/articles/andreas_von_aulock. Accessed: February 5, 2016.

2 Some sources report that the U.S. forces had received a false report about the number of German soldiers in Saint Malo, predicting them to be in the thousands. The GIs found fewer than one hundred Germans in the city when they entered. Hundreds of civilians were locked behind closed gates. Other reports state the actual number of German troops in Saint Malo was as high as 12,000. Some information found at: http:// www.ihr.org/jhr/v02/v02p301_Beck.html; and http://www.historylearningsite.co.uk /world-war-two/world-war-two-in-western-europe/the-battle-for-brittany/. Accessed: January 22, 2016.

3 Some information found at: War Department, *Field Artillery Field Manual: Firing*. Washington, D.C.: United States Government Printing Office, 1939.

4 Quoted from: http://www.historylearningsite.co.uk/world-war-two/world-war -two-in-western-europe/the-battle-for-brittany/. Accessed: January 21, 2016.

CHAPTER 51

1 Some information found at: http://ww2today.com/17-august-1944-a-shattered-city -festung-st-malo-surrenders; http://www.wwiithenandnow.com/index.php/france /normandy-d-day/saint-malo. Accessed: January 21, 2016; and http://www.ihr.org/jhr /v02/v02p301_Beck.html; and http://www.bbc.com/travel/story/20141210-danger-saint -malo-and-the-highest-tides-in-europe; http://europeupclose.com/article/st-malo -france/. Accessed: December 15, 2015.

2 To view a video of Allied troops liberating Saint Malo, please see: http://ww2today .com/17-august-1944-a-shattered-city-festung-st-malo-surrenders. Accessed: January 21, 2016.

3 Information found at: http://www.jugon-les-lacs.com/en/home.html. Accessed: January 21, 2016.

CHAPTER 52

1 Some information from: http://www.2worldwar2.com/fallschirmjager.htm. Accessed: December 16, 2015; and https://www.ibiblio.org/hyperwar/USA/USA-E-Breakout /USA-E-Breakout-30.html. Accessed: January 23, 2016.

2 Some information found at: War Department, *Field Manual: Military Sanitation*, July 1945.

3 Some information found at: War Department Field Manual: Military Sanitation, July 1945.

4 Some information found at: War Department, *Medical Field Manual*, Reference date March 5, 1941; and War Department, *Basic Field Manual: First Aid for Soldiers*, April 7, 1943.

CHAPTER 53

1 Some information found at: http://www.90thidpg.us/Reference/Manuals/E5R1%
20Flamethrower%20Manual.pdf. Accessed: March 13, 2016.

2 Some information found at: War Department, *Field Artillery Field Manual: Firing.* Washington, D.C.: United States Government Printing Office, 1939.

CHAPTER 54

1 Description of Ramcke found at: https://archive.org/stream/BattleDiary/BattleDiary
_djvu.txt. Accessed: January 24, 2016.

2 Some information found at: http://www.specialcamp11.co.uk/General%20der%
20Fallschirmtruppe%20Hermann-Bernhard%20Ramcke.htm; http://alain.liscoet
.pagesperso-orange.fr/recit3an.htm; http://ww2db.com/battle_spec.php?battle_id=113;
http://www.historylearningsite.co.uk/world-war-two/world-war-two-in-western-europe
/the-battle-for-brittany/; http://www.history.army.mil/brochures/norfran/norfran.htm;
http://www.historylearningsite.co.uk/world-war-two/world-war-two-in-western-europe
/the-battle-for-brittany/; and http://www.combatreels.com/viii_corps.cfm. Accessed:
December 16, 2015.

3 Some information found at: War Department, *Field Manual: Military Sanitation,* July
1945.

CHAPTER 55

1 Found at: http://news.bbc.co.uk/onthisday/hi/dates/stories/august/25/newsid_3520000
/3520894.stm. Accessed: January 28, 2016.

2 Some information found at: http://www.historynet.com/world-war-ii-the-liberation
-of-paris.htm. Accessed: January 28, 2016.

3 Some information found at: http://www.historynet.com/world-war-ii-the-liberation
-of-paris.htm. Accessed: January 28, 2016.

4 Quoted from: http://www.historyplace.com/worldwar2/defeat/attack-russia.htm. Accessed: January 23, 2016.

5 Some information/quotes from: https://books.google.com/books?id=ASVTaalp5wgC&pg
=PA4&lpg=PA4&dq=Hitler's+losses+in+summer,+1944&source=bl&ots=rj7uEUh
rAi&sig=RvCM1yLAkF4Sewz05gBPje3-8lI&hl=en&sa=X&ved=0ahUKEwjH4JScrOP
JAhVk5YMKHcqZADIQ6AEIJDAD#v=onepage&q=Hitler's%20losses%20in%20summer
%2C%201944&f=false. Accessed: December 17, 2015.

CHAPTER 56

1 By mid-September, the Allies were speeding across France, having liberated Paris on
August 25, and pushing into Belgium, attacking on a broad front, defeating German
resistance, and getting ready to march into Germany. So rapid was their advance, however, that they were running seriously low on fuel and supplies.

2 Found at: http://www.metrolyrics.com/ill-be-home-for-christmas-lyrics-christmas
-song.html. Accessed: December 16, 2015.

3 The Battle of the Hürtgen Forest began in mid-September with heavy firing a few miles southeast of Aachen, Germany. The battle lasted through mid-December 1944, and didn't officially end until February 1945. More than 24,000 Americans were killed, captured, or wounded. Another 9,000 suffered serious health problems, including trench foot, combat fatigue, etc. The 333rd Field Artillery Battalion did not participate in this battle. Found at: http://hurtgen1944.homestead.com. Accessed: February 16, 2016.

CHAPTER 57

1 Information about the MP44 found at: http://militaryhistory.about.com/od/smallarms /p/stg44.htm. Accessed: February 28, 2016.

2 Found at: http://www.historyplace.com/worldwar2/hitleryouth/hj-boy-soldiers.htm. Accessed: February 28, 2016.

3 On May 1, 1945, Hitler Youth leader Artur Axmann, commanding an HJ battalion of boys and girls in Berlin, abandoned them, fleeing to the Alps to save his own life. Found at: http://www.historyplace.com/worldwar2/hitleryouth/hj-boy-soldiers .htm. Accessed: February 28, 2016.

4 The Volkssturm and the Volksgrenadier are often confused, since both were organized by Hitler in the autumn of 1944. The Volkssturm consisted of old men and young boys and some girls recruited from the Hitler Youth. They were often led by veteran soldiers, under the command of the SS, and equipped with powerful new automatic weapons. The Volksgrenadier divisions came under the command of the Wehrmacht and consisted of broken or destroyed infantry divisions, convalescent soldiers recently discharged from hospitals, Luftwaffe and Kriegsmarine personnel, workers from industry and railways, and every available male, aged 16 to 60. Some information found at: https://books.google.com/books?id=Ja2kCAAAQBAJ&pg=PA505&lpg =PA505&dq=What+is+the+difference+between+Volksgrenadier+and+Volkssturm? &source=bl&ots=EdMmKgfyr-&sig=bkejqYlVNlDV6o3XbW5RZm8BC7w&hl=en &sa=X&ved=0ahUKEwj295qVkZvLAhWJ6yYKHQ70DhIQ6AEITTAG#v=onepage &q=What%20is%20the%20difference%20between%20Volksgrenadier%20and% 20Volkssturm%3F&f=false. Accessed: February 28, 2016.

CHAPTER 58

1 Found at: http://community.worldheritage.org/article/WHEBN0005572961/183rd% 20Volksgrenadier%20Division%20(Wehrmacht); http://www.geocities.ws/orion47.geo /WEHRMACHT/HEER/Generalleutnant2/LANGE_WOLFGANG.html. Accessed: January 25, 2016.

2 Generalleutnant Lange commanded the 183rd Volksgrenadier Division from September 15, 1944, to February 25, 1945. He was captured in the Ruhr Pocket and placed in captivity from April 15, 1945, to October 2, 1947. Found at: http://www .geocities.ws/orion47.geo/WEHRMACHT/HEER/Generalleutnant2/LANGE _WOLFGANG.html. Accessed: January 25, 2016.

3 Information from "Battle Experiences of the 183rd Volksgrenadier Division," SHAEF report, October 1944. Found at Eisenhower Library, Abilene, KS. Accessed: October 2015.

4 The 183rd Volksgrenadier Division was poorly trained and equipped. It was destroyed at Geilenkirchen at the end of November 1944. Found at: http://community .worldheritage.org/article/WHEBN0005572961/183rd%20Volksgrenadier%20 Division%20(Wehrmacht). Accessed: January 25, 2016.

5 A SHAEF report's information received from enemy POWs states that: "According to a fairly large number of PWs interrogated, most of the [enemy] replacements [during the period September–November 1944] were 16-18-year-olds . . . Prior to joining the division, they had had 4–6 weeks basic training, and the training they got with the division was fairly rigorous. As expected, most of the personnel is straight German, with only a sprinkling of Alsatians and Silesians, while a good proportion of officers and NCOs are veterans of France." The report also found that the enemy's panzer division's main deficiencies were: lack of training in combined arms, potential lack of gasoline, potential lack of small arms, reduced tank element, and probably lack of battle replacements. Found at: Supreme Headquarters Allied Expeditionary Force Intelligence Notes: Office of Assistant Chief of Staff, G-2. Found at Eisenhower Library, Abilene, KS. Accessed: October 2015.

6 Information found in: The October 12, 1944, Kampfgrüppe Stoessel Report, of the 462 Division in the METZ sector, obtained by SHAEF. Supreme Headquarters Allied Expeditionary Force Intelligence Notes: Office of Assistant Chief of Staff, G-2. Found at Eisenhower Library, Abilene, KS. Accessed: October 2015.

7 Sparks is referring to the "Tuskegee Airmen" training at Tuskegee Institute in Tuskegee, Alabama, under its Civilian Pilot Training Program. Found at: http://www .archives.gov/publications/ref-info-papers/105/index.pdf. Accessed: February 18, 2016.

8 Some information from: http://scalar.usc.edu/nehvectors/stakeman/walter-white -investigates-in-world-war-ii?path=walter-white-and-the-naacp-through-world -war-ii-and-trumans-election. Accessed: March 8, 2016.

9 Some information found at: http://digital.archives.alabama.gov/cdm/ref/collection /voices/id/3482; http://www.shsu.edu/~his_ncp/AfrAmer.html; https://books.google .com/books?id=k1L6c3gQjT0C&pg=PA36&lpg=PA36&dq=Governor+Chauncey +Sparks+reaction+to+War+Department&source=bl&ots=4Lw6df4drs&sig=t5mO9AUg 5b7H99V3mNAO9IsgWIY&hl=en&sa=X&ved=0ahUKEwif2sC00YnLAhXI7i YKHU_eC_AQ6AEIMjAD#v=onepage&q=Governor%20Chauncey%20Sparks% 20reaction%20to%20War%20Department&f=false; http://cisupa.proquest.com/ksc _assets/catalog/1538_PapersNAACPPart9SerB.pdf; and http://www.archives.gov/pub lications/ref-info-papers/105/index.pdf; and Walter White, "Observations and Recommendations of Walter White on Racial Relations in the ETO," February 11, 1944. NARA, RG 107, Box 447. Quoted in: Charissa J. Threat, *Nursing Civil Rights: Gender and Race in the Army Nurse Corps*, Urbana: University of Illinois Press, 2014, p. 46.

CHAPTER 59

1 Found at: http://news.blogs.lib.lsu.edu/2014/12/22/battle_of_the_bulge_middleton/. Accessed: January 27, 2016.

2 Information found at: http://www.washingtonexaminer.com/the-american-hero-who -saved-chartres-cathedral/article/2552585. Accessed: January 27, 2016.

3 The citizens of Leves, at the place where Colonel Griffith was killed, set up a plaque dedicated to the colonel. Found at: http://www.washingtonexaminer.com/the-american -hero-who-saved-chartres-cathedral/article/2552585. Accessed: January 27, 2016.

CHAPTER 60

1 More than 500 French Resistance fighters, as well as 127 civilans, died in their struggle to help free Paris from the small pockets of Germans that occupied the city. Paris was finally liberated on August 25, 1944. Found at: http://www.history.com/this -day-in-history/liberation-of-paris. Accessed: January 28, 2016.

2 Found at: https://translate.google.com/translate?hl=en&sl=fr&u=http://www.ajpn.org /commune-Saint-Quentin-2691.html&prev=search. Accessed: January 28, 2016.

3 The French in Saint Quentin had also fought the Germans in 1914, during the First World War. Information found at: http://www.firstworldwar.com/battles/guise .htm. Accessed: January 28, 2016.

4 Quoted from: Sergeant Bill Davidson, *Yank* magazine, September 29, 1944, pp. 9–10.

CHAPTER 61

1 Found at: http://www.history.army.mil/brochures/ardennes/aral.htm. Accessed: January 29, 2016.

2 Found at: http://www.history.com/news/8-things-you-may-not-know-about-the -battle-of-the-bulge; http://www.history.army.mil/brochures/ardennes/aral.htm; http:// www.historylearningsite.co.uk/world-war-two/world-war-two-in-western-europe/the -battle-of-the-bulge/; and http://news.nationalgeographic.com/news/2014/12/141214 -battle-of-the-bulge-hitler-churchill-history-culture-ngbooktalk/. Accessed: January 29, 2016.

3 Note: Hitler's plan included:

Sepp Dietrich's Sixth Panzer Army leading the attack and capturing Antwerp, cutting off the Allies' support at the port.

Manteuffel's Fifth Panzer Army attacking American forces, capturing the primary roads and rails of Saint Vith, and advancing to Brussels.

Brandenberger's Seventh Army attacking the southern flank, preventing American reinforcements from attacking the Fifth Panzer Army.

Holding in reserve the Fifteenth Army in case it was needed.

Some information found at: http://www.historylearningsite.co.uk/world-war-two/ world-war-two-in-western-europe/the-battle-of-the-bulge/. Accessed: January 29, 2016.

CHAPTER 62

1 Found at: http://www.houffalize.be/index.php?option=com_flexicontent&view=category& cid=80:l-histoire-d-houffalize&Itemid=514&lang=en. Accessed: January 28, 2016.

2 Found at: http://www.history.army.mil/books/wwii/7-8/7-8_12.htm. Accessed: January 30, 2016.

3 Some information found at: http://www.battleofthebulgememories.be/stories26/32-battle
-of-the-bulge-us-army/727-bleialf-is-overrun.html. Accessed: February 7, 2016.

4 Some information found at: http://www.museum-mm.org/the-siegfried-line/; http://
www.history.army.mil/books/wwii/Siegfried/Siegfried%20Line/Maps.htm; and http://
lostimagesofww2.com/photos/places/siegfried-line.php. Accessed: February 3, 2016.

5 Note: To learn more details about the German-built West Wall, please see: http://www
.museum-mm.org/the-siegfried-line/. To view a map of the West Wall, please see: http://
www.history.army.mil/books/wwii/Siegfried/Siegfried%20Line/Maps.htm.

6 Found at: http://www.thehistoryreader.com/modern-history/december-16-1944
-ardennes-offensive-begins-abysmal-failure-allied-intelligence/. Accessed: February 7,
2016; and http://historynewsnetwork.org/article/120359. Accessed: February 10, 2016.

CHAPTER 63

1 Note: In college, Skorzeny belonged to the Schlagende Verbindung (a dueling society),
becoming a noted fencer. In 1928, a fellow fencer sliced his cheek, a wound that left a
deep and lifelong scar. He called it "the scar of honor." Skorzeny credits his courage and
war success to that painful dueling experience: "My knowledge of pain, learned with
the sabre, taught me not to be afraid. And just as in dueling, you must concentrate on
your enemy's cheek, so, too, in war. You cannot waste time on feinting and sidestepping.
You must decide on your target and go in." Found at: http://szorzeny.greyfalcon.us/
oskorzeny2.htm. Accessed: January 29, 2016.

2 Some information found at: http://www.history.com/news/8-things-you-may-not-know
-about-the-battle-of-the-bulge; http://www.bbc.com/news/uk-northern-ireland
-30571335; https://www.jewishvirtuallibrary.org/jsource/biography/Skorzeny.html; and
http://szorzeny.greyfalcon.us/oskorzeny2.htm. Accessed: January 29, 2016.

PART 4

1 Winston Churchill: quoted from: http://www.worldwar2tributes.com/view_quotes.php.
Accessed: March 22, 2016.

CHAPTER 64

1 Firing missions for October include: October 5: 10 missions; October 6: 8 missions;
October 7: 19 missions; October 9: 12 missions; October 10: 20 missions; October 11:
24 missions; October 12: 29 missions; October 13: 16 missions; October 14: 9 missions;
October 15: 7 missions; October 16: no missions; October 17: 6 missions; October 18:
no missions; October 19: 6 missions; October 20: 57 missions; October 21: 6 missions
(three German robot bombs reported); October 22: 3 missions (4 robot bombs reported);
October 23: 6 missions (4 robot bombs reported); October 24: 11 missions (7 robot
bombs reported); October 26: 7 missions (3 robot bombs reported); October 27: 4
missions (11 robot bombs reported); October 28: 24 missions (5 robot bombs reported);
October 29: 21 missions (8 robot bombs reported); October 30: 6 missions (4 robot
bombs reported); October 31: 10 missions (7 robot bombs reported). Information from
documents and after-action reports found at the Eisenhower Library, Abilene, KS,
October 2016.

2 Rob Shomo, son of the late George Shomo, has traced his family's ancestory back to its slavery roots in Monmouth County, near Red Bank, New Jersey. Slaves from Africa and the Caribbean were brought to Monmouth County in the late 1600s. Slave populations grew rapidly. By 1800, slaves made up 5.8 percent of New Jersey's population. Disobedient slaves were severely punished by their white landowners: flogged, hanged, and burned on stakes. Slavery there was permanently abolished in 1846. Some information obtained in a telephone interview with Rob Shomo; and also found at: http://exa .gmnews.com/news/2007-03-08/Front_page/034.html; http://www.womenhistoryblog .com/2008/02/slavery-in-new-jersey.html. Accessed: February 10, 2016.

CHAPTER 65

1 Some information found at: http://www.historynet.com/drones-dont-die-a-history -of-military-robotics.htm; http://io9.gizmodo.com/11-jaw-dropping-weapons-from -world-war-ii-you-probably-511010752; and http://www.stelzriede.com/ms/html/sub /marshwvr.htm. Accessed: February 3, 2016.

2 Some information found at: http://www.history.army.mil/books/wwii/7-8/7-8_7.htm. Accessed: February 18, 2016.

3 The 106th "Golden Lions" was the last of 36 infantry divisions to be activated in World War II. It was repeatedly stripped of manpower, losing thousands of men and hundreds of officers when they were needed elsewhere. The division's men, leaving New York and arriving in England on November 17, 1944, were only partially trained. They relieved the Second Infantry Division in the Schnee Eifel on December 11. Commanded by Major General Alan W. Jones, they were stationed at the West Wall and ordered to hold the front line. Found at: http://usdefensewatch.com/2015/11/the-desperate-hours -the-demise-of-the-106th-infantry-division-during-the-opening-desperate -hours-of-the-battle-of-the-bulge/; and http://www.history.army.mil/html/forcestruc /cbtchron/cc/106id.htm. Accessed: February 11, 2016.

4 Found at: http://www.indiana.edu/~league/1944.htm. Accessed: February 3, 2016.

CHAPTER 66

1 Found at: http://www.history.com/news/8-things-you-may-not-know-about-the -battle-of-the-bulge. Accessed: February 16, 2016.

2 After the war, Germans admitted how much they feared American spotter planes appearing overhead. They knew it would only take minutes before American artillery would strike. They had no place to hide from the deadly results. Found at: http:// hubpages.com/education/ArtilleryBattalions. Accessed: March 17, 2016.

3 Hitler spoke without using a script at this meeting on December 11 and 12, 1944. Stenographers who were responsible for recording the original meeting did so poorly. The scene written above was created from a number of available recorded sources.

4 Some information found at: https://books.google.com/books?id=3ZNVME6-LHAC& pg=PA44&dq=What+happened+in+Hitler's+Dec.+11,+1944+meeting?&hl=en&sa=X& ei=P36VVZO7KMOWygTt2IGYDA&ved=0CEsQ6AEwCA#v=onepage&q=What% 20happened%20in%20Hitler's%20Dec.%2011%2C%201944%20meeting%3F&f=false;

http://www.historylearningsite.co.uk/world-war-two/world-war-two-in-western-europe
/the-battle-of-the-bulge/; https://www.jewishvirtuallibrary.org/jsource/biography
/Dietrich.html; http://www.history.com/news/8-things-you-may-not-know-about
-the-battle-of-the-bulge; and http://www.britannica.com/biography/Josef-Dietrich.
Accessed: July 2, 2015.

CHAPTER 67

1 Some info from: https://books.google.com/books?id=3ZNVME6-LHAC&pg=PA44&
   dq=What+happened+in+Hitler's+Dec.+11,+1944+meeting?&hl=en&sa=X&ei=P36V
   VZO7KMOWygTt2IGYDA&ved=0CEsQ6AEwCA#v=onepage&q=What%20
   happened%20in%20Hitler's%20Dec.%2011%2C%201944%20meeting%3F&f=false.
   Accessed: July 2, 2015.

2 Found at: https://books.google.com/books?id=rvQHaNuTyj4C&pg=PT115&lpg=
   PT115&dq=%22Your+great+hour+has+arrived.%22&source=bl&ots=fVzGiqFbON&
   sig=dSfRTUT9mXulZSeNy5YHTMSXbFc&hl=en&sa=X&ved=0ahUKEwik4tfp
   -MfLAhUEKCYKHVosB00Q6AEIIDAB#v=onepage&q=%22Your%20great%
   20hour%20has%20arrived.%22&f=false. Accessed: March 17, 2016.

CHAPTER 68

1 At the West Wall, Hitler's initial assembled assault force by December 15 was more
   than 200,000 men (in 13 infantry and 7 panzer divisions), nearly 1,000 tanks, and almost
   2,000 guns. Five more divisions and 450 more tanks followed, moving forward in a
   second wave. Found at: http://www.history.army.mil/brochures/ardennes
   /aral.htm. Accessed: February 10, 2016.

2 The Germans prepared for the Ardennes attack in secret, mostly at night, in the cold
   weather and thick fog of the Ardennes Forest. It is incredible they were able to gather
   so many pieces of artillery, tanks, and equipment into place, with supplies and ammunition; assign targets; and coordinate the advances of the infantry and armor without
   alerting the Allies.

3 Some information found at: http://historynewsnetwork.org/article/120359; https://
   books.google.com/books?id=QsEJplqzN2AC&pg=PR44&lpg=PR44&dq=Hitler's+move+
   into+the+Ardennes&source=bl&ots=kXswUnbVKv&sig=qAIPvyaval-XgzXsRvTt
   -8XkYHs&hl=en&sa=X&ved=0ahUKEwj2seHcxeHKAhXG5yYKHdR5CG8Q6AEIO
   TAE#v=onepage&q=Hitler's%20move%20into%20the%20Ardennes&f=false; https://
   books.google.com/books?id=OSiJ_JB8JzwC&pg=PA475&dq=Where+was+Eisenhower+
   on+Dec.+14,+1944?&hl=en&sa=X&ved=0ahUKEwjHv6-kyuHKAhUMRyYKHdoD
   CEYQ6AEIIzAB#v=onepage&q=Where%20was%20Eisenhower%20on%20Dec.%
   2014%2C%201944%3F&f=false. Accessed: February 5, 2016.

4 Found at: http://www.marlenedietrich.org.uk/id3.html. Accessed: February 5, 2016.

5 Marlene Dietrich, a German-American actress and singer, born in Schönberg in 1901,
   traveled with the USO during World War II, entertaining the troops in Europe with
   songs, magic tricks, and raunchy jokes. She was devoted to the Allied troops, visiting
   wounded soldiers in hospitals, giving shows, performing in shimmering, translucent

gowns, and traveling from dawn to dusk, often working 16-hour days. In 1947, she was awarded the Presidential Medal of Freedom for her entertainment of the troops. She died in Paris on May 6, 1992. Found at: http://www.tcm.com/tcmdb/person/50375% 7C107577/Marlene-Dietrich/biography.html; http://www.marlenedietrich.org.uk/id3 .html. Accessed: February 5, 2016.

6 The after-action report for the 333rd Field Artillery Battalion, December 1, 1944, to December 16, 1944, reads: "Throughout this period the battalion was located in the vicinity of Schönberg, Belgium. The mission of the battalion at this time was to reinforce the fires of the 38th Field Artillery Battalion, of the 2nd Infantry Division. To accomplish this mission both observed and unobserved missions were fired . . . [T]he unobserved fires consisted of harassing and interdiction fires, along with various 'Time on Targets' fired on call. . . . On 12 December 1944, the mission of the battalion was changed to reinforce the fires of the 590th Field Artillery Battalion, of the 106th Infantry Division. The same type of firing was done in fulfillment of this mission as had been done for the 38th Field Artillery Battalion." Quoted from: the after-action report for the 333rd Field Artillery Battalion, December 1, 1944, to December 16, 1944. January 1, 1945 report: Commanding General, Third United States Army. Departmental Records Branch, A.G.O. Pentagon.

7 Found at: https://www.warhistoryonline.com/war-articles/70-years-ago-stormy-day -december-15-1944-glenn-miller-disappeared.html; and http://www.history.com/this -day-in-history/legendary-bandleader-glenn-miller-disappears-over-the-english-channel. Accessed: February 6, 2016.

CHAPTER 69

1 The second observation post in Bleialf was commanded by Lieutenant Elmer King.

2 Some information found at: http://www.battleofthebulgememories.be/stories26 /32-battle-of-the-bulge-us-army/727-bleialf-is-overrun.html. Accessed: February 28, 2016.

3 At this time, the Allied front line was held by the U.S. Army VIII Corps (the 106th Infantry Division, Twenty-eighth Infantry Division, the Ninety-ninth Armored Division, and the Fourth Infantry Division). Saint Vith was the 106th Division's headquarters. Bastogne was VIII Corps headquarters. Some information found at: https://blog .fold3.com/tmih-battle-of-the-bulge-begins-december-16-1944/comment-page-2/. Accessed: February 16, 2016.

4 The Canadians and the British were stationed at the front in the north, and the Americans in the south along the Siegfried Line. A thin, weak line of troops guarded the space in between, in the belief that the Ardennes Forest would naturally block a possible German attack. Found at: https://www.archives.gov/publications/prologue /2014/winter/bulge-final.pdf. Accessed: February 16, 2016.

5 Some information found at: https://books.google.com/books?id=rvQHaNuTyj4C&pg =PT115&lpg=PT115&dq=%22Your+great+hour+has+arrived.%22&source=bl&ots =fVzGiqFbON&sig=dSfRTUT9mXulZSeNy5YHTMSXbFc&hl=en&sa=X&ved =0ahUKEwik4tfp-MfLAhUEKCYKHVosB00Q6AEIIDAB#v=onepage&q=% 22Your%20great%20hour%20has%20arrived.%22&f=false. Accessed: March 17, 2016.

CHAPTER 70

1 The after-action report regarding the 333rd Field Artillery Battalion reads: "At 0300 the enemy fired extensive artillery preparation barrage in the vicinity of Bleialf, Germany. This preparation continued until approximately 0530, after which the enemy attacked with tanks supported by infantry." Quoted from: Headquarters, 333rd Field Artillery Battalion, January 1, 1945, APO 403, U.S. Army. The after-action report regarding the 333rd Field Artillery Group reads: "The enemy was reported as making early and rapid progress. By 1100 hours the enemy had penetrated Bleialf." Quoted from: Headquarters 333rd Field Artillery Group, Action Against Enemy, Reports After/After Action Reports, Commanding General, Third U.S. Army, APO 403, January 5, 1945. From Eisenhower Library, Abilene, KS.

2 Found at: http://www.thehistoryreader.com/modern-history/december-16-1944 -ardennes-offensive-begins-abysmal-failure-allied-intelligence/. Accessed: February 7, 2016.

CHAPTER 71

1 The military definition for a spoiling attack: "A tactical maneuver employed to seriously impair a hostile attack while the enemy is in the process of forming or assembling for an attack." Quoted from: http://www.militaryfactory.com/dictionary/military -terms-defined.asp?term_id=5020. Accessed: February 9, 2016.

2 Found at: http://www.history.com/news/8-things-you-may-not-know-about-the -battle-of-the-bulge. Accessed: February 16, 2016.

3 Found at: https://www.eisenhower.archives.gov/research/online_documents/ardennes _battle_bulge/033_037.pdf. Accessed: February 16, 2016.

4 Found at: http://www.historylearningsite.co.uk/world-war-two/weapons-of-world-war -two/tiger-tank/. Accessed: March 6, 2016.

5 The 88mm proved the best-known piece of artillery during World War II. An antiaircraft and antitank weapon, it was used by the Germans in France, North Africa, and Russia, and during the Battle of the Bulge. Found at: http://www.achtungpanzer.com /88mm-flak-series-flugabwehrkanone.htm. Accessed: February 7, 2016.

CHAPTER 72

1 Freezing temperatures present a multitude of problems for soldiers. "Men are subject to chilling, frostbite, freezing, and snow blindness. When cold, they are less alert. Without proper shelter and covering they lose sleep and weaken. Their fingers may become numb from cold, resulting in poor handling of their weapons. They seek sheltered locations and huddle together for warmth. There are occasions requiring violent exertion which result in their becoming overheated, followed by periods of inactivity during which they may freeze . . . [W]hen the air is still and dry, they are likely to consider the temperature higher than it actually is and become careless in their precautions against frostbite." Quoted from: *Operations in Snow and Extreme Cold*, War Department Basic Field Manual, November 1944, War Department, U.S. Government Printing Office: Washington, D.C., p. 2.

2 The army discouraged beard growth and instructed the men to shave every evening before retiring to reduce skin chapping. Moisture from the breath collects in the beard and plays a part in freezing the face. Found at: *Operations in Snow and Extreme Cold*, War Department Basic Field Manual, November 1944, War Department, U.S. Government Printing Office: Washington, D.C., p. 37.

CHAPTER 73

1 Some information found at: http://gazette.com/66-years-after-battle-former-enemies -trade-war-stories/article/102001. Accessed: February 12, 2016.

2 Quoted from: Rick Atkinson. *The Guns at Last Light*. New York: Henry Holt and Company, 2014, pp. 439–40.

3 Some information found at: http://www.historylearningsite.co.uk/world-war-two/ military-commanders-of-world-war-two/dwight-eisenhower/; http://www.u-s-history .com/pages/h1789.html; https://www.kshs.org/p/general-eisenhower-of-kansas/13002; http://query.nytimes.com/mem/archive-free/pdf?res=990DE1D61038E33BBC4F52D FB467838F659EDE; https://books.google.com/books?id=gy9EgF80YnYC&pg=PA136& lpg=PA136&dq=Where+was+Eisenhower+on+December+15,+1944?&source=bl&ots =Ns7I6ZHq9Z&sig=SXy6Uec_6wNhlJlqReRE4byfNpY&hl=en&sa=X&ved=0ahUKEwj YuZzv5uPKAhXG1CYKHWcZAQ04ChDoAQgoMAI#v=onepage&q=Where% 20was%20Eisenhower%20on%20December%2015%2C%201944%3F&f=false; and http://www.thehistoryreader.com/modern-history/december-16-1944-ardennes -offensive-begins-abysmal-failure-allied-intelligence/. Accessed: February 6, 2016.

CHAPTER 74

1 Found at: http://www.history.com/news/8-things-you-may-not-know-about-the -battle-of-the-bulge; http://www.history.army.mil/books/wwii/7-8/7-8_7.htm. Accessed: February 16, 2016; http://www.nationalww2museum.org/see-hear/collections /focus-on/bulge-70th.html?; http://www.historylearningsite.co.uk/world-war-two /world-war-two-in-western-europe/the-battle-of-the-bulge/; and http://warfarehisto rynetwork.com/daily/wwii/sherman-tanks-tiger-tanks-the-battle-of-the-bulge/. Accessed: March 1, 2016.

2 The after-action report lists that Bleialf had been penetrated on December 16 at 1100 hours and a breakthrough was made on December 17 at 0800 hours. The two infantry regiments of the 106th—the 422nd and 423rd—were encircled and cut off by the enemy on December 16–17. Attempts to break out failed. General Jones officially surrendered on December 19. Later, after the collapse of the 106th Infantry Division, General Bradley said, "The Schnee Eifel battle represents the most serious reverse suffered by American arms during the operations of 1944–1945 in the European theater." Found at: http://usdefensewatch.com/2015/11/the-desperate-hours -the-demise-of-the-106th-infantry-division-during-the-opening-desperate -hours-of-the-battle-of-the-bulge/; and http://www.history.army.mil/html/forcestruc /cbtchron/cc/106id.htm; http://www.history.army.mil/books/wwii/7-8/7-8_7.htm. Accessed: February 11, 2016.

CHAPTER 75

1 German soldiers, especially scared young men, were encouraged to take (what we now call) crystal meth before a battle. Crystal meth causes a person to feel a false sense of well-being, heightened energy, hyperactivity, aggressiveness, irritability, and delusions of power. It can cause bizarre, erratic, violent behavior. This may help explain the wild, feral behavior of the attacking German soldiers. Found at: http://news.nationalgeo graphic.com/news/2014/12/141214-battle-of-the-bulge-hitler-churchill-history -culture-ngbooktalk/; http://www.drugfreeworld.org/drugfacts/crystalmeth/the -deadly-effects-of-meth.html. Accessed: February 16, 2016.

CHAPTER 77

1 To hear the sound of a .50-caliber machine gun, please see: http://soundbible .com/373-50-Caliber-Machine-Gun.html. Accessed: March 18, 2016.

2 Some information found in military reports: Headquarters 333rd Field Artillery Group, Action Against Enemy, Reports After/After Action Reports, Commanding General, Third U.S. Army, APO 403, January 5, 1945. From Eisenhower Library, Abilene, KS.

CHAPTER 78

1 Found at: David Cooke and Wayne Evans, *Kampfgrüppe Peiper at the Battle of the Bulge*, Mechanicsburg, PA: Stackpole Books, 2005, p. 20.

2 Some information found at: http://www.historylearningsite.co.uk/malmedy_massacre .htm; http://www.historyplace.com/worldwar2/timeline/malmedy.htm; and http:// historynewsnetwork.org/article/120359. Accessed: March 6, 2016.

CHAPTER 80

1 The soldiers were from the First SS Division.

CHAPTER 82

1 Paraphrased from: The Bible, Psalm 23, KJV.

EPILOGUE 1

1 Found at: interview with the Langer family; http://www.wereth.org/en/news-events /detail/herman-langer-died-on-friday-june-21-2013-388-12. Accessed: February 10, 2016.

2 Some information from: https://books.google.com/books?id=z2htBQAAQBAJ&pg =PA137&lpg=PA137&dq=Two+Fronts,+One+War,+Wereth+massacre&source=bl&ots =yzEK6mrL8h&sig=QabwQol8kbQJ3uJMzyG5432FuUI&hl=en&sa=X&ved =0ahUKEwibs6vqnPXKAhWDbT4KHffPDjEQ6AEIHDAA#v=onepage&q=Two% 20Fronts%2C%20One%20War%2C%20Wereth%20massacre&f=false. Accessed: February 12, 2016.

3 Found at: http://www.usatoday.com/story/news/nation/2013/11/07/wereth-black -soldiers-battle-of-bulge-army-world-war-ii-history/3465059/. Accessed: February 16, 2016.

4 Four main investigators combed and examined the massacre scene: First Lieutenant Herbert Peterfreund, First Lieutenant John Polachek, Major Baldwin, and Major William F. Everett.

5 Found at: http://www.historynet.com/the-wereth-11-a-little-known-massacre-during -the-battle-of-the-bulge.htm. Accessed: February 18, 2016.

6 Found at: http://archive.defense.gov/news/newsarticle.aspx?id=33014; https://army .togetherweserved.com/army/servlet/tws.webapp.WebApp?cmd=ShadowBoxProfile& type=Person&ID=354430. Accessed: February 11, 2016.

7 Found at: http://www.secondworldwarhistory.com/battle-of-the-bulge.asp. Accessed: February 12, 2016.

8 Some information from: http://research.omicsgroup.org/index.php/333rd_Field _Artillery_Battalion_(United_States); http://tmg110.tripod.com/usarmyh8.htm; https:// books.google.com/books?id=z2htBQAAQBAJ&pg=PA137&lpg=PA137&dq=Two+ Fronts,+One+War,+Wereth+massacre&source=bl&ots=yzEK6mrL8h&sig=QabwQol8k bQJ3uJMzyG5432FuUI&hl=en&sa=X&ved=0ahUKEwibs6vqnPXKAhWDbT4KHff PDjEQ6AEIHDAA#v=onepage&q=Two%20Fronts%2C%20One%20War%2C% 20Wereth%20massacre&f=false. Accessed: February 12, 2016.

9 Found at: http://www.history.com/this-day-in-history/victory-in-europe. Accessed: February 11, 2016.

10 Found at: http://www.google.com/search?client=safari&rls=en&q=military+desegre gated&ie=UTF-8&oe=UTF-8. Accessed: February 11, 2016.

11 Found at: https://www.trumanlibrary.org/9981a.htm. Accessed: February 11, 2016.

12 To read Executive Order 9981, please see: https://www.trumanlibrary.org/9981a.htm.

13 Found at: http://americanhistory.si.edu/brown/history/1-segregated/segregated -america.html. Accessed: March 19, 2016.

14 Found at: http://www.army.mil/article/126907/Massacred_Wereth_11_Honored_at _Belgian_Ceremony/. Accessed: February 10, 2016.

15 Found at: https://books.google.com/books?id=arI0HSFXwLkC&pg=PA510&lpg =PA510&dq=medical+report+on+Wereth+11+men+massacred+Dec.+17,+1944&source =bl&ots=HQgY6gf102&sig=-PWN5lJxH_wz6yP5V-M71wfnxII&hl=en&sa=X&ved =0ahUKEwiuuZXvkfDKAhVI1h4KHcvFDIoQ6AEIJDAB#v=onepage&q=medical% 20report%20on%20Wereth%2011%20men%20massacred%20Dec.%2017%2C% 201944&f=false. Accessed: February 10, 2016.

16 Found at: http://archive.defense.gov/news/newsarticle.aspx?id=33014. Accessed: February 10, 2016.

17 Found at: http://www.wereth.org/en/home. Accessed: February 10, 2016.

18 Quoted from: http://archive.defense.gov/news/newsarticle.aspx?id=33014. Accessed: February 10, 2016.

19 Found at and quoted from: http://www.wereth.org/en/news-events/detail/20th-and -10th-anniversaries-memorial-dedication-389-12. Accessed: February 16, 2016.

20 Some information found at: http://www.wereth.org/en/history; http://www.usatoday .com/story/news/nation/2013/11/07/wereth-black-soldiers-battle-of-bulge-army-world

-war-ii-history/3465059/; http://www.post-gazette.com/ae/movies/2010/11/07/The
-Next-Page-Soldiers-honor-restored-The-Wereth-11-of-WWII/stories/201011070264.
Accessed: February 10, 2016. To view an interview online with Hermann Langer, please
see: http://www.wereth.org/en/home.

21 Quoted from Representative Gerlach. Found at: http://www.historynet.com/the
-wereth-11-a-little-known-massacre-during-the-battle-of-the-bulge.htm.

22 Quoted from Congressman Fattah. Found at: http://www.historynet.com/the
-wereth-11-a-little-known-massacre-during-the-battle-of-the-bulge.htm.

23 Found at: http://www.wereth.org/en/history. Accessed: February 10, 2016; and http://
www.usatoday.com/story/news/nation/2013/11/07/wereth-black-soldiers
-battle-of-bulge-army-world-war-ii-history/3465059/. Accessed: February 28, 2016.

EPILOGUE 2

1 Some information found at: http://findgrave.org/harmon-kelsey-california-690558/;
https://books.google.com/books?id=SQGFChkQZ2gC&pg=PA250&lpg=PA250&dq
=Colonel+Harmon+S.+Kelsey&source=bl&ots=j5UHUPL99V&sig=LthUmzu
CulW1DshJs8kE5_XwWnA&hl=en&sa=X&ei=P5lfVa7ILIOwsAXSjYL4BQ&ved
=0CBQQ6AEwAA#v=onepage&q=Colonel%20Harmon%20S.%20Kelsey&f=false;
http://www.google.com/search?client=safari&rls=en&q=Colonel+Harmon+S.+Kelsey,+
WWII&ie=UTF-8&oe=UTF-8. Accessed: February 12, 2016.

2 Some information obtained in a personal interview with Sergeant Shomo and found
at: http://files.usgwarchives.net/ok/greer/obits/greerobits/mcleodwe.txt. Accessed:
February 2, 2016.

3 Received and used by permission from Robert Hudson Jr.

4 Found at: http://www.newstribune.info/article/20120305/News/303059990. Accessed:
February 16, 2016.

5 Found at: http://www.tulsaworld.com/news/state/one-of-the-wereth-buried-in-okla
-grave/article_f2f61d32-a7cf-5ef2-96da-f80908c4f9a2.html. Accessed: February 16, 2016.

6 Found at: http://townhall.com/columnists/paulgreenberg/2014/10/28/saving-private
-turner-n1911171/page/full. Accessed: February 16, 2016.

7 Found at: http://djournal.com/news/in-memoriam-monument-honors-black-wwii
-soldiers-sacrifice/. Accessed: February 16, 2016.

8 Some information found at: http://www.wereth.org/en/history; http://www.wereth.org
/en/news-events/detail/herman-langer-died-on-friday-june-21-2013-388-12; http://
www.army.mil/article/126907/Massacred_Wereth_11_Honored_at_Belgian_Ceremony/;
and http://www.usatoday.com/story/news/nation/2013/11/07/wereth-black-soldiers
-battle-of-bulge-army-world-war-ii-history/3465059/. Accessed: February 10, 2016.

9 Quoted from: http://www.history.com/this-day-in-history/fdr-dies. Accessed: February
12, 2016.

10 Some information found at: http://www.nytimes.com/learning/general/onthisday/bday
/1011.html; https://en.wikipedia.org/wiki/Eleanor_Roosevelt. Accessed: February 12, 2016.

11 Some information found at: http://www.historylearningsite.co.uk/world-war-two /military-commanders-of-world-war-two/dwight-eisenhower/; http://www.u-s-history .com/pages/h1789.html; and http://starship.python.net/crew/manus/Presidents/dde/ ddeobit.html. Accessed: February 6, 2016.

12 Some information found at: http://www.combatreels.com/viii_corps.cfm. Accessed: January 31, 2016; http://www.87thinfantrydivision.com/Commentary/000020/000020. html; and http://www.spokeo.com/Troy+H+Middleton+1. Accessed: February 12, 2016.

13 Some information found at: http://www.nytimes.com/learning/general/onthisday/bday /1111.html; and http://www.history.com/this-day-in-history/old-blood-and-guts-dies. Accessed: February 12, 2016.

14 Some information found at: http://www.biography.com/people/omar-bradley-9223568; and http://www.history.com/topics/world-war-ii/omar-bradley. Accessed: February 12, 2016.

15 Some information from: http://militaryhistory.about.com/od/1900s/p/World -War-Ii-Field-Marshal-Bernard-Montgomery-Viscount-Montgomery-Of-Alamein. htm; and http://www.historylearningsite.co.uk/world-war-two/military-commanders -of-world-war-two/field-marshal-bernard-montgomery/. Accessed: February 12, 2016.

16 Found at: http://www.history.com/this-day-in-history/legendary-bandleader-glenn -miller-disappears-over-the-english-channel. Accessed: February 6, 2016.

17 Found at: http://www.blackpast.org/aah/miller-doris-dorie-1919-1943. Accessed: October 3, 2015; and http://americacomesalive.com/2012/02/20/dorie-miller-1919-1943 -hero-of-world-war-ii/#.VhFddigvEso. Accessed: October 3, 2015.

18 Found at: http://www.jesseowens.com/about/. Accessed: October 17, 2015.

19 Some information found at: http://www.history.com/topics/world-war-ii/adolf-hitler; https://www.jewishvirtuallibrary.org/jsource/Holocaust/hitler.html; and http://learn ing.blogs.nytimes.com/2012/05/07/may-7-1945-nazi-germany-surrenders-in-world -war-ii/?_r=0. Accessed: February 12, 2016.

20 Some information found at: https://www.jewishvirtuallibrary.org/jsource/Holocaust /goebbels.html; http://www.biography.com/people/joseph-goebbels-9313998. Accessed: February 12, 2016.

21 Some information found at: http://www.ushmm.org/wlc/en/article.php?ModuleId =10007112; http://www.biography.com/people/hermann-göring-37281; and http://www .history.co.uk/biographies/hermann-goering. Accessed: February 12, 2016.

22 Found at: http://www.specialcamp11.co.uk/General%20der%20Fallschirmtruppe% 20Hermann-Bernhard%20Ramcke.htm. Accessed: February 14, 2016.

23 Quoted from: http://germanhistorydocs.ghi-dc.org/sub_document.cfm?document_id =1560. Accessed: February 14, 2016.

24 Some information found at: https://www.jewishvirtuallibrary.org/jsource/Holocaust /himmler.html; http://www.biography.com/people/heinrich-himmler-9339448; and https://www.jewishvirtuallibrary.org/jsource/Holocaust/Lebensborn.html. Accessed: February 14, 2016.

25 To read Himmler's "Procreation Order," please see: http://germanhistorydocs .ghi-dc.org/sub_document.cfm?document_id=1560. To read some responses by critics against it, please see: http://germanhistorydocs.ghi-dc.org/sub_document.cfm?document _id=1561. Accessed: February 14, 2016.

26 Found at: http://militaryhistory.about.com/od/WorldWarIILeaders/p/World -War-Ii-Field-Marshal-Gerd-Von-Rundstedt.htm; http://biography.yourdictionary .com/karl-rudolf-gerd-von-rundstedt. Accessed: February 14, 2016.

27 Some information from: http://www.historylearningsite.co.uk/world-war-two/military -commanders-of-world-war-two/walther-model/; and http://militaryhistory.about.com/ od/WorldWarIILeaders/p/World-War-Ii-Field-Marshal-Walter-Model.htm. Accessed: February 14, 2016.

28 Some information found at: http://www.gutenberg.us/articles/gustav_knittel; and http:// www.post-gazette.com/ae/movies/2010/11/07/The-Next-Page-Soldiers-honor-restored -The-Wereth-11-of-WWII/stories/201011070264. Accessed: February 14, 2016.

29 Some information found at: http://www.historynet.com/massacre-at-malmedy-during -the-battle-of-the-bulge.htm; http://www.waffen-ss.no/peiper.htm; http://www.historynet .com/massacre-at-malmedy-during-the-battle-of-the-bulge.htm; and https://www.jew ishvirtuallibrary.org/jsource/ww2/malmedy2.html. Accessed: October 15, 2015.

30 The Malmédy Massacre: By January 1945, Allies had driven the Germans out of Belgium, back to the Siegfried Line. Using mine detectors, the U.S. troops found and examined the slain GIs killed near Malmédy, their bodies frozen and covered with two feet of snow.

At the end of the war, in a courthouse at Dachau, Joachim Peiper and Sepp Dietrich, as well as 74 SS men of Kampfgrüppe Peiper, were tried in a war crimes tribunal for the Malmédy Massacre. On July 11, 1946, the judges gave 41 defendants, including Peiper, the death penalty. Twenty-two of them, including Dietrich, received sentences of life imprisonment, ranging from 2 to 20 years. Not long after, however, the trial got caught up in controversy; most death sentences were commuted and life sentences reduced. By the early 1950s, most of the convicted SS men were released. Found at: http://members .iinet.net.au/~gduncan/massacres.html; http://www.historyplace.com/worldwar2 /timeline/malmedy.htm; and http://historynewsnetwork.org/article/120359. Accessed: February 10, 2016.

31 The Stavelot Massacre: The day after the Malmédy Massacre, on December 18, 1944, the same SS unit of Kampfgrüppe Peiper brutally executed 130 Belgian civilians in the village of Stavelot: 67 men, 47 women, and 23 children. Some information found at: http://members.iinet.net.au/~gduncan/massacres.html; and http://www.wwiithenand now.com/index.php/belgium/ardennes/stavelot-and-sur. Accessed: February 14, 2016.

32 Some information from: http://spartacus-educational.com/GERmanteuffel.htm; http:// www.britannica.com/biography/Hasso-Freiherr-von-Manteuffel; and http://www .historyofwar.org/articles/people_manteuffel_hasso.html. Accessed: February 14, 2016.

33 Some information found at: http://www.ww2incolor.com/forum/showthread.php/12968 -Funeral-of-Josef-quot-Sepp-quot-Dietrich; https://www.jewishvirtuallibrary.org /jsource/ww2/malmedy2.html; https://www.jewishvirtuallibrary.org/jsource/biography

/Dietrich.html; and http://www.britannica.com/EBchecked/topic/1057227/Josef-Dietrich. Accessed: February 14, 2016.

34 Some information found at: https://books.google.com/books?id=3ZNVME6-LHAC&pg=PA117&lpg=PA117&dq=Colonel+Max+Hansen&source=bl&ots=GbKLq5QrFO&sig=kD3sLhJ4qOiQre8orYCgicU8t1g&hl=en&sa=X&ei=zgFmVaiUM4nQsAWCkoGYCA&ved=0CEEQ6AEwDA#v=onepage&q=Hansen&f=false. Accessed: March 12, 2016.

35 Information from: http://www.stalingrad.net/german-hq/generals-and-divisions/biography_paulus.htm; http://query.nytimes.com/mem/archive-free/pdf?res=9C00EED9163CE43ABC4953DFB7678388649EDE; and https://www.jewishvirtuallibrary.org/jsource/biography/Paulus.html. Accessed: December 7, 2015.

36 Found at: http://www.history.com/this-day-in-history/general-fromm-executed-for-plot-against-hitler; and https://www.jewishvirtuallibrary.org/jsource/biography/Fromm.html. Accessed: October 13, 2015.

37 Found at: http://www.116thpanzer.com/forum/m/836079/viewthread/4409928-generalmajor-siegfried-von-waldenburg. Accessed: February 3, 2016.

38 Found at: http://worldlibrary.org/articles/harald_freiherr_von_elverfeldt; https://books.google.com/books?id=YlCYMciy7zQC&pg=PP23&lpg=PP23&dq=Major+General+Baron+harald+von+Elverfeldt&source=bl&ots=pgo3o5E9Hu&sig=paV8s2gmkUYjQxag9lMLIXm5lO8&hl=en&sa=X&ved=0ahUKEwizlMnrzNzKAhVI6yYKHaV7Cy4Q6AEITzAM#v=onepage&q=Major%20General%20Baron%20harald%20von%20Elverfeldt&f=false. Accessed: February 3, 2016.

39 The plan to capture bridges over the Meuse River was never accomplished.

40 Some information found at: http://www.bbc.com/news/uk-northern-ireland-30571335; http://www.historylearningsite.co.uk/world-war-two/world-war-two-in-western-europe/the-battle-of-the-bulge/; and http://szorzeny.greyfalcon.us/oskorzeny2.htm. Accessed: January 29, 2016.

41 Some information found at: http://www.biography.com/people/winston-churchill-9248164. Accessed: February 15, 2016.

42 Some information found at: http://www.history.com/topics/joseph-stalin; and http://www.biography.com/people/joseph-stalin-9491723. Accessed: February 15, 2016.

43 Some information found at: http://www.telegraph.co.uk/culture/film/3558716/Claus-von-Stauffenberg-the-true-story-behind-the-film-Valkyrie-starring-Tom-Cruise.html. Accessed: October 13, 2015.

44 Some information found at: http://www.telegraph.co.uk/culture/film/3558716/Claus-von-Stauffenberg-the-true-story-behind-the-film-Valkyrie-starring-Tom-Cruise.html; and https://www.jewishvirtuallibrary.org/jsource/Holocaust/julyplot.html. Accessed: October 13, 2015.

45 Some information and quotes from: http://www.theguardian.com/century/1940-1949/Story/0,127827,00.html; and http://spartacus-educational.com/GERmorrellT.htm. Accessed: February 15, 2016.

46 Found at: http://www.dailymail.co.uk/news/article-2317588/Adolf-Hitlers-confidantes-days-extraordinary-seen-interviews.html. Accessed: February 14, 2016.

47 Quoted from: http://racialinjustice.eji.org/timeline/1940s/. Accessed: December 1, 2015.

48 Found at: http://racialinjustice.eji.org/timeline/1940s/. Accessed: March 18, 2016.

49 Some information found at: http://www.archives.gov/research/african-americans/ww2
-pictures/; http://exhibitions.nypl.org/africanaage/essay-world-war-i.html; http://www
.oxfordaasc.com/public/features/archive/0508/index.jsp; http://www.gilderlehrman
.org/history-by-era/world-war-ii/essays/patriotism-crosses-color-line-african
-americans-world-war-ii; and http://www.nationalww2museum.org/assets/pdfs/african
-americans-in-world.pdf. Accessed: March 18, 2016.

50 Some information found at: http://www.footvitals.com/injuries/trench-foot.html; and
http://www.mayoclinic.org/diseases-conditions/frostbite/basics/complications/con-
20034608. Accessed: February 16, 2016.

APPENDIX 1

1 Used with permission of Robert Hudson Jr., March 15, 2016.

EPIGRAPH

1 Found at: http://archive.defense.gov/news/newsarticle.aspx?id=33014. Accessed: February 10, 2016.

INDEX

Printed in the United States
by Baker & Taylor Publisher Services